Family Sacrifices

Family Sacrifices

The Worldviews and Ethics of Chinese Americans

Russell M. Jeung, Seanan S. Fong,
and Helen Jin Kim

OXFORD
UNIVERSITY PRESS

OXFORD
UNIVERSITY PRESS

Oxford University Press is a department of the University of Oxford. It furthers
the University's objective of excellence in research, scholarship, and education
by publishing worldwide. Oxford is a registered trade mark of Oxford University
Press in the UK and certain other countries.

Published in the United States of America by Oxford University Press
198 Madison Avenue, New York, NY 10016, United States of America.

CIP data is on file at the Library of Congress
ISBN 978–0–19–087592–3

1 3 5 7 9 8 6 4 2

Printed by Sheridan Books, Inc., United States of America

CONTENTS

FIGURES

ACKNOWLEDGMENTS

Family Sacrifices: The Worldviews and Ethics of Chinese Americans details the love and indebtedness that Chinese Americans feel toward their families, and we similarly wish to acknowledge and reciprocate the love, support, and help of our family, friends, and students in this writing of this project.

First, I (Russell) wish to thank my co-authors, Seanan Fong and Helen Kim, for their remarkable contributions, insights, and enthusiasm for this book. They saw the significance of highlighting Chinese American voices and the relevance of their *liyi* worldviews, and both were inspiring conversation partners.

We also extend our deep gratefulness to our stellar research team: Sharon Lau, Steven Rozzi, and Annastasia Wong. Their perspective on the second generation who were coming of age was invaluable, as they helped us analyze the interviews and develop the key themes that emerged. Special thanks to Alice Liu, who not only prepared the charts found here but also analyzed the survey data and helped us identify major trends.

Several students from San Francisco State University Asian American Studies, as well as others, assisted in the outreach and transcription of hours of interviews: Jonathan Cunanan, Mariam De Guzman, Julissa Delos Santos, Jessie Huynh, Scott Leong, Bryan Tamsir, and Daniel Yu.

Our colleagues in the Asian Pacific American Religious Research initiative, the Asian North American Religion, Culture and Society section of the American Academy of Religion, and the Religious Studies section of the Association of Asian American Studies provided us with their generosity, wisdom, and feedback. We co-wrote an article with Brett Esaki, whose parallel research on Japanese Americans complemented this study. Young Lee Hertig published some of our findings in ISAAC's *Christianity Next*. Other colleagues include Melissa Borja, Rita Nakashima Brock, Joe Cheah, Carolyn Chen, Himanee Gupta-Carlson, Jane Iwamura, Khyati Joshi, Grace Kao, Mike Karim, Uriah Kim, Jeffrey Kuan, Kwok Pui-lan, Daniel Lee, Benny Liew, Rachel Lim, Jerry Park, Sharon Suh, Justin Tse, Timothy Tseng, Janelle Wong, Gale Yee, and David Yoo.

This research project originated while I was on a Fulbright Fellowship in Taiwan, where Chinese Popular Religion was vibrant. SF State's Department of Asian American Studies and the College of Ethnic Studies provided a great home that validated my examination of Chinese American spiritualities.

Last but not least, I dedicate this book to my own Chinese American family that includes Koreans and Chin Burmese. Joan and Matthew, thank you for our deeply meaningful rituals of mealtimes and bedtimes, vacations and church. Life with you gives me stability, nurturance, and hope. I am blessed to have Bethsy and Bonny, and now Deborah and baby Naomi complete our family. My parents, Bernice Jeung and the late Albert Jeung, are themselves models of Chinese Americans who sacrifice everything for the sake of their children. I hope that we can honor this love and that of our ancestors.

I (Seanan) would like to acknowledge the students and faculty at Harvard Divinity School who offered their support and critique of portions of this book, especially my senior seminar leader, Eunyung Lim, and faculty advisor, Diana Eck. I would also like to extend my gratitude to Stephanie Paulsell, Dan McKanan, Michael Puett, and Dudley Rose at Harvard, as well as Scotty McLennan and Lee Yearley at Stanford, who provided invaluable encouragement to understand and serve the perspectives and needs of an often-overlooked community of which I am a part. Finally, I would like to recognize the experience and wisdom of my own family, especially of my parents, Dennis and May Fong, in forming the inspiration behind this effort.

I (Helen) want to thank my co-authors, Russell Jeung and Seanan Fong, for inspiring and challenging my thinking, from first interviews to final edits. Russell, thanks for opening doors for us to collaborate and for invaluable mentorship. Seanan, thanks for sharing your insights since our time at Harvard Divinity School. I am grateful to the national network of Asian American religious studies scholars as well as my colleagues and mentors at Emory and Harvard who expressed enthusiasm for this project. Finally, to our interviewees: because of you, I now think twice about how to see and where to look for Americans' most cherished values and ethics—thank you.

CHAPTER 1

✧〜✧

Introduction

Chinese American Familism and the Theory of Liyi

THE ATHEIST

If nothing's going to happen afterwards, why are you wasting your energy doing it?

Scott Lai, an attorney in the San Francisco Bay Area, had just dismissed the idea of lighting incense for ancestors. While growing up in a primarily white and black neighborhood in Columbus, Ohio, Scott celebrated some Chinese customs, such as Chinese New Year festivities. His family, however, eschewed practices "imbued with religion." The Lai family was not one to practice "superstitious" customs such as ancestral veneration.

Scott's parents had moved to the Midwest from Taiwan. His mother worked part-time jobs as a real estate agent and school bus driver, while his father obtained his graduate degree in mechanical engineering at Ohio State University and worked as an engineering firm manager. His father's engineering mindset helped to shape Scott's worldview:

> My dad is very much an empiricist; he very much subscribes to the scientific method.
> I don't think he does so explicitly. But in seeing the way he operates in the world, he
> tends to deal with hard facts, realities, what can be adjusted or manipulated. He's an en-
> gineer by training, so I think some of that comes out there.

When Scott and his sister were adolescents, Scott's father encouraged them to test religions to see if they were true or not. When Scott's sister professed belief in the Christian God, his parents were "very encouraging of it," but when she stopped attending church, they were similarly supportive. Eventually conversations with friends of different religions and extensive reading about metaphysics led Scott to decide that he was an atheist:

> In the strictest hyperlogical sense, I suppose you could say I am agnostic, but I am one hundred percent functionally an atheist. And as a matter of belief, I don't believe in the existence of an "omni-three" God. That's kind of the Abrahamic tradition of the omnipotent, omniscient, omnipresent. . . . I don't really believe in a spirit as any kind of independent entity without a physical form.

As an atheist, Scott represents one of three categories that sociologists employ to classify religious "nones," a demographic loosely defined in terms of a lack of religious belief or affiliation. Yet at the same time that Scott identifies as atheist, he holds onto a commitment far more important than his atheism: family. In spite of an abusive childhood that led to his eventual estrangement from his father, Scott expressed a strong devotion to family:

> You know, my grandma called me the other day, as she's worried about everything. And I said, "You know, grandma, I'll take care of you financially for the rest of your life." That's not a problem. To me, it wasn't like a big deal, nor did it feel like an obligation.

His family commitment did not stop with his grandmother, but extended to his nephew:

> This is my family, and I would do that for them. It is more important to me that she live well than I have extra money. My brother is having a baby, and I made the same promise to his new kid. At some point, he was going to lose the house, and I told him I would support his son through college. So I feel very, very devoted to the people that I still recognize as my family.

Although Scott does not plan to have his own family, he values his extended family to such an extent that he would pay for his nephew's upbringing and education. While Scott's atheist beliefs mark him as a religious none, family devotion motivates his most meaningful actions and responsibilities.

THE AGNOSTIC

Laura Chan, a businessperson who moved to the San Francisco Bay Area for her career in advertising and marketing, is unsure whether God or a universal spirit exists. She grew up in Quincy, Massachusetts, as a latchkey child; her parents worked around the clock at a Chinese restaurant, seldom taking vacations, even on holidays. The Chan family practiced Buddhism and aspects of Chinese Popular Religion, attending a temple and maintaining a home shrine filled with statues, including that of Guanyin (觀音), the Buddhist bodhisattva of mercy. Laura's mother burned incense every morning and even advised Laura to change her cell phone number because it included the unlucky number four.

Yet concerning spiritual matters, Laura takes a this-worldly, pragmatic approach. As she put it, "If things happen, they'll happen. I'm not relying on some statues of god to keep me safe." She criticized her father's attempt to use a traditional Chinese healing practice to cure her brother of a diabetic seizure:

> You're relying on something that you don't really have proof of! My dad took this yin yang thing—a spider web, like an octagon with a mirror—but this was all metal and was a keychain. He started using it and rubbing ointment on his head.
>
> I'm like, "That is not going to do anything! He needs a glass of orange juice!" My brother is diabetic—he needs sugar, not something to be rubbed against his forehead.

At the same time she debunks her parents' traditional approaches toward healing, she continues some customs because her parents were so devoted to aspects of Chinese Popular Religion, such as *fengshui* (風水). For instance, she arranges her furniture in appropriate ways to ensure good energy flow and avoids taboo practices during the Chinese New Year. In fact, although she does not subscribe to the logic of the practice, Laura wears red and does not wash her hair on the first day of the New Year, lest her luck run out.

Laura's beliefs place her squarely in the subcategory of "agnostic" when describing her place among religious nones. Yet, like Scott, Laura reveals a more important underlying commitment to her family. She continues to maintain practices of Chinese Popular Religion in order to show her respect to her mother. Moreover, even though she moved to the West Coast for the sake of her career, she expressed a willingness to move back to the East Coast for the sake of her family. She explained that her parents were retired and that she wanted to support them:

> I was going to move back to keep them company. There was an empty nest. They were always alone, so I said I was going to move back after two years. I think that's what they expected.
>
> That's the difference between American culture and Chinese culture: the kids are always expected to take care of [the] parents. I would take care of them if my brother didn't step up. I'd do my best to alleviate the stress.

Though Laura is professionally ambitious and wants the freedom to "grow as an individual, personally and professionally," she is willing to relinquish her career and personal desires to live with her elderly parents in Massachusetts. Even with all of her personal dreams, Laura puts her parents' well-being first.

THE SPIRITUAL BUT NOT RELIGIOUS

Wendy Tong, an acupuncturist in the San Francisco Bay Area, maintains a privately spiritual lifestyle. Her parents migrated from Burma and obtained jobs as an auto mechanic and an assembler for medical equipment. She grew up living with extended family in one house where everyone spoke Cantonese; her grandfather, with whom she loved to watch Chinese gung fu movies, raised her. In the house, her grandmother prayed at two altars— one downstairs for the ancestors and one upstairs for Guanyin. Though it required a 40-minute drive, her mother attended a Buddhist temple every week. Her mother also studied to become a *fengshui* expert, learning to arrange the physical space in people's homes to optimize the flow of *qi* (氣, vital energy pervading the universe), or spiritual energy.

Until her late twenties, Wendy would chant Buddhist sutras nightly before bedtime, and she kept a vegetarian diet for a period out of respect for living beings. Just as Laura does not wash her hair on Chinese New Year's Day, Wendy did not wash her hair for a month after she gave birth. Wendy could not fully articulate the significance of this choice, but she still practiced it because "it was too hard to fight back" against her family's advice and the taboo was "just easier to go with it."

Wendy makes her living based on the manipulation of *qi*, the life force that flows throughout the universe. As an acupuncturist, she helps her patients achieve balance and harmony in their bodies. She follows a Daoist philosophy of balance, believing, "If I can get one person to physically have their body energy to work more harmoniously, then it will make the world a little bit more harmonious in a little way somehow." In her metaphysical understanding of the world, it contains multiple realities that affect the well-being of humans and nature. She does not believe that science can prove everything, because not everything is physical. Instead, as she articulated, "there are a lot of things in life that are not necessarily physical, like the sense of beauty can come from the depth of the soul. I believe in souls for people and animals." Indeed, she believes in reincarnation and the role of powers beyond her control:

[Life works in ways where] one third is in heaven, one third is in earth and one third is in your hand. One third of it is kind of predetermined: heaven. And one third of [life is shaped by what's] environmental: earth. And one third is under your influence: your hand.

Just as she tries to act compassionately and justly because she feels it is right to do so, she also recognizes that heaven governs one-third of the circumstances in her life.

Despite the differences between her beliefs and those of Laura and Scott, Wendy places a similar emphasis on family as her ultimate source of values. For Wendy, the significance of the family bond even relates to one's physical body. She told her white husband that she did not like tattoos because one's body belongs to a longer familial lineage: "It's because your body is not yours. Specifically, individually yours. It is borrowed from the lineage—your parents' sons and your sons' father—and it's not just yours."

Wendy stressed that the most important life events, including birthdays and holidays, should be spent with extended family. She said, "I think having some kind of tradition in the family is to connect [the lineage]." Family parties are the rituals and traditions that connect her to her lineage, which is something she wants to pass on to her son:

I want him to value family. I think he will, because he has a lot of family visiting him all the time. Our parties include family. So I would hope that he wouldn't feel the need to celebrate things with just his friends, and that he would include his family into celebrations.

Amid the constellation of Wendy's many spiritual beliefs, family ties are what she finds most important to transmit to the next generation. Scott, Laura, and Wendy represent how second-generation Chinese Americans are diverse not only in socioeconomic background, geographic upbringing, and dialect, but also in their nonreligious affiliations, beliefs, and practices.

THE ETHIC AND WORLDVIEW OF CHINESE
AMERICAN FAMILISM

Chinese Americans are the ethnic group with highest rate of religious nones, with over half (52%) reporting no affiliation with any religion. Scott, the atheist, is a strict empiricist who does not believe in supernatural forces. Laura, the agnostic, does not discount the possibility of the supernatural but tends toward a "commonsense" approach. Wendy, the "spiritual but not religious," actively believes in *qi* and the soul. Yet amid their differences, nonreligious Chinese Americans do share a common, lived tradition: Chinese American familism. Scott, Laura, and Wendy understand their family history, key relationships, and most cherished obligations through a remarkable, singular narrative of family sacrifice. They are similar in their willingness to sacrifice almost everything for their families. They each live out Chinese American familism, a lived tradition that prioritizes family interdependence and right relationships, through the meaningful rituals of being family.[1]

Through 58 in-depth interviews and national survey data, *Family Sacrifices: The Worldviews and Ethics of Chinese Americans* argues that Chinese American familism operates to provide (1) ultimate values about the purpose and meaning in life for Chinese Americans, (2) ethics to guide their relationships and behaviors, and (3) core identities that offer self-understanding and belonging.[2] As a hybridized and transpacific lived tradition, Chinese American familism has its roots in Chinese Confucianism and Chinese Popular Religion. Through the processes of migration and adaptation, this lived tradition has continuously transformed and has become distilled. Within a postindustrial, racialized, and multicultural American context today, it pervades how second-generation Chinese Americans conceptualize and maintain their human relationships and responsibilities, as well as how they embody, enact, and transmit the practices of family.

Is Chinese American familism a religion for Chinese Americans who self-identify as unaffiliated or simply do not know how to identify with a traditional religion? If it is, how do we categorize those who are religiously affiliated, yet who also practice elements of this familism? The issue of categorizing Chinese Americans by religious affiliation—as well as how to categorize Chinese American familism—raises theoretical issues for the study and analysis of this ethnic group. Unfortunately a review of theories of American religious nones and the conceptualization of Asian American religions offers little in addressing these empirical quandaries. In fact, what is needed is an indigenous, Chinese perspective that can offer an alternative lens and theory to understand religious nones and familism. *Family Sacrifices* aims both to outline the contours of Chinese American familism and to introduce the conceptual framework of *liyi* (禮義, rituals and right relations) to understand familism better. To highlight further these concerns, we first survey the religious affiliations of Chinese Americans to reveal the diversity and seeming contradictions of this group's beliefs and practices.

CHINESE AMERICAN RELIGIOUS
AFFILIATION: DIVERSITY AND CHANGE

Similar to other Asian ethnic groups in the United States, diversity, change, and nonconformity to mainstream American religious categories mark Chinese Americans' religiosity. Although the great majority (70.6%) of Americans identify as Protestant or Catholic Christians, only 25% of Chinese Americans do. Instead this ethnic group has one of the highest proportions of Buddhists (13.9%) in the nation. Moreover, as we profiled in the introductory vignettes, Chinese Americans are the most likely of all Americans to identify as a religious none, just as Scott, Laura, and Wendy do. The religious diversity of this ethnic group, the high proportions of religious nones, and the maintenance of Chinese American familism each present theoretical issues for the study of this group. In order to provide an overview of the religious backgrounds of Chinese Americans and to illuminate their seemingly paradoxical beliefs and practices, this section highlights their religious affiliation and the key factors shaping their religious diversity: nativity, generation, and socioeconomic status.

According to the Pew Research Center's 2012 Asian American survey, over half of this group (51.8%) do not identify with any religious tradition or group.[3] Instead 8.7% of Chinese Americans are atheist, 5.9% are agnostic, and 37.2% are nothing in particular. We consider those who check "nothing in particular" as including those who are "spiritual but not religious." In contrast, 26% of Asian Americans in general and 23% of all Americans are religious nones.[4]

Among those who do claim a religion, 12.8% of Chinese Americans are Evangelical, 4.5% are Mainline Protestant, 7.6% are Catholic, and 13.9% are Buddhist. Overall, about three out of ten Chinese Americans (31.3%) are Christian. Almost one in ten (9.5%) affiliate with other religions such as Daoism or Islam, but their sample size was too small to include.

Certainly, the religious context in which individual Chinese Americans are born and raised is the primary determinant of their religious affiliation. Since three out of four Chinese are born in Asia, they grow up in countries where atheism or Chinese Popular Religion dominates. For example, atheism is the predominant religious category in China, where 73.5% identify as nonreligious.[5] In Taiwan, folk religion predominates, and 44.2% of Taiwanese identify with this folk religion.[6] In the Pew sample, 25.0% were born in the U.S., 46.4% were from China, 5.8% were from Hong Kong, 13.2% were from Taiwan, 1.9% were from Vietnam, and 7.7% were from other nations. Overall, 60.7% of Chinese Americans from the People's Republic of China state that they are religiously unaffiliated, but only 47.3%

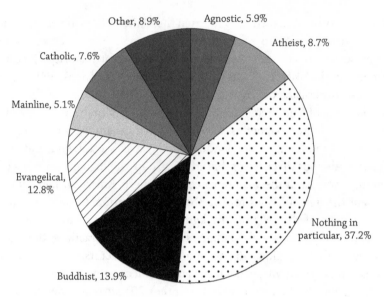

Chinese American
Religious Affiliation

Other, 8.9%   Agnostic, 5.9%

Atheist, 8.7%

Catholic, 7.6%

Mainline, 5.1%

Evangelical,
12.8%

Nothing in
particular, 37.2%

Buddhist, 13.9%

Figure 1.1 Chinese American Religious Affiliation

from the United States are religious nones. Chinese Americans from Taiwan are 2.5 times more likely to be Buddhist than those from Hong Kong or the United States. Immigrants from Hong Kong are more likely to be Catholic than those from any other country.

These percentages, however, belie the amount of religious change occurring within the Chinese American population. Migration to the United States creates such deracination and disruption that almost half of Chinese Americans (45.5%) are likely to adopt new religious beliefs and identities. Among immigrants, those who were Mainline Protestant, Evangelical, or agnostic were most likely to have converted to those affiliations. In contrast, only 34% of the U.S. population overall convert.[7] Nearly seven out of ten Chinese American agnostics (69.0%), six out of ten Chinese American Evangelicals (58.7%), and six out of ten of atheists (57.4%) had changed from their childhood religious affiliation. In contrast, only 20.2% of Buddhists had come to their religion through conversion, as had 36.4% of Catholics.

Generational acculturation to the American religious scene, which is primarily Christian, spurs religious change as well. As the 1.5 and second generation come of age in the United States, they are more apt to identify as Christian (29%) than are their immigrant parents (23.3%). How they

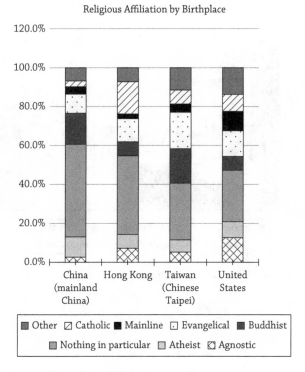

Religious Affiliation by Birthplace

Figure 1.2 Religious Affiliation by Birthplace

acculturate and to what they acculturate depends on the period of immigration. Those whose families came before the 1965 Immigration Act tended to convert to Protestant Christianity, such that over half of third-generation Chinese Americans affiliated with this group. The rate of Protestant Christians within the Chinese American community before 1965 increased from 8.0% of immigrants to 44.3% of the second generation and 51.8% of the later generations. However, in the post-1965 period, only 21.6% of immigrants were Protestant Christian, as compared to 19.1% of the second generation. More recently, in fact, generations who were born after 1965 are apt to identify as religious nones. The rate of religious nones in this group has increased from 51.3% of immigrants to 63.0% of the second generation. Both eras saw significant shifts in the religious affiliation of Chinese Americans across generations.

Chinese American religious groups also vary greatly by socioeconomic status, as evidenced by their educational attainment. Buddhists are the most likely of all Chinese American religious groups not to attend college; 23.8% do not have even a high school diploma. Fewer than half of Chinese American Buddhists obtain a college degree. On the other hand, about

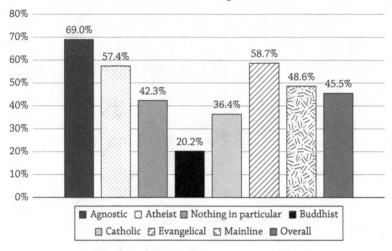

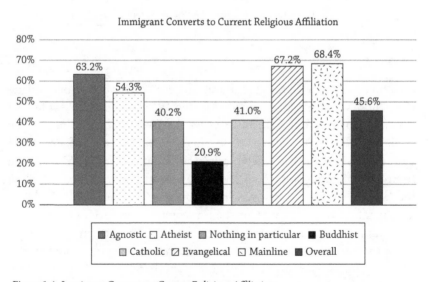

Figure 1.3 Converts to Current Religious Affiliation

Figure 1.4 Immigrant Converts to Current Religious Affiliation

three-fourths of agnostics (76.5%) and Catholics (75.9%) graduate with a bachelor's degree or higher.

To summarize, Chinese Americans belong to a range of religious categories, with no one category having a majority. They have high rates of religious change, as 44% of the community reported converting, and

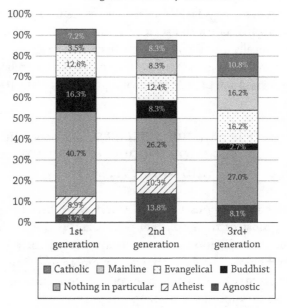

Figure 1.5 Religious Affiliation by Generation

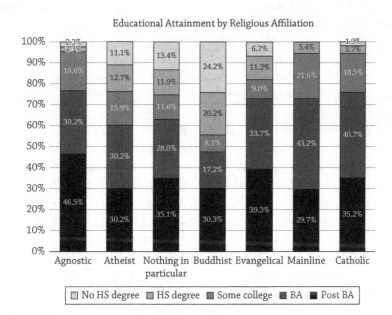

Figure 1.6 Educational Attainment by Religious Affiliation

the number of religious nones has increased by 12% from the first to the second generation. Key factors related to religious affiliation are birthplace, generational status, and socioeconomic status. What makes this diversity theoretically puzzling, though, is that Chinese Americans' religious affiliations—including those who are unaffiliated with any religion—do not necessarily correspond to their beliefs and practices, to which we next turn.

CHINESE AMERICAN BELIEFS AND PRACTICES BY RELIGIOUS GROUP: HETERODOX AND NONSYSTEMATIC

Quite obviously, religious Chinese Americans differed from the non-religious in most of their spiritual beliefs and practices. Interestingly, though, religious affiliation does not always directly correspond to strict orthodox adherence in belief or practice. Chinese American Evangelicals and Buddhists may hold to heterodox beliefs, and Chinese American religious nones may affirm the existence of spiritual beings. The amalgamation of beliefs that Chinese Americans adhere to, even when seemingly contradictory, reflects a Chinese religious repertoire that challenges Western paradigms of religion. This religious repertoire, the toolkit used for spirituality and religion, assumes a plurality of religious beliefs and enables adherents to take a utilitarian approach toward religious practice. This section first examines Chinese American belief in God or a universal spirit. It then shows the percentage of Chinese Americans, especially in comparison to Chinese in Asia, who believe in the supernatural forces found in Chinese Popular Religion, including ancestral spirits, and *qi*.

Those belonging to religious traditions hold to beliefs that the nonreligious do not. Catholics (94.5%), Evangelicals (92.5%), and Mainline Protestants (84.8%) overwhelmingly believe in God or a universal spirit. Of the Buddhists, 70.3% believe in God, compared to 63.5% of all Chinese Americans. Among religious nones, only 45.4% of those believing in "nothing in particular" like Wendy and 22.2% of atheists such as Scott— although by definition, they should not—believe in God. Interestingly, over two-thirds of agnostics (69.8%) such as Laura report that they do believe in a God or a universal spirit.

Instead of a monotheistic notion of God or a universal spirit, Chinese traditionally assume the existence of spirits, gods, and *qi*, a spiritual force that is immanent in the universe. Chinese Popular Religion is an umbrella term for the folk beliefs and practices of the majority of the Han Chinese population. It includes individual folk beliefs, such as fortune-telling

Belief in God by Religious Affiliation

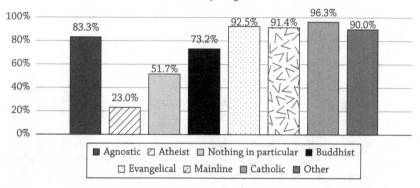

Figure 1.7 Belief in God by Religious Affiliation

practices, efforts to ward off bad luck or evil spirits, and *fengshui*, a system which directs and harmonize the flow of *qi*. It also consists of communal beliefs in local deities, including the earth god (Tudi, 土地), sea god (Mazu, 媽祖), and city god (Chenghuang, 城隍), as well as ancestor veneration.[8] Despite over 60 years of Communist rule that suppresses religion, Chinese in China have begun to practice Chinese Popular Religion again. According to Fenggang Yang and Anning Hu, "At least 55.5% (578 million) of adults in mainland China have engaged in at least of one of the two folk religion types."[9] In Taiwan, even more Chinese adhere to these practices, with 85% participating in individual folk beliefs and 88% in communal folk beliefs.

Compared to Chinese in China and Taiwan, Chinese in the United States overall are less likely to believe in the supernatural forces of Chinese Popular Religion. About four in ten (42.3%) believe in *qi*. On the other hand, Chinese Americans have a greater belief in ancestral spirits (44.8%) than those in China (17.5%).

The beliefs of Chinese American Mainline Protestants and Catholics best indicate the salience of Chinese Popular Religion. About half of Catholics (51.0%), Mainline Protestants (50.0%), and agnostics (51.3%) believe in ancestral spirits. In comparison, 44.8% of the overall Chinese American sample do. Evangelicals and atheists have the lowest rates of belief in these spiritual forces and beings, but substantial proportions of even these groups maintain Chinese beliefs: about one-third of Evangelicals (34.4%) and one-fourth of atheists (27.6%) believe in ancestral spirits.

Other evidence indicating the significance of Chinese popular religion in the lives of Chinese Americans is the maintenance of shrines in their homes and their continuation of Chinese New Year customs and taboos. Four out of ten Buddhists (38.0%) have a home shrine. Interestingly, one in ten nonreligious Chinese Americans have a shrine for prayer, in spite of claiming

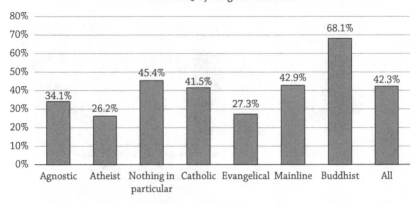

Figure 1.8 Belief in *Qi* by Religious Affiliation

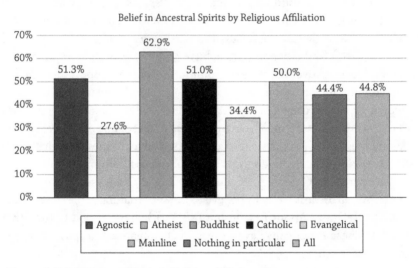

Figure 1.9 Belief in Ancestral Spirits by Religious Affiliation

no religious affiliation. This group may continue to practice ancestor veneration, which differs from the Evangelicals (2.2% having a shrine) and the Mainline Protestants (0%).

An important tradition with religious rituals for the Chinese is Chinese New Year. Overall 85.3% of Chinese in the United States celebrate this festival. Almost all of the Buddhists (95.7%) host some sort of celebration, in contrast to 77.1% of Mainline Christians. Surprisingly, atheists are the next largest religious category that hosts Chinese New Year festivities, at 88.5%.

To summarize, Chinese Americans hold to an array of beliefs and traditions from both Chinese Popular Religion and Judeo-Christian

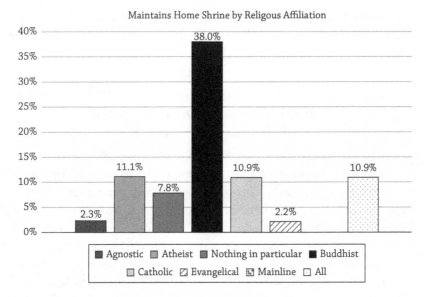

Figure 1.10 Maintains Home Shrine by Religious Affiliation

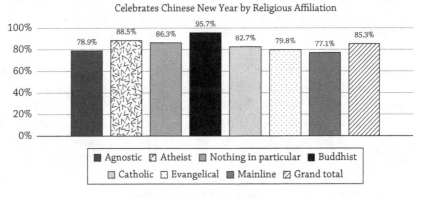

Figure 1.11 Celebrates Chinese New Year by Religious Affiliation

theologies. Although Buddhists and Christians tend to adhere to the tenets and religious practices of their traditions, they also incorporate those of Chinese Popular Religion and each other's theologies. For example, 48.9% of Buddhists and 24.0% of Catholics state that they believe in astrology. The nonreligious too are not necessarily nonbelieving or nonpracticing. The fact that one out of four Chinese American atheists believe in ancestral spirits, as do one in three Evangelicals, hints that Chinese Americans may be more heterodox, hybridized, and utilitarian in their approach toward religion than other Americans. For this group, Western categories of religion are not necessarily appropriate for capturing the spiritual lives of Chinese

Americans. Examination of American sociological accounts for religious nones, and the Western paradigm of religion to which these accounts belong, reveal these shortcomings.

AMERICAN SOCIOLOGICAL EXPLANATIONS FOR RELIGIOUS NONES

American sociologists of religion have just begun to account for the dramatic rise in religious nones since the 1990s. This emergent field has developed typologies and social characteristics of this group. For example, the Pew Research Center has divided the umbrella group of religious nones into three subgroups: atheists, agnostics, and "nothing in particular." The "nothing in particular" category has been further conceptualized and categorized with the use of a range of terms: "unchurched believers,"[10] "humanists,"[11] "spiritual but not religious,"[12] and "liminals."[13] They have found that American religious nones are more likely to be male, unmarried, college educated, and residing in the West.[14] Four other characteristics mark the religiously unaffiliated and provide explanations for their growth in the past two decades: (1) demographic shifts, (2) religious socialization, (3) political trends, and (4) cultural turns toward individualism.

First, the rise of the nones is attributed to generational replacement as millennials enter adulthood and older Americans, who are more religious, pass away. The Pew Research Center argues, "These generational differences are consistent with other signs of a gradual softening of religious commitment among some (though by no means all) Americans in recent decades."[15]

Second, sociologists Joseph Baker and Buster Smith assert that the religious socialization of those who are unaffiliated significantly correlates with their subsequent religious identification as adults.[16] Religious nones are more than three times more likely than the religiously affiliated to have an unaffiliated mother or father, who long serve as their primary reference group. Their parents' nonaffiliation, in turn, shapes the extent to which they bring—or do not bring—their own children to religious institutions.[17] For example, religious nones were much less likely than those religiously affiliated to attend organized religious services as 12-year-olds.

Third, Michael Hout and Claude S. Fischer observe that American religious nones tend to retain traditional religious beliefs but are disenfranchised by organized religion.[18] They are likely to be political liberals who have disaffiliated from religion and have been alienated by the incursion of conservative Christian politics within the past few decades. Similarly, Baker and Smith find that both atheists and unchurched believers share strong opposition to religion in the public sphere.[19] Thus, the growth of religious nones is a political act of disaffiliation, an expression of antipathy both toward organized religion in general and toward some churches' stances on divisive issues such as same-sex marriage.[20]

Fourth, the overall privatization of religion within the United States has promoted the development of personal spirituality, which may be independent of traditional religions. Peter Berger has maintained that increased pluralism destabilizes religious belief and organizations. The availability of alternatives to a single, unified religious worldview opens new options, including secularism and individually crafted spirituality.[21] As religious institutions decline, Americans continue to retain spiritual beliefs and individual religious practices in a bricolage fashion, which Robert Bellah et al. have called "Sheilaism."[22] Among millennials, the increase in religious individualism in the United States is an overall cultural trend that follows secularization trends in Europe.[23]

These explanations address the recent increase in the number of religious nones, and they account for some of the ways that Chinese Americans may have acculturated to the American religious context. Chinese Americans are overwhelmingly college educated, and the majority live on the West Coast, so their educational attainment and geographic location affect their religious beliefs. Chinese Americans who migrated before 1965 tended to convert to Christianity, but today they may have less pressure to do so. Consequently almost two-thirds of Chinese Americans under 30 years old (65.6%) are unaffiliated, a rate greater than the overall American trend for young adults. In terms of politics, 70% of Chinese Americans voted to reelect President Barack Obama in 2012. Chinese Americans, like other politically liberal Americans, may dislike the conservative politics of Christians and disaffiliate from organized religion.

Nevertheless, these theories about the recent rise in American religious nones do not comprehensively explain why Chinese Americans have been historically religiously unaffiliated, nor do they explain the high proportions of religiously unaffiliated in China. Indeed, both a better understanding of religion from a Chinese perspective, as well as a methodology to collect data on Chinese American religious affiliation and behaviors, are necessary.

THE UNEASY FIT BETWEEN THE WESTERN PARADIGM OF RELIGION AND CHINESE AMERICANS

One problem with American sociological accounts of religious nones is the Western paradigm of religion that undergirds these theories. Under this paradigm, the conceptualization of religion focuses on belief and belonging. Since American Judeo-Christian faith traditions emphasize belief in religious teachings and in membership in denominations, these paradigmatic assumptions about religious participation have been valid and reliable. The rise of religious nones is thus assumed to relate to nonbelief and nonbelonging. For instance, the title of Baker and Smith's article "None Too Simple: Examining Issues of Religious Nonbelief and Nonbelonging in the United States" reflects this paradigm.

This dominant religious paradigm of belief and belonging assumes binaries between belief and nonbelief, belonging and nonbelonging. Hence, the spiritual but not religious category assumes a bifurcation of two concepts: religion is tied to organized, traditional faith institutions, and spirituality is connected to hybridized, individualistic orientations toward the transcendent.[24]

Asian American sociologists of religion also employ the belief and belonging paradigm, especially when studying Christianity. Fenggang Yang includes four elements in his definition of a religion, which highlights belief: (1) a belief in the supernatural, (2) a set of beliefs regarding life and the world, (3) a set of rituals manifesting the beliefs, and (4) a distinct social organization of moral community of believers and practitioners.[25] Carolyn Chen prioritizes belonging, defining religion as "living traditions of meaning grounded in institutionalized communities."[26] Their definitions of religion apply to world religions, including Christianity and Buddhism. However, these works are not useful in explaining why so many Chinese Americans report being nonreligious. How do Chinese Americans who do not belong to institutionalized religions find meaning and belonging, which Chen suggests is the primary function of religion for Taiwanese immigrants?

Overall, this paradigm of belief and belonging, and the subsequent categorization of affiliation by this concept of religion, do not adequately capture how Chinese and Chinese Americans do religion. For example, Chinese Popular Religion assumes a variety of beliefs, values, and practices. However, surveys of religion rarely name ancestor veneration or belief in *fengshui* as a religious affiliation. Furthermore, they tend to require respondents to select only one, exclusive religion rather than allowing them to check all that apply. Consequently, Chinese who engage in practices of multiple religious traditions are at a loss about how to name themselves. Both theoretically and methodologically, a Judeo-Christian framework of belief and belonging is an uneasy fit for Chinese and Chinese Americans.

These issues with the Western paradigm of religion require a different theory to distinguish and capture the religious sensibilities and values of

Chinese Americans. Categorization as religious nones does them a disservice; as indicated earlier, they lead lives of devotion and commitment—even the atheists. Instead, what is needed is an indigenous, Chinese perspective that better accounts for this ethnic group's religious repertoire, that is, their toolkit for spirituality and religion. This repertoire, in contrast to the Western paradigm of religion, assumes individuals can hold to a plurality of beliefs; it also enables them to take a utilitarian approach toward religious practice.

THE NEED FOR A CHINESE POINT OF VIEW

In arguing for an indigenous Chinese perspective in relation to the Western concept of religion, the Chinese sociologist Fan Lizhu raises the issue of "reverse analogical interpretation." She asserts that using one religious culture to understand another religious culture is often inadequate:

> Only through emphasizing the concepts, expressions, and symbols fundamental to Chinese beliefs can we appropriately convey the significance of Chinese religious activities. Through attaching great importance to native religious practices and beliefs, we may resolve the dilemmas induced by relying solely on Western religious theories and models in the interpretation of Chinese religion.[27]

Chinese terms analogous to spirituality or religion, such as *tian* (heaven, 天), *yuanfen* (fated connection, 緣分), and *ming* (personal destiny, 命) are difficult to translate but continue to permeate almost all aspects of Chinese culture and reflect a distinctive Chinese religious culture. Indeed, Chinese concepts such as harmony find daily expression in varied dimensions of life, including traditional medicine, ancestral veneration rituals, augury, and geomancy.[28] We need to appropriate these terms and others for their usefulness in examining and explaining the ultimate values, ethics, and relationships of Chinese Americans.

Fan Lizhu recounts how previous scholars of Chinese religions have attempted to identify indigenous Chinese terms to represent Chinese experiences and worldviews. Wang Zhixin theorizes that the experience of religion in China could be understood as "moralization by sacred ways," a phrase derived from a passage in the *Zhou Yi* (周易, *Book of Changes*).[29] The sociologist C. K. Yang identifies the Chinese notion of the *dao* (道) as best encompassing this society's spirituality.[30] The *dao* is the transcendent way or cosmological principle that governs the universe, including the human world. Another term connoting religion as a path or way is *men* (門), a door to enlightenment and salvation. These are not simply other words for "religion," but rather attempts to better capture and do justice to experiences, assumptions, and worldviews that the Western concept of religion is ill equipped to handle.

For our research on nonreligious Chinese Americans, we believe the Chinese concept most apt for studying this group's experiences is *liyi*. To explicate this concept, we first analyze its genealogy to understand its roots, and then abstract the concept from its roots to appropriate it for our current scholarly context.

DEFINITION AND GENEALOGY OF *LIYI* AS A MORAL BOUNDARY SYSTEM

Prior to the late 1800s, traditional Chinese thought did not have a Western understanding of religion in terms of beliefs about the supernatural. Instead, in discriminating among groups according to their ultimate concerns, scholars paid more attention to the values and virtues embodied by those groups, the rituals that developed those values and virtues, and the norms of how to treat one another within relationships. The indigenous Chinese concept of *liyi* (禮義), which served as a moral boundary system, historically focused on these key features to distinguish Chinese from non-Chinese.

Liyi itself is a compound composed of two uniquely Chinese concepts, *li* (禮) and *yi* (義). Sinologists often translate the first word in the compound, *li*, as "ritual propriety," though its meaning encompasses a range of Western concepts, including "ceremony, ritual, decorum, rules of propriety, good form, good custom."[31] As a concept, *li* captures the way life *should* be conducted, from everyday manners at a meal to formal state ceremonies. As the Chinese historian Ben Schwartz explains, *li* refers to "prescriptions of behaviors, whether involving rite, ceremony, manners, or general comportment, that bind human beings and the spirits together in networks of interacting roles within the family, within society, and with the numinous realm beyond."[32] Confucian thinkers defined *li* in opposition to the concept of *su* (俗, custom), which sinologists often render as "custom." Activities were *li* if they were rooted in ethical principles and had the capacity to transform the practitioner; activities were *su* if they were followed simply out of habit.[33] Confucians also defined *li* in opposition to *fa* (法), rendered as "law," and *xing* (刑), rendered as "punishment." As opposed to trying to regulate society using the external threat of coercion, that is, *xing*, they advocated establishing peace and order through proper, ritual behavior. Such behaviors would inculcate appropriate values and attitudes to be internalized by the people.[34]

Sinologists render *yi* (義), the second part of the compound, as "righteousness," though it more specifically refers to the righteousness of carrying out one's responsibilities and duties given one's roles and relationships.[35] Classical Chinese thought viewed certain cardinal relationships as particularly important: between ruler and subject, parent and child, spouses, older and younger siblings, and friends. *Yi* embodied the proper and mutual discharge of responsibilities defined by the relationship. For example, a parent's *yi* was to raise and educate one's child. The child's *yi* was to listen to one's parents and support them in their old age. *Yi* was defined in opposition to the concept of *jian* (姦), rendered as "betrayal" or "selfishness."[36] To fail to fulfill one's responsibilities to those with whom one is in a relationship is to betray and fail them in favor of one's own selfish profit.

The pairing of *li* and *yi* occurred at least by the Warring States period (475–221 BCE) and became a key notion in classical Chinese discourse for boundaries defining who is human. Early Confucian texts cited *liyi* as a foundation for humanity: "That by which humanity becomes humanity is *liyi*."[37] *Li* and *yi* formed a powerful combination because of their mutual relevance. *Li* was the means by which *yi* could be practically and properly embodied in the concrete world, while *yi* was necessary to guide the normativity of the actions that constituted *li*.[38] As claimed in the *Analects (Lunyu,* 論語), "The gentleman considers *yi* to be basic, and uses *li* to carry it out,"[39] and in the *Mencius (Mengzi,* 孟子), "*Yi* is the way, and *li* is the door."[40]

By the Han dynasty (206 BCE–220 CE), *liyi* had become a moral boundary system, as evident in the famous Chinese historian Sima Qian's seminal work, the *Records of the Grand Historian (Shiji,* 史記. According to Sima Qian, what distinguished Chinese from barbarians was that barbarians lacked *liyi*. For example, the Huns "do not understand ritual and moral duty," rendering them distinct from Chinese.[41] This deployment of *liyi* discourse to demarcate groups along moral boundaries matured in the thought of Han Yu (768–824 CE), whose writings reacted against the flourishing of Buddhist and non-Confucian Daoist teachings and practices of the time. Han Yu developed a notion of moralized Chineseness based on *liyi* that "became central to the discourse of barbarian inferiority."[42] However, in the modern era, *liyi* discourse was displaced by competing discourses introduced from the West, including "religion" (*zongjiao,* 宗教), "culture" (*wenhua,* 文化), and "nation" (*minzu,* 民族).

APPROPRIATING *LIYI* AS A
THEORETICAL FRAMEWORK

While historically *liyi* discourse functioned as a moral boundary system, we use it as a theoretical framework to work in parallel with the Western paradigmatic concept of religion for understanding human phenomena. Within their own particular cultures, both *liyi* and "religion" historically served as tools to categorize people and demarcate groupings. European religious scholars, when confronted by religious others, asked a set of questions that grew out of Christian concerns: What are their beliefs, and are they orthodox? What religious bodies do they belong to, and do they belong to the true church? Confucians too employed *liyi* discourse to ask questions of the "other": What ritual practices do they think ought to be followed? What roles and relational responsibilities do they think ought to be honored? The Western paradigm of religion eventually shed its outward Christian appearance. However, as we have argued, discourse about religion, with its paradigmatic focus on belief and belonging, encountered its limits outside its originating context of the West.[43] Here the questions that the Western religion paradigm asks must be supplemented by alternative angles of inquiry.

As we are using it, then, a theory of *liyi* is an alternative approach to understanding people's ultimate concerns. Just as "religion" is not a set of beliefs in itself but rather a conceptual schema for organizing our understanding of the world, so *liyi* is a concept that helps scholars understand what to ask when they study group phenomena. Specifically, the theory of *liyi* examines (1) what moral practices, or *li*, a given group ritually maintains and values and (2) how they understand and rightly act in their most important relationships, or *yi*. Just as Confucius and Durkheim considered human ritual to be the lived expression and reproduction of symbolic meanings, *liyi* interrogates rituals as the embodiment of Chinese American ultimate concerns.[44]

The *liyi* framework is particularly useful for understanding Chinese American phenomena. To understand *li*, we must examine the rites, ceremonies, festivals, and interpersonal practices Chinese Americans hold dearest. In deconstructing the meanings of these rituals for the individuals, as well as the values they rehearse in them, we see the highest ideals held by Chinese Americans. These rituals can be formal, such as practices of ancestor veneration at gravesites, or informal, such as weekend family gatherings for *yumcha* (飲茶), meals of *dimsum* (點心, small dishes) that reinforce respect for family members. Again, we seek to understand and explain the lived values, not necessarily the beliefs or truth claims that are abstracted.

Similarly for *yi*, attention should be given to the relationships that Chinese Americans have, how they nurture and maintain them, and how they impute meaning to these interactions. By inquiring into their relationships with other people and paying attention to how they talk about those relationships, we can grasp how they understand and live out their relational responsibilities. Using a *liyi* framework, we thus are attuned to how relationships reflect ethical concern and moral responsibilities rather than to how one might belong to one faith tradition, denomination, or sect.

This theory of *liyi* makes sense of the high percentage of Chinese American religious nones who adhere to spiritual practices, as well as those who belong to religious traditions yet still venerate their ancestors. It also points to why Chinese American familism is such a stable and enduring value system for this group, even when transplanted in a new context. By prioritizing values and relationships, this Chinese lived tradition structures Chinese Americans to live out their ultimate priorities around family sacrifices and responsibilities.

Methodology and Sample

To explore the worldviews of Chinese American religious nones, we began by interviewing second-generation adults, ages 21 to 40. This group has the highest percentage of religiously unaffiliated among Chinese Americans, and possibly any ethnic age cohort. The second generation consists of Chinese born in the United States whose parents were born overseas. By focusing on this generation, we can examine the influence of the American context on Chinese traditions and perspectives, as well as the values and practices passed down from the immigrant generation.

Our 58 respondents were drawn from a nonprobability sampling technique through the networks of the researchers. Those who were interviewed first were asked to refer other possible respondents. Through this snowball method, we were able to obtain a national sample, with 19.0% from the East Coast, 15.5% from the Midwest, 10.3% from the South, and 55.2% from the West Coast. The sample was 43.1% male and 56.9% female; 79.3% were single and 20.7% were married.

Of the 58 respondents, 22.4% were atheist, 51.7% were agnostic, and 25.8% were deemed spiritual but not religious. Those in the last category espoused belief in supernatural forces and engaged in spiritual practices to connect with these forces.

Overwhelmingly, this sample of the second generation had similar experiences as Chinese Americans. All of their parents spoke a Chinese dialect in the home, and over two-thirds (67.2%) sent their children to Chinese-language school. Almost everyone (87.9%) celebrated the Chinese New Year holiday with their family, and 79.2% of their parents participated in ancestral veneration. In addition, 77.5% said their parents engaged in *fengshui* practices.

Socioeconomically, 65.5% of the sample had parents with professional backgrounds and 34.5% were from working-class backgrounds. Those from working-class backgrounds were immigrants from Guangdong province or Southeast Asian countries who entered through family visas or refugee status. All our respondents had obtained a college degree, reflecting the high level of Chinese American educational attainment. Each stated that they experienced racism during their youth.

The interview data were supplemented with results from the 2012 Pew Research Center Asian American survey. The largest survey about religion conducted with the Asian American community, it asked questions ranging from religious beliefs to political beliefs, from opinions about national issues to values about ethnic status. Chinese Americans made up the largest percentage of those surveyed, at 20.7%.

Chapter Outlines

Family Sacrifices: The Worldviews and Ethics of Chinese Americans introduces two major concepts. First, although the majority of Chinese Americans affiliate as religious nones, they are bound by a familism that operates as the central narrative in their lives, providing meaning, ethics, and identity. Second, an indigenous Chinese perspective, a *liyi* framework, is necessary to identify, explain, and analyze how Chinese American familism functions in the lives of this ethnic group. This book employs *liyi* as a conceptual tool to trace the sources of Chinese American familism, its transmission to the second generation, and its translation to their American context. In detailing the *yi* of Chinese Americans (the right ways to relate to and value others) and their *li* (the rituals they hold most important), *Family Sacrifices* portrays the major role familism plays in Chinese American lives.

Chapter 2, "Ancestral Roots: Chinese American Nonreligiousness and Familism," offers a genealogical exploration of how Chinese traditions have shaped Chinese Americans' current religious affiliations and their familism. Through their religious repertoire based in Chinese Popular Religion, Chinese adopted a plurality of beliefs for their own utilitarian purposes. Given this mixture of beliefs and practices that have no names, Chinese tend to identify as "nothing in particular" when asked about their religious affiliation. Another factor contributing to the high rates of Chinese American religious nones is Confucian thought, which oriented the society toward religious skepticism and toward an agnostic, symbolic interpretation of religious rituals. These twin approaches toward religion are the roots of modern-day Chinese atheism and agnosticism, and both reinforced the primacy of familial relations in Chinese society. These two traditions have undergone changes through modernization, migration, and the religious context in which they took root, and the latter part of chapter 2 surveys how these traditions have transformed through the processes of Chinese state modernization, acculturation to the American context, and racialization.

Chapter 3, "Transmission: Chinese American *Liyi* Socialization," describes trends in the upbringing of Chinese Americans and how significant family practices (*li*) inculcate moral values and obligations (yi) that they hold highest. Family background and class factors have a large role in whether Chinese American religious nones are atheist, agnostic, or spiritual but not religious. Nonetheless, similar family upbringing and group practices instill a familism with ethics of group loyalty and mutual responsibility for kin.

Chapter 4, "Translation: Chinese Popular Religion and Confucianism in the U.S.," identifies how the American context transforms Chinese familism into a distinct, hybrid tradition that carries on. In the face of formative religious and racialized experiences that identified Chinese *liyi* practices as Orientalized, exotic, or other, Chinese Americans still maintained their familial values and some practices. However, as they acculturated to their environment, they abandoned specific Confucian values and Chinese Popular Religion practices. Either their immigrant parents did not see these values and practices as important enough to transmit, or the second generation reinterpreted their family values to make them their own.

Chapter 5, "The *Yi* of Family Sacrifice: Chinese Americans' Highest Values," details what Chinese Americans value the most: maintaining right relationships within their families. Both Pew Research Center data from 2012 and our interviewees indicate that being a good parent is the top goal of Chinese Americans, whether married or single. Among their primary aims in life, Chinese Americans under 30 tend to be "maximizing world-changers," meaning that they want to make a difference in their careers and in the world. Those who are over 30 commonly are "expressive balancers," seeking to juggle multiple concerns for self-fulfillment. Both groups employ familism as a way to frame their ultimate life's purpose. Their understanding of their immigration history, their current main relationships, and their plans all revolve around the theme of family sacrifice.

Chapter 6, "The *Li* of Chinese American Familism: Ritualizing Family, Food, and Fun," continues the description of how this ethnic group maintains the value of family relationships through key rituals. From formal rituals, such as life cycle rites of marriage and death, to informal ones, such as family vacations and mealtime table traditions, Chinese Americans learn about, embody, and reproduce the ultimate value of being family. Even their understanding of ethical relations, that is, how they should relate to others, is derived from how they relate to family members.

We conclude the book with the theoretical implications of employing a *liyi* framework to understand Chinese Americans and Asian Americans in relation to identity, mental health, and political organizing. We also explore how this framework might be useful in explicating the nonreligious growth of other groups, especially American millennials.

CHAPTER 2

༄

Ancestral Roots

Ancestral Roots: Chinese American
Nonreligiousness and Familism

WHY AM I A HEATHEN?

Born and raised a heathen, I learned and practiced its moral and religious code; and acting thereunder I was useful to myself and many others. My conscience was clear, and my hopes as to future life were undimmed by distracting doubt.

    —Wong Chin Foo, "Why Am I a Heathen?," *North American Review* 145 (1887)

In an 1887 issue of the *North American Review*, the Chinese American activist and writer Wong Chin (1847–1898) Foo proudly defended his status as a "heathen" in his article "Why Am I a Heathen?" Rather than a mark of inferiority, he argued, his heathenism was a symptom of a clear conscience unclouded by fear of the supernatural. He scoffed at demands for religious membership, stating, "Unlike Christianity, 'our' Church is not eager for converts," and he found Christian debates on doctrine baffling: "I was bewildered by the multiplicity of Christian sects, each one claiming a monopoly of the only and narrow road to heaven." His Chinese "heathenism" instead held him to a set of public and private moral commitments—to family, to charity, and to the public—which he found more important than "fussing about religion." Indeed, Wong prioritized "the moral code controlling and regulating the relations and acts of individuals towards 'God, neighbor, and self'; and this intelligent 'heathenism' was taught thousands of years before Christianity existed or Jewry borrowed it. Heathenism has not lost or lessened it since."[1] Wong intended to defend Chinese Americans against European American anti-Chinese xenophobia and exclusion. As a perspective from a nineteenth-century religious none, his article is a forebear to the views of our contemporary subjects. Like the nonreligious Chinese Americans Laura, Scott, and Wendy in the previous chapter, Wong defied simple categorization centered around belief and belonging. Instead, he defined his identity around moral commitments, taking issue with the ethical practices and relationships lived out by the Christians he saw around him. For Wong, his *liyi*—the moral rituals and right relationships he prioritized—rather than his nonreligious status mattered.

Where did this orientation come from? Wong himself attributed both his nonreligious status and his moral orientation to his Chinese heritage, even as he identified as an American. Today as much as yesterday, both Chinese American nonreligiousness and the *liyi* of Chinese American familism have their historical and transpacific roots in China. This chapter traces how Chinese American nonreligiousness can be traced to three sources: (1) Chinese Popular Religion's nonaffiliated and nonexclusionary nature, (2) Confucian supernatural skepticism, and (3) *liyi* Chinese identity, which opposed religious membership. Together they help to explain why 52% of the Chinese American population identify as nonreligious yet also maintain a distinct ethic and worldview of familism. By detailing these three transpacific, historic sources of Chinese American nonreligiousness and familism, and their use across sociopolitical contexts, we reveal how they are historically rooted and culturally specific. Moreover, by utilizing *liyi* as a theoretical framework, we identify the key aspects of Confucianism and Chinese Popular Religion that have changed in the past century and how they shape immigrant Chinese Americans so that they identify as nonreligious.

CHINESE POPULAR RELIGION
AND CORRELATIVE COSMOLOGY

Let's say in this world, there's good luck floating around. If you try to bring that good luck into your life with numbers or with actions, then maybe you'll be one of those people to bump into that and to get it, whereas other people may fall into a different route.

—Julia Tom, advertising executive from San Mateo, California

Julia Tom typifies how many nonreligious Chinese Americans inherit and maintain vibrant practices involving supernatural elements or entities. Although she takes these practices seriously, Julia does not identify them as religious: they are not tied to a particular set of religious doctrines or affiliations even as they serve a useful role in her life. In her case, Julia preserves "luck" by avoiding inauspicious numbers. For example, she had serious reservations about interviewing for a job whose office address contained the number 44, a number that suggests death in Chinese numerology. She worried, "Holy crap, does this mean I'm going to be stuck here? . . . It's not just a number to me, I do feel something." These luck-based practices, which are components of Chinese Popular Religion, play an influential role in her life.

Over many centuries, the mutual interaction of popular customs and elite intellectual thought formed a recognizable tradition of Chinese Popular Religion. "The population of traditional China, from government officials to artisans and farmers," shared this tradition widely.[2] Components of Chinese Popular Religion include (1) ritualized relationships with gods, ghosts, and ancestors; (2) acceptance of the spiritual efficacy of religious practices; and (3) assumptions about the role of otherworldly forces, such as fate, karma, and *qi* (vital energy).[3] Unlike the practices transmitted by organized sects of Buddhism and Daoism, Chinese popular practices were "diffused," dependent upon secular institutions such as the family, the village, and the state for their maintenance and transmission.[4] Like Julia, people deployed these practices as part of their repertoire of supernatural practices to enhance their lives.[5] Notably, this repertoire assumes that an individual can hold to a plurality of beliefs and practices that are not exclusive to or affiliated with any one religion. This section covers the origins of three primary practices most often mentioned by our respondents: ancestor veneration, *fengshui*, and luck-based customs.[6]

The most often mentioned practice from this repertoire was ancestor veneration. About 8 out of 10 (79.2%) reported their parents practicing this tradition, especially at funeral services, death anniversaries, the tomb-sweeping festival day of Qingming, and Chinese New Year. To perform ancestor veneration, descendants *baibai* (拜拜, bow in respect, often three times) and offer incense and sometimes food, drink, or paper money to deceased ancestors. Ancestor veneration has had a central place in Chinese culture "from the earliest periods for which we have information," and its motivations have been diverse, with popular beliefs comingling with elite interpretations since ancient times.[7] Common to each of the varied aims of ancestor veneration was a sense of the "continuity of ties . . . between the living and their dead ancestors," expressed from the Bronze Age to modern times and "central" to Chinese society throughout.[8]

A pragmatic motivation for the veneration of the ancestors was to feed and care for the *hun* (魂, the immaterial soul) of the deceased, which continued to exist in this world even after the *po* (魄, the material soul) was buried. If ancestors were not provided for, they could become hungry, wandering ghosts that might bring ill fortune to their descendants.[9] On the other hand, elite interpretations, reflecting Confucian influences, linked ancestor veneration with moral cultivation, in particular as a ritual that promoted and expressed *xiao* (孝, filiality).[10]

Ancestor veneration assumed a plurality of supernatural beings and deities. Chinese practiced this ritual without one clear, orthodox belief or purpose, but alongside a concern for other gods and spirits. Oracle bone inscriptions from the Shang dynasty in the second millennium BCE, when ancestor worship is first attested, also indicate the worship of deities and the "high god" Shang-ti.[11]

While ancestor veneration had roots as far back as the Bronze Age (by 1700 BCE), *fengshui* and luck-based practices of Chinese Popular Religion drew upon correlative cosmology, which also evolved through a mutually reinforcing interaction between popular conceptions and elite thought. Correlative cosmology assumes that things with similar properties can influence each other; by manipulating one, it is possible to manipulate the other. With roots in concepts widely shared among the Chinese people, the influential philosopher Zou Yan (305–240 BCE) systematized the concepts of correlative cosmology as he articulated the principles of *yinyang* (陰陽, dual contrary but complementary forces) and *wuxing* theory (五行, the "five phases" of should be of wood, earth, water, fire, and metal).[12] The scholar Dong Zhongshu (179–104 BCE) refined these principles, which became dominant in the elite thought of the Han dynasty (206 BCE–220 CE). This paradigmatic passage of a classical text from that era captures Chinese metaphysics:

> Things of the same kind summon each other, those with the same vital energy join together, sounds that match resonate. Thus if you strum a gong note other gong will resonate; if you strum a *jue* note another *jue* will vibrate. Use a dragon to bring rain; use the form to move the shadow.[13]

Through these elite texts, these principles of correlative cosmology permeated Chinese society at all levels, such that they are found with remarkable consistency among Chinese populations studied by anthropologists in the 20th century.[14]

The practice of *fengshui* (geomancy) best demonstrates Chinese correlative cosmology. Of our respondents, 77.5% reported that their parents arranged their homes according to *fengshui*. The principles of *fengshui*, which literally means "wind and water," attempt to harness "the topographical forces of nature for the benefit of man" (Rawski, 1988, p. 25) by manipulating the arrangement of space, or one's place within it; one also manipulates the flow of *qi* through one's life. For example, some of our respondents remembered their families ensured that their homes were situated and oriented in the proper direction given the landscape, or avoided having mirrors or stairways opposite doors lest good *qi* be deflected out. Analogous principles apply to health and traditional Chinese medicine, through which the manipulation of one's physical body affects one's *qi* and thus one's health.

Correlative cosmology undergirds Chinese conceptions of fate and luck, which govern the lives of humans. In Chinese popular practice, *ming* (destiny) is the set of one's predestined opportunities and limitations based on the actions of cosmic forces upon one's life. Through astrology and divination, one's *ming* can be somewhat predicted, but it is most often employed as a pragmatic, post hoc rationalization for life's events and material conditions.[15] Similarly, each person has a certain amount of *yun* (運, constitutive luck), which shapes periodic cycles of good or bad fortune.[16] Through correlative cosmology, however, individuals can also invite better *yun* or avoid bad *yun*. As reported by our respondents, for example, certain numbers are auspicious and others are inauspicious according to how they sound. *Ba* (八), the word for the number 8, is similar in sound to *fa* (發), the word for becoming rich. It is therefore a lucky number, desirable for car license plates and home addresses. On the other hand, *si* (四), the word for 4, sounds like *si* (死), the word for death. As a result, this number is avoided. Days of the year can also be lucky or unlucky based on their features as described in the Chinese almanac (tongsheng, 通勝), which correlates a number of astrological and natural events based on the principles articulated by Zou Yan and Dong Zhongshu centuries ago.[17]

One of the most common and vivid ways our respondents experienced luck-based practices in their lives was in the celebration of traditional Chinese festivals. Almost nine out of ten immigrant families (87.9%) in this study celebrated Chinese New Year, a time to usher in blessings and prosperity for the upcoming year. By invoking words and symbols that "correlate" with auspicious things like prosperity and harmony, families invite good fortune through instances of "luck talk." Examples are speaking aloud positive greetings, posting couplets with good wishes on doors, having conversations about propitious matters, and eating foods whose names resemble auspicious words. Positive expressions include "Good Health!," "Forward Steps in the New Year!," "Surplus Every Year!," and "Happy and Prosperous New Year!"[18] Negative comments about topics such as sickness and death are avoided, as the words themselves might bring ill upon the family. Breaking things during the New Year festival also "correlates" with unfortunate circumstances that might occur in the upcoming year. To counteract these negative comments and occurrences, individuals may deploy luck talk.

The Chinese religious repertoire, as evidenced by Chinese Popular Religion, thus allows individuals to practice a plurality of rituals that are not necessarily competing or exclusive to one belief system. Consequently, this cosmology enables respondents like Julia to maintain "nonreligious" identities—that is, identities free of allegiances to theological doctrines and institutional affiliations—even while availing themselves of the tools of their religious toolkit.

A TRADITION OF SUPERNATURAL SKEPTICISM

[My parents] don't believe in superstition. So, I think, to them, there should be a reason behind the things that you do. . . . The cultural ones are so that you have a tie to who came before you be- cause certain traditions produce good things, [such as] bringing families together. But then, as for the superstitious ones, if nothing's going to happen afterwards, why are you wasting your energy doing it?

—Scott Lai, attorney from Columbus, Ohio

Scott Lai, introduced in the previous chapter, describes a tradition of skep- ticism toward the supernatural that he inherited from his parents. In the world of thought in traditional China, this skepticism existed alongside the Chinese religious repertoire described in the previous section. Unlike in the Christian West, where skepticism about the divine was rare and cer- tainly not normative, skepticism about supernatural entities and forces was long an intellectual and religious option in China.[19] As an enduring strain of Chinese thought, particularly within the Confucian tradition, supernatural skepticism is thus another important part of explaining Chinese American nonreligiousness today. Among our respondents, 19.0% identify as atheists and 48.3% as agnostics, indicating the skeptical tradition among Chinese Americans.

The Chinese skeptical tradition dates back to one of China's most influ- ential figures, Confucius (551–479 BCE). When asked about serving the spirits of the dead, Confucius replied, "While you are not able to serve men, how can you serve their spirits? . . . While you do not know life, how can you know about death?"[20] Confucius strictly abstained from speaking ex- tensively about the supernatural and refused to speculate on otherworldly concerns: "The subjects on which the Master did not talk, were: extraordi- nary things, feats of strength, disorder, and spiritual beings."[21] By his silence on the supernatural Confucius, established a precedent of agnosticism to subsequent generations of interpreters.

Sometimes that agnosticism veered toward the atheistic. An early and highly influential Confucian thinker, Xunzi (c. 310–c. 235 BCE), re- lated the story of a man who died from overexertion after running from a shadow mistaken for a devil, alongside the case of a person wasting a drum and a pig in trying to use them to cure a disease. Xunzi concluded that any sort of belief in supernatural entities is a mistake made in the wrong frame of mind, when one is "suddenly startled, or at a time when [one is] not sure, or confused. This is thinking that something exists when it does not, or that it does not when it does, and so making a [mistaken] judgment."[22] He denied the existence of supernatural beings that intervened in the human world.

Whether agnostic or atheistic, this skeptical understanding of the supernatural had implications about the role and function of religious rituals. Like Scott's parents' belief that "certain traditions produce good things," Chinese thinkers emphasized that rituals should be carried out for the benefit of humanity rather than for the benefit of supernatural beings. In the *Analects*, Confucius stressed the importance of carrying out the actions of respect and ritual, even while maintaining distance from the supernatural: "While respecting spiritual beings . . . keep aloof from them."[23] Confucius believed in the value of ritual "for the living human beings who participated in them rather than in their magical power to affect the spirits . . . remaining averse to any kind of supernaturalism."[24]

Further elaborating this pragmatic, human-oriented understanding of ritual, Xunzi described the dangers of ritual: too much emphasis on the supernatural was a detriment to humankind. In a potent passage, Xunzi criticizes those who take natural omens too seriously: "When stars fall or trees groan, the people of the whole country are afraid. We ask, 'What does it mean?' I answer: it doesn't mean anything!"[25] Instead, Xunzi emphasized that human failures—uncultivated fields, bad harvests, high grain prices—should be of concern. Rulers who place too much attention on worshipping the gods at the expense of people are both unwise and immoral.

This early Confucian notion of pragmatic skepticism fully blossomed in the influential work of Wang Chong (27–c. 100 CE), a Confucian scholar who championed the skeptical tradition against the supernaturalistic trends of the Han court. Most famously, Wang Chong compared humans on the earth's surface to fleas in the folds of clothing: "If fleas wanted to influence what humans thought, and screamed into our ears, we would not even hear them; likewise, it would also be absurd to imagine that Heaven and Earth could understand the words or wishes of mere humans."[26] In the tradition of Xunzi, Wang Chong attacked attention to the supernatural as a distraction from true concerns. Citing history, he argued that unwise rulers in history sought comfort in ghosts and sacrifices, forgetting about the importance of their own behavior: "The conclusion is that man has happiness in his own hands, and that the spirits have nothing to do with it. It depends on his virtues, and not on sacrifices."[27]

By the end of the Song dynasty (960–1279 CE), supernatural skepticism had become a part of orthodox Chinese thought that challenged the aforementioned practices of Chinese Popular Religion. In the flowering of Neo-Confucian thought during that period, Xunzi's skeptical understanding of ritual unmistakably manifested in the work of Sima Guang (1019–1086 CE), Cheng Yi (1033–1107 CE), and Zhu Xi (1130–1200 CE). Sima Guang believed that rites were important not because a dead soul would care, but rather because those rites were essential to performing filiality. In fact, he criticized Buddhist services because they posited the distracting idea that dead bodies could suffer punishment.[28] Along the same skeptical lines, Cheng Yi dedicated efforts to proving *fengshui's* fallacies.[29] Zhu Xi, known as the greatest Neo-Confucian thinker, sought to standardize ritual practice for both elites and commoners through his widely circulated liturgical guidebook, *Family Rituals*. In addressing the topic of ritual, Zhu and his contemporaries "did not debate what ancestors were or how they were affected by offerings of food or drink. Rather, they analyzed ancestral rites in terms of their symbolism, especially the ways they symbolized the hierarchy of society."[30] Because of the influence and popularity of books like *Family Rituals*, a skeptical understanding of ritual was accessible and pervasive within Chinese society across social strata.

The skeptical tradition's influence in orthodox Chinese thought continued through subsequent dynasties. At the end of the Qing dynasty (1644–1912 CE), the last imperial dynasty, reformers attempting to modernize Chinese society found inspiration in China's ancient skeptical tradition as a bridge to European Enlightenment secularism.[31] Hu Shih (1891–1962), one of the most prominent figures of that period, saw modernization as the culmination of the skeptical tradition's emphasis on the human over the supernatural. Deemed backward and inimical to national progress, Chinese supernatural practices waned among the urban and educated classes as the government adopted Western categories of religion to name those practices superstitious. In Communist China, the state's "atheism-based regulation of religion" increasingly suppressed supernatural practices until it eventually banned all religion during the Cultural Revolution (1965–1968).[32]

Scott's atheist parents, who grew up in Taiwan before moving to the United States as adults, were undoubtedly shaped by such societywide currents of secularization that ultimately traced back, at least partly, to the long Chinese tradition of supernatural skepticism. They passed on the attitudes of their generation to their own children, inculcating both a mistrust of supernatural beliefs and a Confucian high view of ritualized, moral behavior.

LIYI CHINESE IDENTITY AT ODDS
WITH RELIGIOUS MEMBERSHIP

Back when we were going to church, we had these prayers to give thanks. We tried to do that at dinner and Dad got really mad. We thanked the Lord for food, but my Dad worked his ass off to get the food, so he yelled, "Why are you thanking God?" Maybe that's the reason why we stopped going to church.

—Kenneth Lam, student from San Leandro, California

Kenneth Lam's anecdote highlights another historical dynamic underlying Chinese American nonreligiousness. For Kenneth's father, adopting a Christian commitment led to dereliction of a family commitment: thanking the Christian God failed to show the appropriate gratitude and respect due to him for his sacrifice for the family. In Chinese history an analogous tension between the demands of religious participation and the maintenance of core human relationships put Chinese identity itself at stake. Because the traditional concept of what we term *"liyi* Chinese identity" tied Chineseness to the rituals and duties of key human relationships, anything that undercut the centrality of those relationships was seen as un-Chinese and worthy of rejection. This conflict would eventually play out in debates around Buddhism and Christianity when they were introduced to China; it would later be mirrored in family dynamics like Kenneth's. This Chinese identity therefore shaped a sense of belonging and identity around *liyi* rituals and values outside of religious beliefs and affiliations. Consequently, this historical discourse obviated the need for religions to serve these functions.

The views of Han Yu (768–824 CE), an influential scholar and official, best represent *liyi* Chinese identity. One of the most important figures in the history of Confucianism, Han Yu wrote the influential work *Essentials of the Moral Way*, which brought together key classical resources to answer the burning questions of his time.[33] In the context of the cosmopolitan, multinational Tang dynasty (618–907 CE), in which the Chinese (*hua*, 華) intermingled with the "barbarians" (*hu*, 胡), those questions included "Who are we?," "What makes us Chinese?," and "What sets us apart?" In this setting, Han Yu's *Essentials* crystallized the traditional self-understanding of a *liyi*-based Chinese identity.

Han Yu's moralized notion of *liyi* Chineseness turned on two key steps. The first was not to base Chineseness on a tribal or racial definition. That is, anybody could be Chinese regardless of descent. In support of this approach, *Essentials* refers to Confucius's own example. In deciding how to compile the histories of the Chinese central states, Confucius would count those who behaved in a civilized way as Chinese and those who behaved in an uncivilized way as barbarian. Thus, Chinese people are those who adopted Chinese behavioral standards of *li* and *yi*.

The second step established these Chinese behavioral standards as fundamentally moral. It canonized the "teachings of the former kings," that is, the Confucian classics, which depicted an idealized ancient civilization. The essence of that morality was the observance and practice of *yi*, proper social relations (*renlun*, 人倫). The seminal Confucian thinker Mencius (372–289 BCE) iterated these key relationships: "Between parent and child, there should be affection; between lord and subject, righteousness; between husband and wife, attention to their separate functions; between old and young, a proper order; and between friends, fidelity."[34] Under this vision of proper civilization, *liyi* relationships formed the foundation of life; thus, the correct maintenance of these human relationships determined one's morality and authentic Chinese identity. Because they involved concrete human relations, Confucian emphasis was on the actual practice of Chinese morality in the tangible world, not in relation to the supernatural.

With such a notion of Chinese identity, anything that interfered with the rightness of one's relationships according to Chinese standards was a threat to one's morals and Chineseness. Buddhism, with its call to otherworldly concerns, improper rituals, celibacy, and monastic life away from the family, fell into that category. As it gained ascendance in China during the Tang dynasty, its encounter with *liyi* Chinese identity gave rise to a vocal tradition of anti-Buddhist rhetoric based on its objections to the ways that Buddhism demanded un-Chinese conduct.

For example, Buddhism violated the right Chinese relationship between subject and superior. According to the Confucian tradition, every subject in the realm—including monks—owed loyalty (*zhong*, 忠) demonstrated through obedience to their ruler. Yet the behavior of Buddhist monastics as "sojourners beyond the limits" implied that monks were "not to be bound by Confucian doctrines of propriety, to whom the moral imperatives governing lord and subject are irrelevant."[35] This conflict erupted in court debates in which Confucians insisted that Buddhist monks prostrate themselves before the emperor like every other subject. One Confucian claimed that common Buddhist practices, such as calling temples by the term "palace," were in fact "reducing the Confucian code of social relationships to confusion" by inverting the subject-to-lord relationship.[36]

Likewise, from the 17th century onward, during the late Ming dynasty (1368–1644) and Qing dynasty (1644–1912), Christianity came under attack as another movement that threatened morals and the very core of *liyi* Chinese identity. The official Yang Guangxian (1597–1669) wrote passionately against Christianity because of its conflicts with the proper relationships between parent and child as well as between inferior and superior. In the work *I Could Not Do Otherwise* (*Budeyi*, 不得已) he wrote, "Jesus' mother, Mary, had a husband called Joseph. But they say that Jesus was not begotten by His father. Moreover, the people who take refuge in their religion are not permitted to present offerings to the ancestral tablets. This is no recognition of the relationship between father and son." He also critiqued Christianity for its disrespect of laws and authorities: "The Lord of Heaven, Jesus, was nailed to death because He broke His country's laws. This was no case of recognizing the relationship between ruler and subject."[37]

A Record of Facts to Ward off Heterodoxy (*Bixiejishi*, 辟邪紀實) was one particularly salacious anti-Christian tract, first produced in 1861 by "the most heartbroken man in the world." Though much of the tract's argumentation simply lewdly characterizes Christians, in some places it makes its appeals to the reader by implicitly invoking the notion of *liyi* Chinese identity. One section responds line by line to a fictionalized missionary named John who claimed that Chinese are depraved because they are nonbelievers:

> Let me ask: this evidence of human depravity, this sinfulness of the Chinese, does it consist in the moral obligations which we uphold, the Confucian teachings? Fortunate it is that the believers are few and the nonbelievers many! If [the Christians] were to get their way in China and draw us all into their evil fold, there would no longer be any place for our posterity.[38]

As this and other works show, Christianity faced opposition because it threatened the foundations of public morality and Chinese civilization itself.

Moralized Chineseness as defined by righteous relationships thus sets itself up in opposition to "religiosity" as exemplified by Buddhism and Christianity. Even as this understanding of Chineseness faced significant challenges in the modern era and, for Chinese Americans, in the process of migration to the United States, a distilled, familized Chineseness would nevertheless duplicate and continue the tension between "religiousness" and human relationships. An early Chinese American example was Wong Chin Foo.

Wong Chin Foo: A Late 19th-Century Chinese American Example

Though separated from America by centuries and continents, the three historical threads discussed are relevant to the Chinese American context, as is made evident in Wong Chin Foo's piece "Why Am I a Heathen?" As the first Chinese American to use the term "Chinese American," Wong was a fierce advocate for the early Chinese American community, in some ways a progenitor of the Asian American movement 70 years after his time. Having spent his education and his career in America, and being one of the first Chinese to adopt U.S. citizenship, he has been considered the "first Chinese American." In "Why Am I a Heathen?," Wong defends why he is not a Christian, explicitly using his Chinese identity to explain his choice. As a representative of one early, fully Chinese American experience, this piece gives clear expression to the historical roots we have described, in relevant dialogue with its American context.

While most of the piece is an attack on Christianity—as Wong understood it—rather than a defense of so-called heathenism, the lens through which he attacks is indicative of the *liyi* discourse employed by Chinese for moral boundaries, especially that of religious skepticism and righteous relations. For example, the difference between the demands of religious membership in the Western cultural context and the *liyi* pluralism in the Chinese context is evident in one section in which he derides Christian evangelism: "Unlike Christianity, 'our' Church is not eager for converts; but, like Free Masonry, we think our religious doctrine strong enough to attract the seekers after light and truth to offer themselves without urging, or proselytizing efforts."[39] Wong thus found it distasteful to seek out newcomers to "join" one's faith; instead, he suggested that the emphasis should be on the rational individual to find and practice the "light and truth."

Wong also reflected the skeptical tradition—in particular, the worldly emphasis encouraged by the early Confucian thinkers—in defending his so-called heathenism:

None of [the religions of China, i.e., Daoism and Buddhism] were rational enough to become the abiding faith of an intelligent people; but when we began to reason we succeeded in making society better and its government more protective and our great Reasoner, Confucius, reduced our various social and religious ideas into book form and so perpetuated them.[40]

He highlighted the virtues of reason, rationality, and religious skepticism over religious belief.

In criticizing Christianity, he hearkened to *liyi* Chineseness, particularly the importance of righteous relationships, especially between parent and child:

On the whole, the Christian way strikes us as decidedly an unnatural one; it is everyone for himself—parents and children even. Imagine my feelings, if my own son, whom

I loved better than my own life, for whom I had sacrificed all my comforts and luxury, should, through some selfish motive, go to law with me. . . . Is this a rare Christian case? Can it be charged against heathenism?[41]

In this critique of American individualism, Wong offered an example of filiality in how he sacrificed for his own child.

To be sure, Wong's story is not the story of every Chinese American; in fact, the same journal featured a rebuttal to his piece just one month later by Yan Phou Lee, another Chinese American, entitled "Why I Am *Not* a Heathen." Nevertheless, Wong's piece demonstrates how these historical roots shaped what it meant to be a nonreligious Chinese *American*. Furthermore, as a forebear of contemporary Chinese Americanness, Wong's identity itself makes the piece an important part of the story of Chinese American nonreligiousness.

Although the roots of Chinese Popular Religion and Confucianism run deep among Chinese Americans, the expressions and contours of these traditions have evolved and transformed over time and space. We turn to three critical factors shaping changes in Chinese traditions: state modernization, migration, and institutional market forces.

State Modernization and Chinese Religious Change

Modernization, the transition from an agrarian society to a modern one through industrialization, has widespread consequences for a society's political and cultural ways of life.[42] Through technological advancement and new modes of production, modernizing nations tend to see urbanization, social differentiation and rationalized organizations, increased social mobility, greater equality, and a push for public participation in sovereign nation-states. Likewise modernization effects great changes in the religious sphere. As the dynamics of industrialized capitalism unfold, sociologists theorize that societies will become increasingly secular in three aspects: decline in the number of religious adherents, functional differentiation of society, and the privatization of individual religiosity.[43] Chinese traditions, including Confucianism and Chinese Popular Religion, underwent these processes as well when China modernized in the 19th and 20th centuries. What stands out in China's religious change over this time period is the role of the government in its attempts to regulate, suppress, and use religion for modern nation-state building. Subsequently, religious and philosophical traditions in China had to reform, adapt, and readjust to survive.

By the end of the 19th century, Western powers and Japan had effectively colonized China as they carved out spheres of influence over different regions. In response to foreign imperialism, Chinese intellectuals outlined three different political strategies to restore national pride: (1) pro-traditionalism in rejecting Western ways and strengthening the country through cultural revival, (2) adopting Western technology to preserve the essence of Chinese civilization, and (3) antitraditionalism. As an example of the first movement, the Boxer Rebellion was led by a religious sect chanting incantations to Daoist and Buddhist spirits who wanted to revive the Qing Empire. They attacked Chinese Christian communities, martyred foreign missionaries, and eventually sieged Beijing's foreign legation district. Ultimately, the Boxer Rebellion was suppressed when an eight-nation force of 20,000 troops took control of Beijing and required China to pay war reparations for the next 39 years.

The second response to foreign imperialism was modernizing China through Western technology while maintaining state Confucianism. While the Boxer movement was gaining momentum in 1898, Emperor Guangxu initiated the Hundred Days of Reform. Confucian reformers, such as Kang Youwei (1858–1927), established changes to the examination system of the state bureaucracy and the education system. At the same time, Kang reinterpreted Confucian texts to make Confucianism less reactionary and viewed some of its classics as forgeries, showing how its teachings might be revised.[44] In this way, state modernization was coupled with the modernization of Confucianism. However, Empress Dowager Cixi engineered a coup d'état of Emperor Guangxu in 1898 and rescinded the reforms of the Hundred Days.

Following the overthrow of the Qing dynasty and the establishment of the Chinese Republic, both President Sun Yat-sen (1866–1925) and President Yuan Shikai (1859–1916) continued the approach of employing Confucianism to legitimize the state.[45] For example, President Yuan legislated a series of reforms at the local level to appropriate temples and their lands and use them for schools and government offices. These acts not only supported the modernizing reforms of local self-government and Western-style education and provided funding for the state, but they also sought to eradicate "superstitions" as outdated and feudal.[46] In Zhili, where he was first named viceroy, the number of temples fell from 432 in 1900 to only 116 in 1915. This reorganization of local power structures, in both discursive and political ways, clearly reflects secularization in the form of institutional religion's decline in civil society.

In contrast to the first two responses to imperialism, antitraditionalist Chinese intellectuals argued that the nation needed to adopt Western ways since its Confucian system was sick, corrupt, and useless. The May 4th movement was one such response to Western imperialism. Following World War I, the Treaty of Versailles gave German rights over Shandong province to

Japan. A student-led nationalist movement held demonstrations, called for Western science and democracy, and denounced Confucianism as a vestige of the past and a feudal ethical code. Its symbolic success, in which Chinese delegates refused to sign the Versailles Treaty, was a historic turning point, especially for the Chinese Communist Party. Uniting students, intellectuals, and the masses, it was a broad-based movement challenging both Chinese Confucian thinking and Western-style liberal democracy.

Overall during this period, Chinese popular religion waned among the urban and educated classes as the government adopted Western categories of religion to name popular religious activities as superstitious. During the Republican era, over half a million Chinese temples were removed under the slogan "Destroy temples to build schools."[47] Yet even as Confucian reformers aimed to rid the nation of popular religious practices deemed superstitious, they themselves failed to help modernize China or to even reform Confucianism itself. Consequently, the Chinese philosophy scholar Sor-Hoon Tan summarizes, "The dominance of Confucianism in Chinese culture cannot be taken for granted after the nineteenth century. . . . While some politicians enlisted Confucianism in the service of authoritarianism, and others argued for Confucian democracy, more people considered it irrelevant."[48]

Confucianism and Chinese Popular Religion faced even greater state opposition once the Communists took over in 1949. The Communist government mandated even stricter policies against religion when they adopted the Marxian notion that religion was the opiate of the people and that religious ideas were distorted, illusionary reflections of social reality. The sociologist Fenggang Yang observes that the state's "atheism-based regulation of religion" increasingly suppressed religion until it eventually banned all religion during the Cultural Revolution. In his biographical account about growing up in China, Yang notes that religion was eradicated in every public sphere: "While religious artifacts were smashed, religious buildings torn down or converted for other use, and religious clergy were forced to return to secular life, gods, spirits, and ghosts were exorcised out of the literature, movies, mass media and other publications."[49] Following the death of Mao, however, the Chinese Communist Party in 1982 reaffirmed religious tolerance and granted legal recognition to Buddhism, Daoism, Islam, Protestantism, and Christianity, but not to any other group.

Since that time, all kinds of religions have seen a strong upsurge, including the revival of temple and home activities constituting Chinese Popular Religion and the resurgence of Confucianism as a state-legitimizing, moral authority in the nation. Chinese Popular Religion, in fact, was no longer termed "feudal superstition" but instead called "folk beliefs."[50]

In response to modernization, and especially state policies to regulate religion, both Confucianism and Chinese Popular Religions have adapted over the past century. One example is New Confucianism, a school of thought that emerged after the May 4th movement's denunciation of Confucianism. In the 1958 document "Manifesto for a Reappraisal of Sinology and Reconstruction of Chinese Culture," leaders of the school privileged culture in the diagnosis to problems posed by Western modernity, such as the lack of value orientation in science. They asserted that the West should learn from China, specifically the "more all-encompassing wisdom" of Confucianism.

Operating largely overseas, the third generation of the New Confucians, as represented by Tu Wei-Ming (born 1940), downplayed the political role of Confucianism, as expressed by imperial state orthodoxy or by politicized Confucianism to support authoritarianism. Rather, he affirmed Chinese culture as essentially Confucian, as a way of life, guiding family, work ethics, and personal cultivation. His creative bridging of humanistic Confucianism to Enlightenment values reflect the attempt to make Confucianism universally applicable. Tu suggests that Confucianism offers a prescription to the pervasive ills of modernity: "A significant and captivating aspect of this alternative East Asian vision of modernity is that of the communal spirit. . . . In this particular connection what Japan and the Four Mini-Dragons symbolize is a less adversarial, less individualistic, and less self-interested but highly energized and fiercely competitive approach to modernization."[51] From being conceived as traditional, conservative, and supportive of authoritarian structures during the May 4th movement, new Confucianism clearly has reoriented the tradition toward a cultural essence envisioned to temper the ills of modernization.

Similarly, Chinese Popular Religion has seen a revival in China since 1979. The sociologists Fenggang Yang and Anning Hu reviewed surveys of China in 2007 and Taiwan in 2009 about three types of folk religion: communal, sectarian, and individual. Communal folk religion includes collective worship of local deities outside the home, such as the earth god, city god, and sea goddess, as well as ancestor venerations of clans. Sects are organized religious groups that work beyond local boundaries, such as Falun Gong (法輪功) *qi* practitioners and Yiguandao (一貫道), a large religious movement. Individual folk religion consists of magic practices such as fortunetelling, numerology, and *fengshui*. Overall, in Taiwan, with greater religious freedom, almost 88% of the surveyed engaged in practices of individual folk religion, and 85% belonged to communal folk religion temples. In contrast, 52% of those in China engaged in practices of individual folk religion, and 20% were adherents of communal folk religion, even though the Chinese government eradicated religion for decades. The authors conclude, "The persistence of folk religion in spite of political suppression cries out for new theoretical explanations."[52]

These two sociologists then examined the trajectories of individual folk practices in Taiwan from 1990 to 2009.[53] They found that adherence to communal folk religion and other practices of individual folk religion, such as amulet practices, have increased slightly. They attribute these changes to shifts in the Taiwanese state's regulation of religion and institutional religion's openness to individual practices. However, the percentage of those with a positive attitude toward ancestor veneration has declined. This trend provides evidence of traditional secularization theory, that Taiwanese society is becoming more "disenchanted" as it modernizes and individuals adopt scientific-rational worldviews. This shift signals changing beliefs about ancestral spirits and the waning of home-based, family ritual.

Migration and Religious Change

Migration, especially across national borders, is a disruptive event that can require changes in individuals' and groups' worldviews, spiritual needs, and religious participation. Because the process uproots immigrants from their homeland moorings, it can create a crisis of meaning so that immigration is a "theologizing experience."[54] Furthermore, as immigrants face disruptions in a new land, they often turn to their religious institutions for social belonging, support for adaptation, protection from discrimination, and preservation of culture.[55] Consequently, some Asians arriving in the United States experience religious revivals, convert at high rates, and engage more in religious activities.[56] For example, Filipino Catholics and Korean Protestants attend church more regularly than any other ethnic group in the United States.[57] On the other hand, the religious landscape in the United States is very different from that of Asia, and access to Chinese religious institutions and professionals is less available. In fact, a study of Canadian immigrants, including Vietnamese but not Chinese, indicated that religious participation declines across ethnicities and religious affiliations.[58] Beyond participation in religious congregations, individual spiritual practices such as prayer and observance of religious holidays may also be affected by the migration process.[59] Even if the communal participation and individual practices are retained, however, the meanings of these rituals for the individuals—especially across generations—might shift in their new contexts.[60]

The sociologist Carolyn Chen, who examined Taiwanese immigrants to the United States, observed that the decline in their practice of Chinese Popular Religion was due to two key factors: separation from extended family and lack of access to temples. Since they no longer lived with their elderly parents or other family members, they were much less likely to maintain household traditions practiced together. She explains:

> Given the importance of family to Taiwanese religious practice, separation from the extended family significantly reduced the religiosity of Taiwanese immigrants in the United States. Half of the respondents claimed that after immigrating to the United States they did not observe any religious practices, even ancestral veneration. . . . None of the respondents kept an ancestral altar in their homes.[61]

In Taiwan, temples and shrines could be found in every neighborhood, but outside Chinese ethnic enclaves these religious spaces were not available. Consequently, Chen's respondents found temple participation to be inconvenient, and thus they stopped attending.

Although the immigrant generation may be able to retain their beliefs and practices, the second generation often adopt new religious patterns as they acculturate to the United States. In particular, the process of racialization heightens Asian Americans' awareness of their racial status, and the discourse of multiculturalism encourages pride in their ethnic heritage. These identities of race and ethnicity intersect with an individual's spiritual background so that new combinations of religious identities emerge.[62] For example, Chinese Americans are often attracted to pan-Asian American Christian congregations, where they may identify as Asian Americans and find the social comfort and pastoral care more suited to their lifestyle affinities.[63]

Acculturating to the American context, second-generation Chinese Americans tend to lose key components of their cultural heritage, including knowledge of customs and traditions, as well as the ability to speak Chinese fluently. Nevertheless, they retain ethnic distinction by taking pride in what the sociologist Nazli Kibria terms "distilled ethnicity." She proposes that this group adopts a sense of ethnicity in "which ethnic culture and identity are pared of nonessential components down to their core essence." In interviewing dozens of Chinese Americans, she found that the "core essence" of being Chinese boiled down to three elements: "an emphasis on family, work, and education."[64] Although these traits may reflect the deep traditions of Confucianism and Chinese Popular Religion, in the U.S. they become generalized values.

These values of distilled Chinese ethnicity are selectively retained, Kibria submits, because they are compatible with the mainstream, middle-class American lifestyle and sensibility. Even as they allowed for easy social integration into the middle class, these values enabled Chinese Americans to maintain a group self-consciousness and pride in their ancestral origins.

These traits are also advantageous for economic mobility in the U.S. and, as such, easily retained.

The migration process from Asia to the U.S., along with generational adaptation, shapes religious change among Chinese Americans. Outside an Asian religious landscape that promotes both individual and communal spiritual practices, as well as a cultural context that reinforces Confucian values, Chinese in the U.S. adapt their religiosity to fit their new environment. Consequently, just as their religious beliefs and values are distilled, their spiritual commitments and practices alter to fit the American religious landscape. Nonetheless, we assert that Chinese Americans continue to hold to the *liyi* tradition of their heritage, albeit in a different form.

The Religious Marketplace and Religious Change

As indicated by Carolyn Chen's observations about the declining practice of Chinese Popular Religion in the United States, the lack of local temples and neighborhood shrines discourages Chinese Americans from participating more often. This argument corresponds to the supply-side theory of religious change, that the capacity of religious organizations to provide spiritual services and promulgate religious teachings is a significant variable in religious change.[65] In an open market, religious groups flourish if they offer products attractive to the consumers, and so religious participation is high.[66] However, "government regulation can affect producers' incentives, consumers' options, and the aggregate equilibrium."[67] How well Confucianism and Chinese Popular Religion fare in the United States depends on how well their institutions and entrepreneurs can market their spiritual teachings and services.

In recent decades Confucianism, Chinese Popular Religion, and other religious groups have seen the growth of religion in China. According to sociologist Yang, a triple religious market exists in China that has created a shortage of suppliers and pent-up demand. While some religions are official (the red market) and others are banned (the black market), most religious activities are ambiguously regulated under a large gray market.[68] As a result of the lack of religious supply, the large market of spiritual seekers in China has spurred pluralization, that is, an increase in the varieties of religious practice.

In the United States, however, the state regulates religion much less and the religious marketplace is dominated by a range of established Christian denominations and institutions. These organizations, especially evangelical ones, are more successful than Buddhist organizations at reaching out and meeting the needs of Asian American spiritual consumers.[69] In addition, with specialized experience, training, and staffing oriented toward young adults and youth, Christian churches and nonprofits are better equipped to serve the Asian American second generation.[70] Over time, generations of Chinese Americans who identify religiously are more likely to be Christian than Buddhist or other religions: 21.0% of the Chinese immigrants are Christian, compared to 23.4% of the second generation and 35.9% of the third generation.[71]

While Chinese American churches and temples are staffed with professionally trained clergy and may be supported by organizational bureaucracies, Confucianism and Chinese Popular Religion have much less institutional structure and backing. In addition Christian, privilege in the United States makes it much easier for individuals to adhere to Christianity than to minority religions.[72] In the religious marketplace of the United States, then, Confucianism and Chinese Popular Religion are disadvantaged in their ability to maintain their share of Chinese American spiritual consumers.

CONCLUSION

Wong Chin Foo wrote over a century ago, "We bring up our children to be our second selves in every sense of the word. . . . It is our motto that if we cannot bring up our children to think and do for us when we are old as we did for them when they were young, it is better not to rear them at all."[73] The moral code of family responsibility remains the main element of the ethical tradition of Chinese American religious nones. Chinese American familism has developed over time from its roots in Chinese Popular Religion and Confucianism. From these twin sources, Chinese are more likely to identify as nonreligious because they are religiously pluralistic and skeptical of the supernatural. Furthermore, they find identity in Chineseness and family more so than they do through traditional religious categories. Rather than assuming that Chinese individuals adopt a particular belief or church for religious affiliation, one might expect Chinese to hold both a plurality of beliefs and skepticism.

Chinese Popular Religion and Confucianism have also transformed in the previous centuries, and Chinese Americans find themselves in a different context to apply these teachings and practices. How they transmit their values and rituals from their Chinese heritage is the subject of the next chapter.

CHAPTER 3

⌒⌒⌒

Transmission

Chinese American Liyi Socialization

INTRODUCTION

I remember in the morning, the first thing in the morning, my mom would come in and give me a red envelope. And she made sure I put it in my pocket and kept it with me all day. I had to wear red, too!

—Sharon Chung, nonprofit director from Newton, Massachusetts

When we're in Taiwan, I think during *saomujie* (掃墓節 , Tomb-Sweeping Day), we would go to my dad's side, my grandpa's grave, and clean it and burn paper money. Actually, my parents and myself, we view it more as tradition and ritual. We don't really believe the food will somehow pass into another realm. I think maybe my grandma kinda' believes that.

I think it's just a ritual thing. I mean, the funny thing being I never knew my ancestors, but it must have been good enough that I'm alive, so I guess it's paying respect to the older generation and then I think it makes my grandma happy.

—Jonathan Hu, shoe salesperson from Albany, California

Sharon's mother made her wear red and carry a red envelope all day during Chinese New Year. She was insistent, so that Sharon might have prosperity throughout the upcoming year. Her mother, a member of the Falun Gong sect, also devoutly lit incense to their ancestors and prayed for protection. According to her mother, these rituals are efficacious in bringing about luck and health. In contrast, Jonathan's family engaged in the very same rituals during a memorial festival, but neither his mother nor his father "really believe." They practice these customs out of tradition, as a sign of their respect for their ancestors.

As these examples illustrate, this chapter details two themes about the *liyi* socialization of second-generation Chinese Americans. First, in inculcating their most significant rituals and their highest values, Chinese American families adhere to practices of Chinese Popular Religion and Confucianism, albeit in varying degrees of frequency and intensity. Nine out of 10 respondents (87.9%) described how their parents celebrated the Chinese New Year, 8 out of 10 (79.3%) venerated their deceased ancestors, and 77.5% understood the metaphysics of earth in the form of *fengshui*. While each of these individuals identified as religious nones, they did grow up with elements of Chinese Popular Religion and Confucianism, whether or not they acknowledged it. From these traditions they inherited the roots of Chinese American familism. Second, their educational and class backgrounds shaped how their parents viewed these traditions—either as efficacious in affecting spiritual forces, as ethnic customs representing Chinese heritage, or as inculcating moral virtues. These differing worldviews and how they passed them down in turn affected their own children's varied affiliations as religious nones.

This chapter first examines the Pew Research Center's findings of differences in educational level that shape what Chinese Americans believe and practice. It then compares how the working-class and professional families from our sample approach the practices of Chinese Popular Religion and Confucianism, especially in terms of ancestor veneration, Chinese New Year, and other "efficacious" practices around luck.

THE IMPACT OF EDUCATION ON CHINESE AMERICAN SPIRITUAL BELIEFS AND PRACTICES

Overall, the less education Chinese Americans had, the more likely they were to believe in and adhere to Chinese Popular Religion. Those with more education were more likely to adopt Western beliefs in God. According to the Pew Research Center, Chinese Americans who did not complete high school were much more apt to assume the presence of *qi* and ancestral spirits in this world. On one hand, about 65.0% of those whose highest education was a high school degree believed in *qi*, and over 50.0% of them believed in ancestral spirits. On the other hand, only about 30.0% of those with college degrees believed in *qi* and 40.0% believed in ancestral spirits.

Those with a high school degree or less also celebrated Chinese New Year and maintained a home shrine at higher rates. This group was 2.7 times

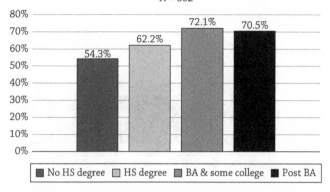

Figure 3.1 Belief in God by Educational Attainment

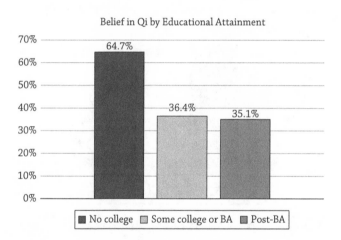

Figure 3.2 Belief in *Qi* by Educational Attainment

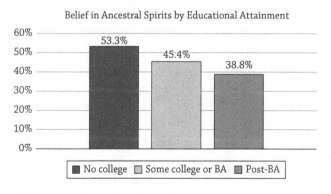

Figure 3.3 Belief in Ancestral Spirits by Educational Attainment

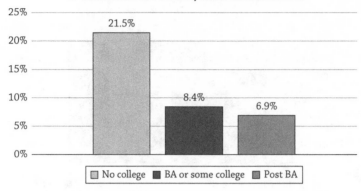

Figure 3.4 Maintains Home Shrine by Educational Attainment

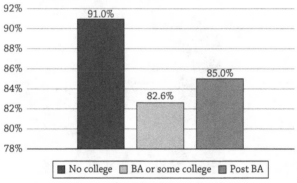

Figure 3.5 Celebrates Chinese New Year by Educational Attainment

more likely than the college-educated group to keep a shrine and also celebrated Chinese New Year slightly more often.

IMMIGRANT PARENTS' EDUCATIONAL AND WORK BACKGROUNDS

As indicated by the national survey, the backgrounds of immigrant parents heavily shaped their subsequent settlement in the United States and how they developed their own worldviews. Our sample of households revealed similar patterns regarding the practice of Chinese Popular Religion and Confucianism. The working-class parents migrated through family reunification visas. They thus generally settled through family linkages in urban areas with higher concentrations of Chinese Americans. Coming from more rural and less educated upbringings, they subscribed to practices of Chinese Popular Religion and could maintain these traditions with the institutional support of local Chinese American communities. In contrast, the professional parents had advanced degrees in engineering or science that led them to careers throughout the United States. Their children were more likely to be raised in suburbs, outside of Chinese American ethnic enclaves. These immigrants were much more likely to hold to scientific worldviews to explain reality and employ Confucianism as a secular ethic in terms of relating to others. This section compares the two groups in terms of education, occupation, and residence to illustrate the different contexts where professional and working-class families live and how they practice Chinese Popular Religion.

Working-Class Households

Working-class immigrant parents were much less educated than the professional parents and thus had blue-collar and service-sector occupations. Eleven of the 16 working-class households had parents who did not complete high school. As a result, they worked as cooks, garment workers, and service industry workers. Many lived with extended family in the same household in low-income or working-class neighborhoods.

Working-class parents grew up in rural areas, such as the Taishan (Cantonese: *Toisan*) region in Guangdong, and met through friends. Kenneth Lam's parents grew up farming and never finished high school. They immigrated through family connections, and his mother worked at the family restaurant: "[My parents' families] are both farmers in Taishan. My dad only went up to fourth grade, something like that, and my mom got to about the same—fourth or fifth grade. They met because my grandparents knew each other and they got introduced." Lacking English and job skills, they had to take jobs in the secondary labor market with inflexible schedules. These jobs sorely affected family life, according to Kenneth:

> Growing up, I had my parents almost never there because of their restaurant. My uncle used to pick up my mom at ten o'clock in the morning and she'd come home at eleven o'clock at night. So I'd see my mom only at breakfast.
>
> My dad worked at a bakery, where they made danishes. He had random shifts, sometimes early morning—four, five in the morning. He also used to gamble a lot so I would barely see him when he came home late. They never had time to raise us, spend time with us in the American way of life.

Since his parents were usually at work, his grandparents raised Kenneth, and he learned to speak Cantonese and Taishanese. He seemed to resent his parents' work schedules, since they deprived him of the American way of life, where families spend time together.

Similarly, Steph Woo's parents grew up in Taishan and had an arranged marriage. They grew up in a village and went to work at the restaurant of a second cousin in Maryland:

> [My parents] grew up in the Taishan area in China. I don't think they knew each other growing up. My father was a friend of my mother's brother and had sort of an arranged marriage, I think. I know my dad didn't have much education. My mom did a little better. I guess she tested higher and she was supposed to have more schooling. But I guess at a certain point, my mother's family didn't have enough money to send her to get advanced schooling so she stopped. She lived at home and she helped my grandmother with sewing. She would take in sewing work for certain people in the neighborhood. And I know they raised chickens and things like that.

Like many of the other working-class families, Steph's parents immigrated through a family reunification visa and went to work in a small, family-owned business. Because of this extended family arrangement, where grandparents would help to maintain Chinese customs, the working-class households more easily kept up with practices and traditions of Chinese Popular Religion than the professional families.

Professional Households

In contrast to the educational background of working-class parents, over 40% of the professional households had at least one parent with a graduate degree. Even more striking, almost every father was either a scientist or an engineer. While this sample is not fully representative of professional Chinese Americans, it does reflect a general demographic trend: professional immigrants from China or Taiwan are much more likely to have graduate degrees in science, technology, engineering, or math, which shapes their scientific worldviews. These families settled throughout the United States, primarily in suburbs and often near university towns, where their children had a middle-class upbringing in predominantly white neighborhoods.

As an example, Peter Hsieh, who grew up in Naperville, Illinois, describes his parents' educational backgrounds that helped them obtain positions in major corporations. Their migration story reflects how they pursued higher education in the United States and then were able to obtain professional careers:

My parents came here for grad school where my dad got a C.S. degree . . . a computer science degree. [Although he got a B.A. in English literature in Taiwan, he] had to put bread on the table. And then he started working at Lucent, or back then it was AT&T Bell Labs. And my mom went to University of Chicago and she got a food science degree. She started working at Swift, which became part of Kraft. [She does] user testing and consumer product testing.

With these high-paying occupations, they settled in a suburb that was rated one of the best places in the nation to raise a family. According to that city's website, it has the best public library in the nation and excellent schools.[1]

Cheryl Teng's parents, too, were highly educated and met at the University of Illinois, Champagne-Urbana. In fact, even her grandparents were very well educated:

My mom was born in Taiwan, and then went to Japan for her master's. She came to America for her Ph.D. My dad was born in Taiwan, and he moved to Hawaii when he was twelve or thirteen. His parents brought him over, when his mother taught Chinese at the University of Hawaii and got a job. Then my dad went to the University of Illinois for his Ph.D. and that's where my parents met. . . . My dad works for Chevron as a chemist; my mom works for the U.S. Department of Agriculture in production.

They settled in Berkeley, California, another university town known for its good schools. Since her parents were a scientist and an engineer and her family lived in an educated environment, she and her siblings developed similar worldviews.

With these divergent educational and professional backgrounds, Chinese immigrant parents understood and adhered to Chinese Popular Religion in contrasting manners. They viewed their traditions on a continuum: one end was the belief in the spirit world and in rituals as efficacious in relating to supernatural forces; the other end viewed these traditions as secularized cultural customs that were symbolic of the values Chinese cherished. These values could be Confucian ethics of filiality, loyalty, and reciprocity, or they could simply be cultural pride in one's Chinese heritage.

Although respondents observed their parents practicing these traditions, and they themselves may have occasionally participated in them, second-generation Chinese Americans had fairly superficial understandings of most of these conventions. They recognized that the customs aimed to bring good luck, but how or why they were conducted in a certain fashion was generally unknown. Nevertheless, some continued to retain these customs as ways to honor their family and, for a few, to relate to the supernatural.

How much they then retained and continued to practice was a function of how their own parents engaged with Chinese Popular Religion.

IMMIGRANT PARENTS AND PRACTICES OF CHINESE POPULAR RELIGION

In general, working-class parents, especially the women, maintained the beliefs and practices of Chinese Popular Religion and were more devout in their adherence to them. The professional parents, because they come from more scientific and educated backgrounds, were more likely to hold to a secularized, rational worldview. The men from this background were particularly atheistic. Thus, while all of the families engaged in some practices of Chinese Popular Religion, the meanings of the rituals to the immigrant parents and the extent to which they practiced them differed widely.

Working-Class Households and the Spirit World

The working-class families engaged in more practices and taboos of Chinese Popular Religion than did the professional families, and they also took these practices more seriously. They placed demands on their children to follow them and more devoutly and regularly engaged in religious rituals. As a result, their children were more open to the possibility of interacting with the spiritual world. They recognized that science itself did not hold all the answers to life's questions and concerns, and that spiritual forces operated in this world.

First and foremost, working-class parents would take time to revere their ancestors at home shrines and other sites. For those following Chinese Popular Religion, this practice is efficacious in providing for the ancestral spirits in the afterlife. Hailing from the Taishan area in Guangdong province, Michael Chen's father worked as a cook at a Chinese restaurant, and his mother, also from Taishan, was a nanny. He grew up in San Francisco, and he recalled the regular family acts of devotion at their home shrine and at the cemetery where his grandparents were buried:

> We had an ancestral altar downstairs and a Guanyin [Buddhist bodhisattva of mercy] separate altar. We would have cemetery days—you know, like offering days—when we would burn money, ghost money. What I remember I had to do was to put up tangerines and then a set of tables. [My mother] gave me the easy stuff because I'm the youngest.

The presence and practice of Chinese Popular Religion in the home made that spiritual reality more salient for working-class children like Michael.

Julia Tom, who grew up on the San Francisco peninsula, where her father from Taiwan operated printing presses, often witnessed her parents offer incense, food, and paper money at funerals. She explained the custom of burning fake paper money and other counterfeit objects for the deceased:

> Basically, it does feel like you're giving them something to have in the afterlife, so they have money. You can even go to the store and buy stuff like a car with a driver, a house. And then you can buy a sushi; it's like cardboard sushi! There's a whole business out of it. And part of it is kinda' fun.

Her parents have a home shrine for her grandmother, who had lived with them and helped to raise Julia. Whenever Julia returns to visit, she makes a prayer and offers gifts to her grandmother at the shrine.

Julia observed that the actual practice of placing offerings is her family's way of respecting, communicating, and making time for her grandmother. All the family participated, including Julia: "We do literally offer—we put out fruits and stuff. We place it out to her, and I guess for the incense, it's almost like offering her my time. I came home and I spent time with her and had a conversation. . . . So it's like our time together." Julia's family makes offerings and speaks with her grandmother because they assume she is actually present. Besides ancestor veneration, Julia also remembered visits to Taiwan, where her family would appease ghosts by throwing red envelopes over bridges.

Not only did Julia's family make offerings to spirits, but they also sought to manipulate spiritual forces of Chinese Popular Religion: fortune, luck, and qi. She observed how her parents avoided specific numbers since fate and luck operate to affect one's destiny. For example, they coded their security alarm with lucky numbers: "They were [into lucky numbers]. Their shop is closed now, but before, the password to their alarm system would be good luck numbers. I guess they kind of, maybe planted the seed [for me to believe in lucky numbers]." She went on to explain her parents' Chinese concept of manipulating luck:

> Let's say in this world, there's good luck floating around. If you try to bring that good luck into your life with numbers or with actions, then maybe you'll be one of those people to bump into that and to get it. Whereas other people may fall into a different route. It's kind of a star thing. [God or Heaven] is not taking a human form, but something is out there, some kind of energy that's guiding things one way or the other.

Her parents, who she says are not very religious, nonetheless went to the extent of picking lucky numbers so that they would be more likely to "bump into" good luck.

Another example of this Chinese assumption that one can increase luck is the use of auspicious dates. As a homemaker in Sacramento, California, the Hong Kong–born mother of Larry So raised her children by devotedly following the Chinese almanac. This book helps to identify auspicious dates for the planning of events. Larry reported that he even changed his wedding date to obey her wish for an appropriate date:

> My mom is big on the fortune book—the almanac that predicts certain days to move into new house, only do this for a healthy baby. My mom was big on it, but I didn't believe in it. But it gets ingrained in your head. [My mother] doesn't like the number four. Funny enough, I set the date [for my wedding] and she said I can't do that date. My dad doesn't believe it, but my dad was taking so much grief that he had to pay to change my wedding date. Just a week's difference cost about one-seventy-five to two hundred dollars!

Larry's mother was so concerned to get a proper wedding date that she nagged her husband to pay extra for another date. Her conscientiousness about lucky numbers and dates came to affect Larry, who became "ingrained" with its practice even though he insists he is an atheist.

Just as Larry's family went to great lengths to follow principles of Chinese numerology, Laura Chan's parents made sure she followed good *fengshui* principles whenever she moved. Having migrated from Taishan and worked as a cook and seamstress, they were "big believers" in *fengshui*, according to Laura. She explained that because her home in Quincy was at the end of a street, her parents replaced some panels at the front of the house with mirrors to reflect back bad energy. In addition, since a neighbor's home overlooked her brother's, they positioned two stone guardian lions at his driveway to offset the negative energy.[2] The family also positioned beds away from mirrors, doorways, and windows. Laura said her mother told her to move to a different apartment that was located in a better position:

> They would tell me [to follow *fengshui*] whenever I moved. When I moved to San Francisco, I lived in the south building, which is higher than the north building. I had an option to live in the north building. My parents wanted me to live in the higher building so nothing higher was pressing on you or competing. You never want to be lower or you don't want anything overshadowing you.

Though her family was on a limited income, they paid to arrange their homes correctly.

The presence of spiritual beings, the efficacy of particular religious practices, and the role of supernatural forces are most clearly highlighted during Chinese festival seasons, such as Chinese New Year and the

Mid-Autumn Festival. The working class celebrated Chinese New Year in a more elaborate fashion than the professional families and rigorously maintained more taboos. As explained, the working-class immigrant parents took great pains to celebrate these *liyi* traditions, particularly in regard to (1) house preparations, (2) dishes with meaning, (3) red envelope blessings for good luck, and (4) taboo prohibitions to avoid bad luck.

Working-Class Households and Chinese New Year

For the upcoming year, Chinese prepare their home and give it a thorough cleaning to sweep away bad luck. No sweeping is done during the New Year festivities, lest good luck is swept away. Decorations, in the forms of wall hangings, flowers, and food displays, have the power to bring blessing and luck. Red posters with couplets are posted around the front doorway to ward off evil spirits. One couplet reads, "Dragon and phoenix bring the prosperity; Peach and apricot blossoms welcome the spring; Blessing on the Land." Households place oranges, signifying abundance, and pomelos, symbolizing family unity, in pyramids on rice containers or tabletops. Potted shrubs and flowers, such as peach blossoms, enliven households and are believed to bring longevity. Families often place red envelopes in plants and fruit displays to bring prosperity for the year.

Sharon Chung's parents migrated from Africa to join their family, and her father opened a martial arts studio in their apartment in Boston's Chinatown. Even though both her parents grew up on that continent, they still adhered to many customs from Guangdong province. Her family made a special point of decorating the house to welcome in the New Year:

> We left lights on that night, as the New Year was coming. And on the front door we would make sure we would hang prosperity things up. That way, the good fortune would find its way to the house. You would leave the light on to show that you want to attract attention. Since it's the New Year, you want the good spirits to come into the house.[3]

After the house was prepared, her extended family would gather on New Year's Eve for a meal with the "requisite foods."

The New Year's Eve reunion meal often consists of "dishes with meaning." Each dish, based on a homonym or its appearance, represents a blessing for the New Year. Dumplings look like Chinese silver ingots, so the more one eats, the more wealth one can receive. The word for "fish" sounds the same as the word for "surplus," so Chinese prepare whole fish for the dinner. They often leave some of the fish uneaten to symbolize this surplus. *Niangao* (年糕), a glutinous rice cake, sounds like "elevating year by year." This dish is eaten so that the family can improve their lot in life. A special Buddhist vegetarian dish has either 10 or 18 ingredients, both lucky numbers. Also known as Buddha's Delight, it includes as one of its ingredients *facai* or *fat choy* (髮菜, a vegetable that looks like black hair), which sounds like "strike it rich" (發財). It is pronounced similarly to the words in the New Year greeting *Gongxi facai* or *Gung hei faat coi* (恭喜發財). Other holidays have their special foods, such as mooncakes for the Mid-Autumn Festival and *tongyuan* (湯圓, glutinous rice balls) for Winter Solstice, dishes that symbolize completeness and reunion, respectively.

Most working-class families ate the same requisite foods for Chinese New Year since each dish had meaning. For example, Laura said, "My parents are Buddhist, so they are really traditional. They had specific days where you can't eat meat, where they'd have veggie days." She described the New Year meal: "I don't know what it's called, but we always had these round taro-like thingies.[4] They'd have these white and round pieces. And we'd always have the steamed chicken,[5] and these noodles that looked like hair. It was brown."[6] Because her family owned a restaurant, they would eat together for their New Year meal after work. This meal was so important that the parents woke up their children to join them for dinner at 2 a.m. They did this so regularly that Laura thought the Chinese tradition was to wake up at 2 a.m. for the New Year.

Visiting and honoring family, as symbolized by the gifting of *hongbao* (紅包, red envelopes), is the most mentioned New Year ritual among our respondents. Respondents recall the New Year as the most important time of the year, as they had reunion meals with family members. In the two weeks of the holiday, Chinese visit the households of other family members and exchange gifts and red envelopes. Red is the color for energy, happiness, and good luck, so the envelope is as important as the money inside. One version of its origin is that, as an answer to a couple's prayers, fairies disguised as coins shone brightly to protect their baby and scared off a demon. News spread of this event, and thereafter coins were placed under children's pillows at night during the New Year. Now, crisp new bills are given to mark the New Year and to wish material blessings on the younger generation.

Grace Chu stated that Chinese New Year was her most vivid memory from her childhood. Her parents both worked in garment factories when they migrated from the Guangdong countryside to reunite with other family in Daly City, just outside of San Francisco. Her father did not complete elementary school, but her mother was able to graduate from high school. She regularly visited her mother's factory in San Francisco's Chinatown, where everyone celebrated the traditions: "I remember around Chinese New Year's was the best. Because there were so many old Chinese ladies [at the garment factory], my mom made a little pouch for me to collect red envelopes!" Within this ethnic enclave, she was immersed in Chinese Popular Religion and the blessings of red envelopes.

Common taboos to be avoided at New Year's celebrations include cutting or washing hair (washing away luck); wearing old clothes or black and white clothes (symbolizing death); using knives or scissors (cutting one's luck); lending or borrowing money (bringing debt); and taking medicine (inviting sickness). In general, avoiding these taboos prevents bad luck in the form of sickness, poor relationships, and financial hardship.

Since her family was so connected to ethnic networks of family and coworkers, Grace was better able to explain the New Year rituals than most of our interviewees. She described the traditions her family kept in order to bring about an auspicious new year:

> My mom and my grandma from my dad's side were really big on the tradition: [we had to get] new shoes, a new haircut, new bed sheets. Clean the entire house. I know cleaning is a fresh start to the year, and I know cutting off your hair is like cutting off the old ends like the past. Pretty much you want to have a fresh everything and tie up all loose ends before that day; everything on that day will reflect the New Year.

Furthermore, her household made sure to avoid taboos that might lead to bad luck. Grace described an accident that occurred during the New Year: "They also believed in omens. I remember one Chinese New Year, a handle broke off of something, like a ladle. My mom freaked out! She just thought it was a sign, and she's still like that. I laugh at her and she just says, 'One day, you'll see!'"

Thus, working-class families hosted a more ritualized (*li*) environment with regular devotions, holy spaces, and special times when key spiritual practices are followed. They created a greater "plausibility structure" for the existence of gods, ancestral spirits, and ghosts.[7]

In sum, the working-class families in this study were devout practitioners of many aspects of the *li* of Chinese Popular Religion. Their daily lives were infused with the presence of gods, spirits, and ancestors who needed to be placated and supported. The regular rituals they conducted, such as ancestor veneration, aimed to be efficacious in communicating with and appeasing these spiritual beings. While the immigrant parents worked hard for what they earned, they also recognized that their lives were governed by supernatural forces, such as fate, luck, and *qi*. They therefore went to great lengths to enhance their luck and to balance life energy. At certain times of the year, especially during the Chinese New Year, these traditions required devout adherence in order to bring good fortune, health, and prosperity to the families.

Professional Households and the Spirit World

Similar to the working-class parents, the professional parents performed rituals of Chinese Popular Religion, especially ancestor veneration and Chinese New Year celebrations. However, they did so as customs to instill virtue or to maintain tradition, rather than to serve as spiritual acts of efficacy. In these cases, they may be termed "culturally religious" in that they practice religious traditions but do so without believing in their supernatural effectiveness.[8] They are like those who call themselves Christians and celebrate Christmas but do so only out of custom instead of belief that Jesus, the son of God, came to earth to save the world. These professional parents were able to reconcile their secular, scientific worldviews with their ethnic Chinese practices by interpreting the traditions as symbolic, cultural acts. These acts both teach and embody what Chinese Americans consider righteous (*yi*), especially in terms of their key relationships.

These parents venerated their ancestors and visited the gravesites of relatives, but did so with a Confucian approach to memorialize the deceased and to pay respect to their family. When their children observe that certain customs fade, they also learn that these practices are merely cultural obligations and not necessarily efficacious spiritual acts. Peter Hsieh, whose parents were born in the People's Republic of China and then moved from Taiwan, explained their reasons for the bow, or *baibai*:

> If they do [ancestor rituals], it's usually because of other family members; I don't think they'd ever do it of their own volition, but mostly for appearances. Like we'd go visit graves and do that because my aunt or uncle would say we have to do this. We *have* to go respect our ancestors.

Knowing that his parents did not willingly visit the graves in order to feed the spirits but did so anyway, Peter also learned that these acts are compulsory in order to save face and to keep up appearances.

Celia Hsiao discussed how her parents, college-educated professionals from Taiwan, did not maintain as many Chinese customs as her grandparents did. They lived in San Francisco where observing Chinese Popular Religion, such as visits to the temple or consulting *fengshui* experts, is made easy with the presence of relatively strong religious institutions. However, her parents—an engineer and a nurse—decided not to practice them: "We did not do many rituals. My dad would tell me stories of rituals he used to do. But he didn't have us do it because he's pragmatic, not superstitious. He doesn't dismiss them but he doesn't need to perform them." She observes that her family acculturated to a Western perspective that is scientific and rational, not "superstitious."

Just as ancestral rituals were conducted for tradition and appearance, some professional families practiced *fengshui* for "practical purposes." Jonathan Hu, whose father obtained a Ph.D. in orthodontics and whose mother graduated with an M.B.A., grew up in Albany, California, near U.C. Berkeley. He was able to explain why the family's furnishings were arranged according to *fengshui*. He first cited the spiritual rationale that his mother taught him:

> I think they believe in the practical aspect of *fengshui*. It makes your house a little bit nicer. You're not supposed to have a mirror in front of your bed because according to the spiritual part of *fengshui* that my mom told me, it's because your soul will wake up at night. And then you'll wander around and the mirror will confuse it.

Then he explained his mother's "practical" use of *fengshui*:

> But I don't think they actually believe it. It's more like when you wake up and see yourself in the reflection, you might scare yourself. That's what I mean [by] more practical side. I think it's more like, "It makes your house looks nice!" Not, "Oh my God, we're going to disturb the balance of the universe or something!"

His parents also made him aware of Chinese numerology, but they don't "really, really believe" in it.

Professional Households and Chinese New Year

The celebration of the Chinese New Year by professional families contrasts with that of working-class families. Professional parents tend to view it as a cultural holiday, not a religious one. For instance, Scott Lai's parents saw Chinese New Year as an ethnic festival and a time for reunions and socializing. After obtaining a graduate degree in mechanical engineering, his father settled the family in Columbus, Ohio. They had large get-togethers and parties with other Chinese American families in the area during the holiday, and Scott said his mother would cook traditional foods. He understood the meaning of some dishes: "It's kind of hard to list everything [we did for Chinese New Year's]. There's lots of red envelopes, and there's tons of food. We do the whole fish, but we only eat half the fish because it represents your prosperity. And it has to be a whole fish." However, the family didn't eat these foods for luck, but to maintain customs. They were explained to him as "traditional" foods that reflect his Chinese heritage: "My mom would cook traditional foods. I couldn't name them all, if you asked me now. And then we would have to observe a lot of different things about a couple particular dishes, that I was told were generally Chinese customs. They could've been family customs, I don't know."

Thus, Chinese parents with scientific backgrounds or with high educational attainment had very different perspectives on Chinese Popular Religion and its rituals. They lit incense and made offerings to their ancestors and dead relatives, not to provide for their souls in the spiritual realm but primarily to pay their respects and gratitude for what the ancestors had done for them and future generations. Visiting gravesites and celebrating holidays were not opportunities to appease spirits or invite luck, but were ethnic customs to affirm their Chinese heritage. Chinese New Year, then, became a secular holiday for family reunions, socializing with co-ethnics, and festive traditions.

Since these parents saw the traditions of Chinese Popular Religion and Confucianism as ethnic customs and not necessarily efficacious spiritual practices, the rituals were optional and selectively maintained. Usually the most fun and celebratory aspects of Chinese Popular Religion, such as eating dishes with meaning and giving *hongbao*, were maintained. Other traditions that were practical and decorative, such as *fengshui* arrangements, were also more likely to be maintained. However, onerous aspects of Chinese Popular Religion, such as visiting gravesites that were far away or not washing one's hair, were easily discarded. Of all the elements in the Chinese religious repertoire, the Confucian ones that deal with family— remembering deceased family, respecting family elders, honoring parents, and gifting children—were the ones esteemed as most important and most likely to be maintained by professional households. Confucianism thus meshed better with the scientific worldview of these families. Instead of a worldview inhabited with gods, spirits, and ancestors, the professional parents, especially those with science and engineering backgrounds and those who were men, had a scientific, rationalist orientation toward the world. From San Mateo, California, Leslie Dong had parents who had graduate degrees in engineering and science. She explained that her mother, a chemist, leans towards being a Buddhist and participates in ancestral rituals. Her mother is not likely to believe in a Christian god because she has too many doubts about the coexistence of a loving deity and evil, suffering, and war. Leslie explained, "I don't think my mom believes in the Christian God. She has questions about whether God really exists because she is a scientist, and she says, 'There's war. If there really was a god, how can there be war?!'" From her mother's point of view, one's worldview should be rational and coherent, instead of based on faith.

Along with prioritizing empiricism and rationality, these parents were skeptical about religious dogma. For example, Irene Hui grew up in San Jose in Silicon Valley, the daughter of a computer engineer and a lab assistant. She described her father's personality: "He's very concrete, he's very smart, he's very scientific. He doesn't dwell very much with emotional things." Both her parents chafed against religious individuals who imposed their beliefs and judged others. Irene shared how her father railed against proselytizers:

> My dad would bring up the topic of evolution, because he's very much a science man. He loves watching *Nova* on PBS, and they once had a documentary called *The Darwin Trials*, about creationism and the whole politics of that, and I remember he loved it! And just commenting on how people should not be imposing their beliefs in the school system, where it's fine if you believe what you believe. But you shouldn't be using your beliefs to teach children the wrong thing.

In addition, Irene mentioned that her mother brought up the idea of judgment and how it was "silly" that not everyone has the chance to go to heaven.

With this empiricist orientation, requiring proof and rationality, these professional parents were much less likely to view their Chinese traditions as efficacious in relating to spiritual beings. Rather, they secularized Chinese rituals and holidays so that they were compatible with scientific worldviews.[9] Nevertheless, the customs were not simply symbolic acts devoid of significant cultural meaning.[10] These key rituals were effective in inculcating esteemed values of right relations (*yi*), as well as a sense of identity and belonging based on the family.

IMMIGRANT PARENTS' RELIGIOUS SOCIALIZATION PRACTICES

What worldviews, values, beliefs, and practices do these immigrant parents pass on to their children, and how do they do so? Very few of the immigrant parents teach or train their children about Chinese Popular Religion, as it is primarily based on practices, not tenets or doctrine. Instead, most model for their children what values they wish to pass on, and only occasionally reinforce verbally the key lessons that they wish to inculcate. As a result, the children have little knowledge about Chinese Popular Religion or the meaning behind its practices. Furthermore, because local Chinese temples primarily serve to host rituals rather than to instruct religious teachings, they also do not pass on Chinese Popular Religion very well. Nonetheless, because working-class parents practice more rituals of Chinese Popular Religion, their children are more likely to participate in them and to have them in their own religious repertoires.

Working-Class Households and Religious Socialization

Compared to the professional parents, the working-class immigrant parents were more successful in passing down Chinese Popular Religion for three reasons. First, their own example of religious devotion modeled for their children a sense of the spiritual world, as opposed to a scientific world-view. They also required their children to participate in spiritual rituals alongside them more often than the professional parents did. Second, the working-class families practiced Chinese religious traditions more often. These parents visited temples more regularly than the professional ones because they lived in areas with greater concentrations of Chinese Americans and Chinese temples. And, because they often immigrated with extended family, grandparents who passed away were buried in the United States rather than in Asia. These families thus visited the cemetery and performed death anniversary ceremonies more often than the professional families. Third, they were strict about maintaining a few specific rituals and beliefs that taught their children the importance of religious devotion. Indeed, the working-class parents displayed greater emotional and financial investment in Chinese Popular Religion than did the professional ones.

Many of the working-class parents daily lit incense for their ancestors and took seriously their responsibility to pray or visit the temple. Rodney Shem, from Fairfield, California, observed the devotion of his Hong Kong–born father, who worked as a bus driver: "[My father] lights incense. Every morning he bows three times in front of a Buddha statue. He has a picture of his mom, too. She's deceased." Sharon, whose ancestors also came from Guangdong, noted, "We would *bai sun* (*baishen*, 拜神): you know, put out stuff for the ancestors. It was something my mom *always* did." Wendy Tong said of her Burma-raised mother's regular practice of visiting the temple, "My mom is very religious. She goes to temple quite often. Her temple is not local. Her temple is forty minutes away. Her temple is in San Bruno and she lives in San Jose. But she goes every week or two." These parents were faithful in their attendance and would occasionally bring their children along. Even if the children did not understand the ceremonies, they at least observed their parents' commitment and practice of their beliefs.

Visits to the cemetery were perhaps more significant to the working class because they were the rare rituals they did as a family. Kenneth Lam's parents worked most of the time, so his family did not even eat together. The rare occasions that they did go out together were to visit his grandmother's gravesite:

My parents would say, "Hey come *bai sun*. Make that day available." I know we bring food always, a lot of food. We'd always burn money, burn the paper money. And then burn incense. And then we *bai sun*, eat the food, and go for dim sum after.

> You know, I was saying how we don't spend time as family? [Cemetery visits were] kind of nice. I like hanging out with my brother, sister, mom, and dad. My brother and sister are really close. We depended on each other back then. I enjoy the time we have to hang out. It wasn't a bad thing, it was a long car drive. It was fun. I value those times.

The cemetery visit reinforced the value of taking care of one's ancestors, as well as valuing one's living family.

Indeed, one of the core values of both Chinese Popular Religion and Confucianism that immigrant parents taught was to honor and respect one's ancestors, as well as the right way to honor them. Michael Chen, from San Francisco, described the seriousness with which his Taishan-speaking parents venerated his grandfather. The ceremony had to be conducted "properly," in recognition that they owe him their lives:

> [My mother] gave me the easy stuff because you know, because I'm the youngest. Stuff that you can't mess up. I think my sisters did the lighting of the candles. Making sure that all the stuff was there properly and was set properly and put out the picture.
>
> My mom would say a few things. I don't know what it would have been. She would kind of speak to the picture and then she would, you know, tell us just to stay quiet and that this is the time for us to respect him and his memories—what he did for the family and stuff. To respect in terms of what he had done for our family, and how he helped your father to bring him to this life and as result, he is the father he is today.

Michael and his sisters were required not only to participate in the gravesite ceremony but also conduct the ritual in the correct manner. The children, as well, were taught to reflect silently on the sacred role of the family.

Along with modeling regular ritual practice, the lengths to which their parents went in order to practice their *li* activity stood out to the children. When Sophia Wong, whose father was a repairman and mother a nanny, went back to her ancestral village in Taishan, she and her extended family hiked one mile to their grandfather's burial site carrying a whole pig. They climbed up a mountainside over dirt roads to reach the cemetery. When asked about the ritual, she said it made a deep impression on her:

> I think it's a very respectful thing. Back there it's the way it is. I guess in a way, to me, it's not just like a custom. That is a belief. It's like something you should do; it's something you're supposed to do. To me I feel like there is an afterlife. What it is, I don't know. But I think that it creates a stronger family bond.

Making offerings to her grandfather was not just a traditional custom, but a "belief" and "something you should do" as an ethical imperative of *yi* righteousness. Similar to Michael's comment about the gravesite visit as a sacred family ritual, Sophia recognized how this event unified her family, both living and dead. In her understanding, this ritual is significant for its embodiment of Confucian filiality.

As described previously, the working-class parents incurred great costs to manipulate their luck and fortune even though they had less money and time to spare. Laura's parents paid for *fengshui* consultants and purchased or rented properties that were more expensive than others in order to have better *qi*. Larry lost deposit money because his mother wanted a different date for his wedding. On the rare times when they could take days off, they would use the time to pay respects to their ancestors. Kenneth noted that the only time his entire family was together was on the special occasions when they visited the gravesite. Susan said that when her family took vacations, they would visit Chinese temples because they did not have any near their home. For Chinese New Year, Laura's entire family would wake up at 2 a.m. just so they could all eat together and enjoy dishes with meaning.

The second-generation Chinese Americans were struck by the emotional intensity, devotion, and fervor with which their working-class parents engaged in Chinese Popular Religion. Michael came to appreciate the deep significance of visiting his grandparents' gravesite, especially to his own parents: "When I was younger, I thought it was nonsense. Why are we spending all this time with dead people? I was not very sensitive to that. Of course, when I got older I started to realize that it is important because *it's important to my parents*". Other working-class children also observed the great influence of Chinese Popular Religion on their parents. Larry said his mother "is big on the fortune book," and Grace shared, "My mom and my grandma . . . were really big on the tradition."

Perhaps what made Chinese Popular Religion most salient was the emotional investment the parents made to its practices. When a ladle broke during Chinese New Year at Grace's home, she vividly recalled how her mother "freaked out." If Rodney took a shower during that festival time, his father would "get really angry." When Laura's brother dropped his chopsticks, her father also "got really angry." The incidents may be small, inadvertent acts, but the parents reacted very strongly to the possible consequences of these omens. The salience and importance of these traditions to their parents certainly made a mark on the children.

Professional Households and Religious Socialization

In contrast to the devotion of working-class parents to Chinese Popular Religion, the professional parents, especially those with a scientific background, conducted Chinese traditions as customs both for fun and to practice and teach good values. In fact, they were more likely to view the role of ritual as Confucians did—as means to develop *yi* virtues of filiality and obedience. Similarly, they raised their children with Confucian religious skepticism: to be open, tolerant, and not too dogmatic. In line with their scientific, evidence-based approach to life, they allowed their children to explore different religious perspectives.

Scott Lai explained why his parents taught him that Chinese traditions were customs rather than efficacious, spiritual practices. When asked about the meaning of his family's Chinese New Year practices, he replied that they were rituals to build family unity: "The cultural ones are so that you have a tie to who came before you because certain traditions produce good things, you know, bringing families together and things like that." Certain customs were selectively maintained to inculcate Chinese values. However, other customs, such as taboos, were discarded because they were seen as meaningless:

> But then, as for the superstitious ones, if nothing's going to happen afterwards, why are you wasting your energy doing it? I mean, my dad is very much an empiricist, very much subscribes to the scientific method. I don't think he does so explicitly, but you know, in seeing the way he operates in the world. He tends to deal with hard facts, realities, what can be adjusted or manipulated. He's an engineer by training, so I think some of that comes out there.

Since his father was an empiricist, he saw the customs as a means to build Confucian values, not to welcome better fortune.

In fact, the children of professional households mentioned Confucianism more than those of the working-class families in describing their religious socialization. For example, Scott interpreted his family's Chinese New Year greetings as a reinscription of Confucian family relationships. He spoke of his parents' aim to instill respect for family members: "We observed the Chinese holidays. We observed, we did them to observe certain Confucian roles, social positions in the family. You know, proper greetings of people. Yeah, [my parents] were very observant of kind of the Confucian aspects of the culture earlier on!" The observance of rituals around family, and not necessarily luck and fortune, was emphasized.

Henry Zhou, whose father had a Ph.D. in nuclear physics, said his family did not give out *hongbao* or decorate during Chinese New Year. He described his parents this way: "They were not religious at all. If anything, they say they follow Confucianism. I think that's more of a philosophy. I guess in general, filiality. Giving respect to parents and doing good things generally." But they did visit his grandparents' gravesite in China, and Henry had to bow three times to their ancestors:

It was a Chinese tradition, everyone else is doing it. The old Chinese idea of filiality, that was it. It was a mixture of respect and cultural tradition. [Visiting the gravesite] taught me to respect my ancestors, and to treat my family well. Remember them for who they are, and think about them every now and then. Without them, I wouldn't be here.

The moral lesson of obligation and gratefulness, that they "wouldn't be here" if it were not for their ancestors, was a common refrain when the second generation spoke of these ancestral practices.

Professional parents were not necessarily antithetical to religion, but they wanted their children to employ a scientific and pragmatic approach toward spiritual matters. For example, Peter Hsieh's parents allowed him to go to a Christian church, especially since many of the Chinese families in that suburb did so. However, at a certain point they became concerned because he was no longer thinking independently. He was surprised at their attitude because he felt that in general, going to church was good for a youth. He shared their response:

"We want you to grow up independent. We don't want you to be brainwashed. You are being brainwashed." They didn't like how I was changing. My mom would always bring up this story. She said, "We don't want you to become a missionary and give away all your possessions and move to Africa." They'd heard stories about friends who did that. But I think that, by what they said, they were worried about me. That I was losing my own person, like I wasn't myself anymore.

While his parents were open to his attending church, they feared that he would be "brainwashed" and follow extreme, dogmatic beliefs. In the end, they valued remaining intellectually independent more than the good behavior preached at the church.

This open attitude led some immigrants to explore and adopt different religious beliefs. Yet again, the parents ultimately valued intellectual inquiry, not necessarily the adoption of higher meaning. For instance, the parents of Serena Zhang of Cleveland, Ohio, were academics. She described her mother's quest for spiritual belief:

My mom is atheist and my dad is atheist or agnostic. They said "No, we don't believe in god." My mom said, "I just have a scientific mind and I tried really hard to believe in a god, but I just can't." I thought it was interesting that she tried.

Thus, most professional parents socialized their children to be scientists—to be intellectually open to religion and to test it—whereas working-class parents socialized their children to be devoted to Chinese Popular Religion.

The class groupings of Chinese Americans highlight each component of *liyi* transmission. The working-class parents focused on *li* rituals because their orthopraxy in relating to the spirit world better enhances their fortune, health, and well-being. The professional parents were less concerned about the efficacy of their ritual practice, but they still valued the *yi* righteousness that their traditions embodied. Whatever their emphasis, Chinese American families maintained the *li* rituals of ancestor veneration and Chinese New Year, which additionally provided our respondents with a sense of identity and belonging.

Spiritual but Not Religious versus Atheists

Like other Americans, the primary factors shaping the religious beliefs, attitudes, and practices of Chinese Americans was their parents' religiosity or nonreligiosity, as well as whether they were socialized religiously or nonreligiously.[11] In our sample, most parents were on different parts of the continuum with regard to the Chinese religious repertoire. One parent might take the rituals seriously in order to affect supernatural forces or pray to spirits; another might see them as customs that were to be maintained out of tradition and appearances; and still another might view them as means of moral instruction. Given this variety, most of their children could understand the different approaches toward Chinese rituals of ancestor veneration, *fengshui*, and Chinese New Year and identified as agnostic. They did not see themselves as religious, but they did not discount the presence of supernatural beings and the role of spiritual forces.

The second generation who became spiritual but not religious (N = 15) had parents who were devout followers of Chinese Popular Religion, Buddhism, or Christianity. Sharon Chung's mother was a strong role model to her in her devotion and dedication to her ancestors and deities, as well as her selflessness. Her mother was raised in Mozambique, and her family passed down the importance of regular, ritualized spiritual practices. She burned incense every morning and prayed at two home altars (one for the ancestors, one for deities), held elaborate meals and made offerings during Chinese New Year and Winter Solstice, and arranged the home according to *fengshui* principles. When they took vacations, they made it a point to visit Chinese temples.

The spiritual environment in her home made it easy for Sharon to acknowledge the importance of her ancestors, the presence of supernatural beings, and the role of fate in her own life. She was open to Christianity and attended church for a while. There she saw more spiritual forces at work in this world. Even though she no longer attends church, she concluded, "I did realize in the process of being in the church that I did feel that there was a Holy Spirit or some kind of spiritualness of being in church. I do believe—feel like—there's something out there bigger than us that's doing something."

Since "something out there bigger than us" is operating, she sees her life as having a destiny that is governed by fate. Occasionally, she said, the "universe" would point her in the direction of her destiny and the paths she should take in life. When she went to visit her grandparents' gravesite, she had an "aha" moment. It related to the sacrifices of her ancestors, her parents' immigration, and her own destiny to be a voice for the Asian American community. She explained, "I went to Zimbabwe, where my grandparents were buried. There were just certain things in my life that were happening, that I felt all these 'aha!' things were happening. Maybe I was here for another reason. Maybe that's why I was put here on this earth." At another time she left her job and was worried about her financial situation. While she was walking out of a grocery store—and she never went shopping in the morning—she looked down and found a "diamond solitaire, about a karat in size." She interpreted the jewel as "a symbol that the Universe was giving to me that [changing jobs was] the right thing to do."

Sharon concluded that her parents deeply affected her own spiritual sensibility, although they did not instruct her to follow the traditions. "My parents are very subtle in what they say. I do feel [my spirituality] comes from somewhere. There's a part of me—what I've learned about Buddhism in school and ancestor worship—that's kind of what my family does. That's a part of me." Consequently, she has consulted palm readers and desires to spend more time "meditating, listening, and taking more quiet time." Doing so would make her more in tune with what the universe has in store for her.

In the same way, 84.6% of the second-generation Chinese American atheists (N = 13) had parents who instilled the same rationality, scientific mindset, and pragmatic approach to life. Cheryl Teng, whose parents are scientists with graduate degrees, said, "[I characterize my parents] as nonreligious because they've never done anything that religious. They are both practical people—both scientists—so it may go against their practical mindset. I guess they need evidence and proof of something to believe it. I'm sure it rubbed off [on me]." Just as her parents had a "practical mindset" in which they needed "proof of something," Cheryl also adopted this scientific worldview for herself. Likewise, Scott Lai's father received his graduate degree in mechanical engineering and adopted a pragmatic mindset toward religion where, "one, it has to make sense, and, two, it has to be functional for you."

Just as the households where Chinese Popular Religion was practiced made it plausible for the second generation to be spiritual but not religious, the secular environment of the homes of atheists made religion, in the Western sense, implausible. Jonathan Hu's parents told him they did not want ancestral, gravesite ceremonies because they saw themselves as "not traditional." They do not have shrines and never told him to go to temples or to pray. He asserted:

> [My nonreligiousness] is due to my parents and the environment that I grew up in. There's religious people in the Bay Area, but I don't feel like they're a majority per se, so it's always been like an insulated community. And my parents never told me, "Well, if you're feeling bad, you gotta pray." They never did that. And there was no prayer in the house. So religion and God and spirits in general has always been this alien concept.

Insulated from God and the spirits, the atheists in this sample, after considering their options, chose to deny the existence of the supernatural.

CONCLUSION

Chinese American households continue to pass down the *liyi* dimensions of Chinese Popular Religion and Confucian ethics, which are the sources of Chinese American familism. Given a family's class and professional background, *li* rituals had different meanings and effects. For the working class, the performance of rituals for their efficacy demanded more frequent and devout adherence. In contrast, the use of rituals for their *yi* virtue by the professional class may have required less strict adherence in form, but still demanded high solemnity and respect.

While their *liyi* socialization shaped the second-generation Chinese Americans, they did not fully adopt or subscribe to the values and practices of their immigrant parents. Instead, they selectively chose to discard and retain *liyi* traditions, and thereby forged their own hybridized worldviews. The next chapter explores how the second generation translates their traditions in the American context.

CHAPTER 4

❧

Translation

Chinese Popular Religion and Confucianism in the United States

I'll do [ancestor veneration for my parents] on my own. I do believe it. I feel like someone is watching out for me. It doesn't hurt; it's more of the type of thinking that I don't want to put all my eggs in one basket, so I do traditional rituals. I don't think my dad's going to bring my future husband to fall in my lap, and meet him on the T. But I think, it doesn't hurt.

— Erica Tseng, financial aid officer from Boston, Massachusetts

E rica, who works at Boston University, explained why she continues her family tradition of lighting incense for deceased family members. She does not believe that her father will specifically answer her prayers for a husband, but she does derive some assurance that "someone is watching out" for her. Even though she believes in fate and karma and wears a Buddha pendant, she states that she is nonreligious. One reason is that, unlike her Christian friends, she "doesn't feel so deeply about one thing that is not tangible." In fact, she says, "I'm jealous of their blind faith, because I don't have that." Authentic religious adherence, according to Western Christian tradition, thus requires two elements: a strong faith and exclusive devotion. Erica, on the other hand, does not feel so deeply about Christianity and "doesn't want to put all [her] eggs in one basket."

The other reason that Erica identifies herself as nonreligious is because the traditions and rituals that she performs are not systematically organized, nor do they have names. Although in *Family Sacrifices* we call this constellation of spiritual assumptions, values, and practices Chinese Popular Religion, it is neither commonly known in the United States nor found on religious surveys. Consequently, Erica may be categorized as "spiritual but not religious," even as she adheres to most of the beliefs and practices of Chinese Popular Religion.

What happens when an Asian spiritual tradition, such as Chinese Popular Religion, is transplanted onto American soil, a nation with a Christian-dominant religious landscape? How much can immigrant parents pass on to their second-generation children, and what are the factors that shape this transmission? In this new context, Chinese Popular Religion and, to a lesser extent, Confucianism get translated, reinterpreted, and reshaped by both generations. Overall, four main factors hampered the transmission of Chinese Popular Religion in the United States.

First, because Chinese Popular Religion emphasizes practice more than belief and has no set doctrines or sacred scriptures, parents rarely teach the explicit meanings behind the rituals. Instead, they model the rituals to their children, who may or may not be expected to continue them as adults. As a result, second-generation Chinese Americans often do not know how to perform the rituals, nor do they understand their meanings. Second, the dissonant acculturation between Chinese immigrant parents and their English-speaking children makes transmission of Chinese traditions difficult. The second generation often cannot communicate well with their parents in the Chinese language. Further, they have adopted American ideals of personal autonomy, equality, and individualism, which challenge Chinese values of hierarchical relationships and veneration of spirits. Chinese Popular Religion, as well as Confucianism, is perceived as too traditional, authoritarian, and strange. Third, the American religious marketplace is not conducive to the propagation of Chinese Popular Religion. Chinese religious institutions and cemeteries have been established only in areas with high concentrations of Chinese Americans. Unless the second generation has the strong presence of extended family, especially elders, they probably do not have much access to Chinese Popular Religion and its practices. The United States privileges Christianity, its discourse, and its communal associations as religious norms. Consequently, Chinese spiritual worldviews, especially those dealing with luck and fate, are viewed as superstitions. Fourth, the racialization of Chinese Popular Religion as exotic and strange is a significant factor in the decline of its adherence by Chinese in the United States. In wanting to acculturate into mainstream society, second-generation Chinese Americans often discard aspects of Chinese Popular Religion that do not fit.

COMPARISON BETWEEN FIRST- AND SECOND-GENERATION CHINESE AMERICANS

The division between the first and second generations of Chinese Americans can be illustrated by the Pew Asian American Survey results. The second generation tend to hold more to a Western belief in God, but the first generation believe in Chinese supernatural elements much more than their children do. For example, over three-fourths of the second generation believe in God, but only about two-thirds of the first generation do.

In contrast, the first generation are much more likely to believe in *qi* (46.7% of the first generation vs. 29.3% of the second generation), as well as in ancestral spirits (Surprisingly, the second generation is more likely to believe in ancestral spirits, even though they were born and educated in the United States where they are less likely to learn about such spirits.).

While their beliefs differ, their practices do not, and thus they indicate a continuation of *liyi* customs. Roughly the same percentages of Chinese American immigrants and second generation maintain home shrines and celebrate Chinese New Year.

The second generation thus differ from their parents in their beliefs regarding Chinese Popular Religion, yet they still generally adhere to them at the same rates as their parents. These trends demonstrate that in the translation of Chinese Popular Religion and Confucianism, the second generation have developed their own understandings of why they continue their ethnic customs. They tend to create their own meaning systems because, often, they do not fully grasp their parents' beliefs and traditions.

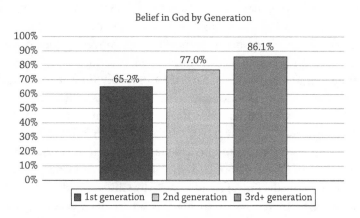

Figure 4.1 Belief in God by Generation

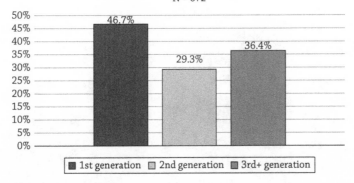

Figure 4.2 Belief in Qi by Generation

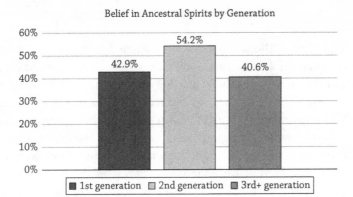

Figure 4.3 Belief in Ancestral Spirits by Generation

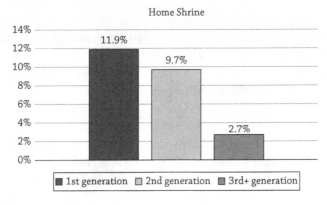

Figure 4.4 Maintains Home Shrine by Generation

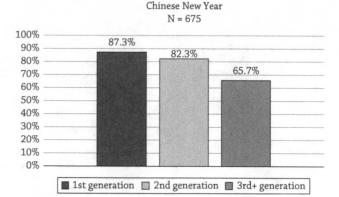

Figure 4.5   Celebrates Chinese New Year by Generation

Rituals Modeled but Not Explained

Although most of the respondents participated in the rituals of Chinese Popular Religion, few had received clear explanations from their immigrant parents of the meanings, histories, and actual mechanisms of how the rituals were to be efficacious. Instead, the children were commanded simply to copy veneration rites or obey rules of luck, *fengshui*, and numerology. If given explanations at all, they were generally cursory, such as that rituals were conducted for "good luck" and taboos were protection from "bad luck." Consequently, very few of the respondents continued these traditions as elaborately, frequently, or devoutly as their parents.

For example, Teresa Owyang's family was proud of their Chinese heritage but did not explain Chinese spiritual traditions. She was raised in Los Gatos, California, by her father, an electrical engineer, and her mother, a systems analyst. They lived in a predominantly white town, but her parents cared enough about passing down their Chinese heritage that they drove over 30 minutes three times a week so that their daughter could participate in a Chinese folk dance group as well as a Chinese-language school. Even though Teresa knew the historical background of each of her ethnic dances, she did not know the meanings of her family's Chinese holidays. She could not even recall the names of the holidays they celebrated: "And Chinese New Year we'd celebrate, the Harvest Moon Festival we'd celebrate. I don't know the names for the other celebrations, but I mean, food-related festivals, we did those." Often the second generation was unaware of when the holidays occurred, and they did not anticipate their celebration. All that Teresa understood about them was that they were associated with specific foods: "And it wasn't necessarily, 'Don't forget this weekend is blah-blah-blah festival.' It was like, 'Today is such and such day. We're supposed to eat *tangyuan*,' so I was like, 'Okay, today I'm gonna' eat *tangyuan*.' I don't think it had rituals, other than the food." For her family, religious festivals that formerly required specific rituals had transformed to ethnic celebrations simply related to food.

Just as religious festivals lost their meaning, so did ancestral rituals. Even if Teresa asked for the reasons for family ancestor rituals, she and her siblings would not receive a clear answer, but an abrupt one:

> We don't do the incense-y thing, or anything, but we do food offering, clean up the grave site, and that's on the death anniversary every year. I take it as custom. I think we've asked before why, and [my mother] just says, "That's what you do!" Honoring the ancestors, she didn't really explain.

In fact, her mother seemed reticent to provide explanations; Teresa said that she learned about the rituals more from watching Chinese movies than from her parents:

> When someone dies, we never did the money burning or anything, but I knew about it because of movies that I watched. And asking about that, my mom told me about how you have to pay for the entrance [to the afterlife]. But it was never, "Let's sit down, and you should know about this tradition, and you should know about this custom!" It was just me asking and it kinda' off-hand being explained to me, "We're just doing the customs, and it's just tradition to do such things."

As described in the previous chapter, her parents explained the rituals as customs done for the sake of tradition.

Compared to Teresa's family, Sophia Wong's working-class family in San Francisco carried on even more of a variety of customs of Chinese Popular Religion, including visits to gravesites and elaborate Chinese New Year practices. These included lighting firecrackers, leaving on the front porch light, hanging tangerines, and not washing one's hair. Nevertheless, after pointing out all the traditions her family maintained, Sophia complained that they were practiced primarily to participate in the ritual, not to affirm a belief: "That's the thing, they never explained like why we do the things we do. We never talked about why. You do it to do it. You're supposed to do it." Her statement succinctly summarizes how Chinese Popular Religion is primarily performative and not doctrinal.

Sophia knows neither the recipe for the special dishes nor the dates for the holidays themselves. Again, like Teresa, she noted that these religious festivals often arrived without her awareness:

> When you go to cemetery or when my mom will make the *joong*, [zongzi, 粽子][1] she doesn't say why or what part of the calendar it lands on, or why she's making it now. I come home one day and she's in the kitchen and the whole kitchen table is covered with all these ingredients to make it. So then, I know it's that time of the year. But I never really think about what time of the year it is.

Sophia concluded, "When I'm living on my own, I won't even know what I'll be carrying on. The fact is that I don't even know how, or why, or when to do certain things." Although her family was very "traditional" in its adherence to customs, her parents did not attempt to instruct her on their meanings. In spite of the fact that Sophia had the desire to carry on the traditions, she remained unaware of their spiritual significance.

Instead of learning about these customs from their parents, the second generation had to take their own initiative and read about them if they wanted to know why they were practiced. Julia Tom, from San Mateo, California, also described the holidays as primarily times to eat. Just as Sophia did not know when or how to make *joong*, Julia also expressed her confusion about that particular dish and its festival: "I guess I would know the festival, but not always the background. There's another festival where you eat the sticky rice. The *zongzi*. I don't know what it's called in English. So we eat that." She paused because she realized she had mixed up the festivals. She said she would have to use the internet to be clear on the traditions.

> What is that one? I hope I'm not confusing the festivals. I may have to Google this afterwards. [The holiday] was pretty much just to prepare a meal and eat. There wasn't really any actions or games or anything that you'd play. It's just, "Yeah, let's get together!," and then you eat.

In sum, second-generation Chinese Americans gain little knowledge about meanings and teachings of Chinese Popular Religion rituals. Although they may have been required to participate in them, they did not understand the background of the customs or the spiritual dimensions by which they were to be efficacious. Instead, their parents and grandparents often told them to mimic certain behaviors, such as bowing three times, or to obey injunctions about numbers, *fengshui*, or luck. As a result, they rarely were able to explain when, why, or how they were supposed to follow Chinese spiritual traditions.

Dissonant Acculturation

Not understanding their parents' worldview is an example of dissonant acculturation, which occurs when children learn English and adopt American ways faster than do their immigrant parents.[2] Besides being unable to communicate well or to pass down traditions, Chinese immigrant parents only slowly adopt Western parenting styles. Because of this, their children viewed the ways of their immigrant parents, which included the practices of Chinese Popular Religion, as old-fashioned and irrelevant to the North American context. Four other examples of dissonant acculturation in which the second generation differed from their parents include (1) loss of Chinese religious terminology, (2) inability to engage fully in Chinese rituals, (3) perception of Chinese household rituals as weird, and (4) perception of Chinese values as antiquated.

Due to a language barrier, Chinese-speaking parents cannot communicate well the complex worldviews and deep meanings of their spiritual traditions. In turn, their second-generation children do not know the terminology of Chinese Popular Religion or Confucianism even if they want to ask questions about these spiritual and philosophical discourses. Indeed, the children often did not know the names of deities in their homes or their functions. For example, Laura Chan, from Quincy, Massachusetts, described the statues in her home:

> We had statues everywhere! They have this temple-like shelf with that statue of a goddess, and they stick red envelopes on the trees around the house. My house looks like a Chinese antique store! More so at Chinese New Year. I don't know who the gods are, except the goddess statue. She was the only female god. Her name was Gwun Yum [Guanyin].[3]

Laura's parents were devout in their prayers to the deities and wanted her to pay her respects to them. Paradoxically, though, they did not teach her about these gods. "I think my mom would be really upset that I don't know [what Gwun Yum does for her followers]. It's funny that they never explained it to me. I never asked." In retrospect, Laura realized that she did not know about Chinese deities, even though she grew up with their statues throughout her home.

Reading and writing Chinese is more difficult than being able to understand that language. Even though the great majority of second-generation Chinese Americans attended Chinese-language school, their literacy levels were still low. Learning how to do chants and rituals through Chinese written texts was nearly impossible. Leslie Dong, who grew up on the San Francisco peninsula, said she could not fully participate in temple rituals when she returned to Taiwan:

I have been to Taiwan probably once a year as a kid, and then now every two or three years, I go back. But whenever we do, my grandfather who still is there likes to take us to the temple near his house. And we go in there, and I'll light some incense, and maybe bow to some of the things in there. I don't really know what it means because I can't read [the chants]. But I'm just going with them and doing things like that.

Blocked from active engagement in temple worship, she could only perform the rituals in a haphazard manner.

In addition to communication barriers, the cultural differences between the second generation's Chinese households and their surrounding North American neighborhoods were stark. Edward Song, who was raised in Calgary, Canada, thought that his mother was "really crazy" for obeying taboos about numbers and table manners. He listed the Chinese "superstitious" customs that she maintained:

She believes in the numbers. Four is a bad number. It's more an avoidance of the bad things—as long as you don't pick the bad numbers. Also, don't stick your chopsticks upright in your rice bowl. Never stick chopsticks or forks upright in the rice bowl! Because to her, that means someone's going to die.

He continued to identify *fengshui* principles that his mother constantly insisted upon that he thought were irrational: "When buying a house— *fengshui*, she had some belief in that. The door cannot directly face the stairs or all your wealth will flow out of the door. She'd say things like this *all the time*" (italics added). Edward noted that she probably learned these beliefs from his grandparents, because his aunts were even "more crazy" than his mother.

Even though his mother regularly reminded him of these prohibitions, she never did explain why, so Edward thought they were irrational. He attempted to ask her why she insisted on certain traditions, but his mother's answers were unsatisfactory. For example, he complained about her requests that he post religious decorations:

She does hang good fortune signs upside down all the time. She'll tell me things to do, but she won't tell me why. When we got married, she'd tell us, "You need to hang the double happiness sign on your wall." And she'll repeat it. If I don't hang this, then my marriage will go bad—is that what she believes?

Not only did he find it challenging that his mother offered no explanation for these traditions of Chinese Popular Religion, but she also used an authoritarian tone in demanding he follow the traditions. He complained of her expectation that he listen to her instructions without question: "I think she's crazy. This [bad luck due to failure to obey taboos] is not going to happen. I used to discuss with her, 'Why?' Her answer would not be rational. It would just be 'It's just bad luck.' End of discussion." Edward viewed practices of Chinese Popular Religion as irrational and strange because they were not fully explained.

Edward's family held conversations about *fengshui* principles or rules about luck at the dinner table, in the privacy of the home. However, in his community, which was primarily white, no one else seemed to maintain such strange customs or hold conversations about luck. Edward elaborated, "We lived in Calgary and I guess I didn't notice this [taboo practice] from other people. It was personal, at the dinner table. It seems unusual; I didn't see anyone else doing it." Given the norms of his Canadian neighborhood, the rituals and taboos of Chinese Popular Religion seemed odd. Second-generation Chinese who grew up in predominantly white areas suffered from this dissonant acculturation more than those who were raised in Chinese ethnic enclaves.

The final example of dissonant acculturation is the prevalent antipathy among our respondents toward having to attend Chinese-language school. Although the second generation may have enjoyed the social aspects of being with other Chinese Americans, they uniformly disliked having to spend extra time in school and receive rote instruction in Chinese. Jonathan Pan was raised in San Mateo on the San Francisco peninsula by his father, an engineer, and his mother, a biotech chemist. He disliked his weekly Chinese schooling so much that he railed against the Confucianism they employed to keep students obedient and diligent. He was also virulently opposed to ancestral veneration because he linked it to Confucianism and school pedagogy:

> Honestly, when I have my own family, I don't plan on doing [ancestral rituals] because it's ridiculous! It's just Confucius-type stuff, and I hate Confucius stuff. I hate Confucius because of my upbringing. It was Confucius this and Confucius that. First grade through eleventh grade—that was all Chinese school. It leads into the Chinese culture, which really screwed me up when I entered white America.

Jonathan pit his Confucian heritage against white American norms, critiquing the humility and hierarchical relationships that the former espouses: "A lot of the Confucian stuff was great at home because that's how my parents are used to communicating and living their life, but terrible for America. And I'm still trying to assimilate myself into white America." He argued that his Confucian upbringing actually hampered him from advancing in American corporate culture, which values bluntness, assertiveness, and directness:

I was getting hammered left and right in the corporate world. People would not have the best perceptions of me, and I had no idea why. A lot of it has to do with because of the way I was brought up as an Asian American, and it really doesn't speak anything about who I am and my work ethic or my performance or anything. Mainstream America has this certain way of behaving. And if you don't learn it, and there was no way for me to learn it because my parents didn't know it either, it makes things a lot harder.

Since his own upbringing failed to prepare him for the corporate world, Jonathan planned to discard ancestral rituals and Confucian norms so that his own children could better compete in the American mainstream corporate world.

As the second generation of Chinese Americans grew up in the United States, they adopted American ways more quickly than their parents had. This adaptation to their host environment and the dominance of the English language led to their inability to grasp the Chinese terminology employed in family rituals and temple worship. So they were at a loss in learning further about Chinese Popular Religion, even if they wanted to explore it. In addition, the prevailing cultural norms of their communities made Chinese orientations toward luck, *fengshui*, and Confucianism seem out of date and out of place. In fact, they recognized that some of the values inculcated by Chinese Popular Religion and Confucianism, such as obedience and respect for authorities, were cultural barriers to overcome in the American corporate setting. In the American religious landscape, Chinese Popular Religion has disadvantages as well.

Religious Marketplace: Extended Family, Institutions, and Christian Privilege

Along with the cultural barriers to passing on Chinese traditions, the American religious marketplace privileges Western religions and disadvantages Chinese Popular Religion and other home-based spiritual traditions. The religious marketplace of the United States includes suppliers of religion, such as churches, temples, and religious entrepreneurs, and consumers of religion, who make up the demand. Using this metaphor of a market, sociologists of religion theorize that suppliers compete within niche markets to meet the demand. Those that are successful increase their share of the market. Even with freedom of religion in the United States and less state regulation of religion compared to other nations, the American religious marketplace is not necessarily open with an even playing field. Instead, certain religious institutions, especially Christian congregations, have more resources, personnel, and volunteers to expand. Larger religious institutions can also shape demand, such that spiritual consumers expect specific types of services from their religions. This section examines this marketplace and how Chinese Popular Religion is positioned within it.

Since Chinese Americans primarily practice Chinese Popular Religion within the home and not at congregational sites, its maintenance and perpetuation relies heavily on key members of the extended family who carry on the rituals, and not on professional clergy. Families in the United States that include elderly relatives are more likely to practice Chinese Popular Religion. Some Chinese immigrants who arrived through family reunification visas came precisely because they had family in the United States to sponsor them. Among our respondents, these immigrants not only had the financial and housing support of relatives, but they also received the spiritual support of their relatives.

For instance, when Grace Chu's parents came to the United States, they moved into her aunt and uncle's home. When Grace was born, she entered a household that included those two couples, as well as her single uncle and her grandmother. Her grandmother was "really big on the tradition," and she made Grace assist in setting up the shrine and offering foods and taught Grace to bow on certain days. This practice was a regular ritual that the grandmother supervised. "We did this once every few months. We stopped doing it as much after my grandma from my dad's side passed away. But she was always on top of all that." Together the extended family reinforced the ancestral veneration rituals.

Michael Chen grew up in San Francisco, the son of a cook and a housekeeper. His grandfather first came to the United States as a paper son using the documents of another person, went back to China to have a family, and then returned to San Francisco to resume working. Michael's father then migrated, also illegally, to join the grandfather. Eventually, the grandfather passed away and was buried in the Chinese cemetery in Daly City. Since Michael had a grandparent's gravesite close by, the family could easily go to pay respects on Qingming, the tomb-sweeping festival when family members tidy their ancestors' gravesites, and on his death anniversary. Michael reported that they went every two months: "We had a home shrine for my grandfather from my father's side. I remember going to do ancestor worship by going to the cemetery. Putting up the food, recognizing his death anniversary. We took turns as kids, going every two months or so." During these rituals his mother taught the children that they should respect their grandfather for giving them life.

Michael's grandmother lived in San Francisco as well. Participating as a pallbearer in her funeral service gave him the opportunity to reflect on her life and that of his other ancestors:

When I started to hear people talk about her, that got me thinking, "Wow, she was this whole person. She had this whole life that I never really knew." That's when I started to appreciate her more. My mom would tell me that [his grandmother and grandfather] worked really hard to get us what we have now and enabled us to have what we have currently.

The presence of grandparents, their practice of traditions, and later the remembrance of their sacrifices helped these immigrant families to maintain the key elements of Chinese Popular Religion.

Those without the nearby physical presence of extended family experienced greater dissonance with ancestral rituals, especially if they adopted American cultural values. As the sociologist Carolyn Chen concluded in her study of Taiwanese American immigrants, the practice of Chinese Popular Religion declined among this group because most did not have extended family nearby.[4] This ethnic community mostly immigrated through education and professional visas. With less family expectation and cultural pressure to continue ancestral practices, Taiwanese American nuclear families abandoned them. Furthermore, since they were far from ancestral gravesites and temples, they had less opportunity and access to participate in religious traditions.

To illustrate, Michelle Li grew up in a suburb of Philadelphia, where her father worked as a researcher and her mother as an accountant. She said that while she was growing up, they did not "practice anything" in terms of religious or traditional customs. However, since her parents moved back to Taiwan for retirement, they have participated much more in ancestral practices. Michelle explained that although her parents do not "really believe" in these customs, they do so now because of the change in their family environment.

> [My parents venerating ancestors] makes sense to me because I feel like, because they're not strongly religious, they, or they don't seem to me, [are not] strongly superstitious. Since they're away, they didn't really believe in it; it was just this extra thing they had to do. They had their own little life in America, no big deal. Now that they're back, it's such a big change. In general, they're so involved with the family. I heard that my grandmother is at their house all the time.

She felt that not participating in ancestor rituals would be outside the norm in Taiwan, especially if they wanted to try to fit in again. In fact, nonpractice would actually be disrespectful in the Taiwanese context: "I think they're just back and they're in it. They haven't been in it for twenty years and of course, it's natural to do these things with them. It would be kind of weird if they came and they're like, 'We don't do that—we're American!'"

Even though her parents privately complained about the expensive funeral arrangements, they went along with the rest of the family's and the grandmother's wishes. For example, the family had to purchase several expensive items for their grandfather's Buddhist funeral. Despite her parents' hesitancy to pay for these rituals, they obliged:

> My parents were like open to the funeral ceremonies, but I think some things were like, "Do we really have to spend extra money on this extra urn thing?" And my uncle was like, "This is normal; this is what you do." And my parents were like, "Okay, whatever makes you happy."

Since taking care of one's ancestral spirits was "normal," her parents made no objection to going along with the rest of the family.

As a child, Michelle acculturated to her Philadelphia suburban setting, where there was only one other Asian household. She recalled how she made her parents give her gifts for Christmas, even though they had no idea how to celebrate this holiday:

> One day I came back from elementary school and I made a stocking just to put gifts in it. I was like, "Mom, Santa Claus is supposed to put gifts in it," but the next day there were no gifts. So we kind of taught them to do these things: "This is what's normal." Mostly for us, they got really into it.

Michelle was disappointed that her family did not celebrate Easter like those around her. She expressed feeling left out: "I always wondered why my parents wouldn't do Easter baskets for me because all my other friends would get baskets with candy in it and all these things." Later, in high school, she fit in better, becoming a cheerleader and being heavily involved in school activities, such as going to dances.

In contrast to "what's normal" in her American life, Michelle came to view her Chinese background as marginalized. She attended Chinese school weekly, but felt that the other Chinese Americans were "kind of dorky." She described her family's Chinese customs, especially those pertaining to luck, as "slightly superstitious, or slightly silly." She believed the rituals of Chinese Popular Religion were culturally appropriate for Asian settings, especially in order to pay respect both to the dead and the living. However, since she and her sister are the only ones in the family left in the United States, she currently finds no need to maintain any Chinese traditions, except for fun ones.

Besides the presence of extended family, certain religious institutions and religious specialists reinforce Chinese Popular Religion. Within Asia, temples and neighborhood shrines are ubiquitous and remind locals of the presence of ancestors, spirits, and deities. Practitioners of Chinese Popular religion can regularly visit cemeteries and memorial halls in homes on death anniversaries and Qingming. *Fengshui* experts, diviners, spirit mediums, self-cultivation teachers, and ritual specialists make up some of the Chinese religious specialists from the Buddhist, Daoist, Confucian, and Chinese Popular Religion traditions.[5] These individuals are readily available at temples and are consulted on a variety of occasions, such as important events and major decisions. However, although these religious specialists are easily accessed in Asia, they are usually found only in Chinese ethnic enclaves in the United States.

The scant number of Chinese religious institutions and specialists in the United States clearly makes the preservation of Chinese Popular Religion difficult and the propagation of the religion even harder. For example, Laura Chan's family in Quincy, Massachusetts, were devout temple worshipers in her early childhood, until the long distance made it difficult to continue: "We used to go to the temple—they used to do it. Then it was like once a week and eventually they stopped. Not really sure why, but it was a half an hour to forty-five-minute drive." Similarly, Rodney Shem's father in Fairfield, California, had to drive an hour to visit a temple. Rodney himself did not enjoy visiting the temple the few times he went because he "didn't like the drive." Put simply, limited physical access to the institutions of Chinese Popular Religion inhibits its development on American soil.

Even if the second-generation Chinese Americans did attend a Chinese temple, this religious institution was not set up to meet the spiritual needs of young adults. Emily Huang's parents were not very religious when she was young, but later they became weekly attenders of a Buddhist temple in San Jose. Her grandparents first started attending, and then her parents joined them. Emily described how the temple met her parents' needs: "My parents started going because I think their friends led them there, probably. I think it was originally a social thing for them; they just started going because there were other people their age and [who] spoke their language who were there." After her parents began to attend the temple through family connections, they remained for ethnic and social ties. As they became more involved, they also derived spiritual edification on the issues they faced in their lives. Emily noted how the temple classes sought to educate persons on how to apply Daoist and Buddhist teachings:

> And I guess their whole thing is about living in a way that's most beneficial to everybody—what they'd consider most appropriate. It's all really abstract, so it's really hard to kind of describe. But as far as I know, I think they're there trying to study how to apply that to their own lives. I know there was one lady who was talking about how she really liked it because it allowed her how to solve some conflict with coworkers.

Although the temple met the social, ethnic, and spiritual needs of her grandparents and parents, it had much less relevance for Emily.

Her parents encouraged her to attend the temple, and Emily admitted that she was not "turned off" by the temple classes. Nevertheless, the temple was not structured to serve the second generation as it was to meet the needs of the first generation. In the first place, the temple could serve only Chinese-speaking individuals. Emily observed, "I think it's usually in Mandarin. Some people only speak Cantonese. I think we've had a Vietnamese lady there before. There was an English class for a little while, but there's not enough people who go there, so they didn't continue that."

In the second place, the temple did not meet the social needs of young adults such as Emily. Although some young persons attended, the temple did not encourage community-building:

> There's definitely people who are younger. I think they sort of hang out together, but they also sit with the adults during the class. It's just one class. Older people. Not really [a youth group]. I mean, I've met some people through there that I'm still friends with. But I guess I don't really hang out with them. I'm not sure if they do anything, outside of just the temple.

Whereas Christian ethnic churches tend to meet multiple needs of the first and second generation, Chinese temples provide spiritual services, at most, only for the second generation.

In addition, Chinese temples are not oriented toward outreach as much as evangelical Christian churches that aim to draw in members. Emily noted that the temple does make efforts to recruit new members, but these attempts are sporadic: "I know they have this big meeting maybe twice a year, where they just try to see if they can get more people. And then, they try to introduce the philosophy to new people. But I don't think they really have too many other big activities like that." Since the temple is not that welcoming to non-Chinese-speaking individuals, and it is not equipped to attract young adults such as Emily, she no longer attends.

Married and living in her own home, Emily continues to meditate and engage in daily self-reflection rituals that she was taught at the temple, which she considers "useful." However, she made a point of mentioning the types of persons who attended the temple, and how this religious practice was not something she would share with her social group:

> I don't really talk about [the temple] with my friends too much. One of my friend's cousin's mom goes sometimes. And some people that are family friends will go, but not my school friends. I wouldn't call it embarrassing, but I definitely feel like it's one of those things you don't normally talk about with friends, at least for me.

This particular Chinese temple attempted to draw new members by offering English-speaking classes and hosting large, introductory events, but it was unable to retain its second-generation Chinese American members because it could not fulfill their combined social and religious needs.

In contrast to the barriers to passing down household religious practices and to attending Chinese religious sites, Christianity and its institutions retain a privileged position in the American marketplace. Almost all the respondents had visited a Christian church, so they became familiar with the language, music, sermons, and fellowship groups of this religion. Indeed, Christianity establishes the rules and the expectations of religion in the United States. It is the basis by which second-generation Chinese Americans evaluate their own family's spiritual worldviews. These rules include the nature of God and the supernatural, how to relate to the supernatural, and how to relate to fellow adherents of the faith.

The Christian view of God as a transcendent being who is a "higher power up there," shapes the second generation's perception of the supernatural, as Tony Chan, an analyst from the San Francisco Bay Area, commented. In this dualistic framework, people live in the worldly and profane plane, while God is in heaven, an eternal and sacred being. God may or may not be knowable, but God is an outside force that animates and moves the universe. This viewpoint clearly contrasts with that of Chinese Popular Religion, in which gods, spiritual beings, and ancestors are immanent and qi infuses the world. Sophia Wong did not consider her family's practice of ancestor veneration religious because she contrasted her deceased relatives with the notion of deities with greater powers. When asked about whether her family tradition constituted a religion, she explained, "No not really. Because they never, it was never like a specific deity. It was just 'Bow to your ancestors.'" Religion, according to this Western perspective, involves worship of specific deities, but bowing to ancestors is simply an ethnic custom.

Along with the expectation that religion related to belief and commitment to God or deities, our respondents had notions about established religion in terms of how individuals were to relate to God and to fellow believers. Their experiences with the Christian church established for them these essential elements and functions of religion. They recognized that Christianity expected weekly worship attendance and conformity to moral norms, provided fellowship and social support, and demanded strict affiliation.

Like many of our respondents, Irene Hui rejected Christianity because of its "established" character as a powerful institution demanding conformity to rules. When away from home at medical school and having just broken up with her boyfriend, Irene looked for a community of friends. With her Christian roommate, she attended a Christian church for a year.

Eventually, though, she dropped out because she disliked the explicit and implicit rules, as well as the judgments made at the church:

> I'm not very comfortable with the idea of established religion. I think it's gone to the point where it's really turned me off. The people, I feel, were being really judgmental. If I didn't go to church one day, they would ask, "Why aren't you going to church?" Just certain concepts of "Here are things that you should be doing and things that you shouldn't be doing."

Besides the perception that established religion employs rules and requires regular attendance, she also found that this church demanded exclusive belief, which she rejected:

> I don't have a problem with the idea of believing in God or having a relationship with God, or praying or speaking to God. I think that, for me at least, I'll do it if I'm very stressed or if I'm very fearful, or I'm going through a lot of things and I think that it's a personal thing for me. But I don't feel the need to have to congregate with a bunch of people and have to prove myself to other people or conform to other people. And I'm kind of okay with the uncertainty.

Religion, for Irene, provides personal support, but she rejected the need for exclusive affiliation and clearly defined truth boundaries. Even though she turns to God in times of distress, she does not see herself as religious because she does not meet the Christian criteria for strong faith.

Karen Lai, who hails from Alhambra, California, found that she could not identify fully as Christian even though her father is Catholic and she agrees with its beliefs:

> I feel like I could go to a Sunday Mass, or I could participate in one, which I've done in the past, because my roommate wanted to go and I went with her. And when I was there, I was able to identify with everything they were saying. They would tell a Christian story, and this idea that you could reflect upon what that saint or person was doing. I would say, "Amen." I would understand the story and everything.

Despite her identification with and assent to all that went on in Mass, she still could not affiliate with Catholicism. She explained, "But at the end of the day, when I go home, I don't feel like a bona fide Christian would say to me that I was part of their sect because I wouldn't necessarily want to abolish all my other beliefs that I have." In contrast to "bona fide" Christians, Karen held to other beliefs, including Greek mythology and reincarnation, which she felt barred her from being a true follower.

In addition to its being an established institution with sets of rules and exclusive theologies, respondents felt that authentic religion involved a high commitment and strong faith. Many became disillusioned with Christianity when they found church members to be hypocritical and not genuine. Peter Hsieh, for instance, attended a Chinese church because many of his friends went and his parents encouraged him to explore different philosophies. He quit after a period because of the duplicity he observed at the church youth group:

> There was just so much rampant hypocrisy. The same friend who would be in church crying, praying about how he needs to be a better person, God loves us all, would ask me to copy my homework at school. I mean, it was just stupid stuff like that.... I was in the mindset that, "Well, if this is real, if this is what you believe, then you know you should believe it." But it looks like no one really believes it. And it was a big turnoff!

True religiosity, for Peter, would be reflected in strong belief and, subsequently, moral behavior consistent with one's beliefs.

Through these examples, second-generation Chinese Americans outlined normative expectations of what religion consisted of: (1) a strong belief in a deity or higher power, (2) relationship and exclusive commitment to this deity, (3) voluntary association with co-believers, and (4) moral behavior consistent with these beliefs. Like other Chinese Americans, they did not affiliate with Christianity because they found they could not believe as firmly, did not want to rely so much on an outside force, and did not want to affiliate with a flawed institution.

Interaction with Christianity had another effect besides dissuading this sample of Chinese Americans from joining the Christian church. It made their Chinese family experiences with ancestors, spirits, and luck seem beyond the pale of religion. Respondents often termed these spiritual practices "superstitious," with the negative connotation that these traditions were pointless and ineffectual. For example, Ben Wong from Atherton, California, shared that his parents and many of his friends followed Chinese "superstitions," such as not putting chopsticks upright in one's rice bowl. In retrospect, he stated, "When you're a kid, a lot of those customs are weird to you." The more he learned about them, the more he found them "sillier and sillier." Now, however, he states, "[I] realize that [I'm] doing this for my great-grandparents. There was a lot of those deep Chinese traditions."

To summarize, Christianity is the dominant institution in the American religious marketplace. Not only does it have the resources, personnel, and established institutions to meet multiple needs of members and nonmembers, but it also structures the rules of the marketplace. Its privileged position enables it to establish what constitutes authentic religion and true worship, what makes up proper religious behavior and appropriate commitment. In comparison, the second generation of Chinese Americans view the practices of Chinese Popular Religion as privatized family spirituality at best, and ethnic superstition at worst. Even as they reject Christianity, none viewed Chinese Popular Religion as an established religion to affiliate with, and they did not see their household practices as constituting a viable spiritual tradition. In fact, they did not even have a name for the constellation of practices and "deep Chinese traditions" in which their families engaged. Thus, they perceived themselves as nonreligious even if they did adhere to practices of Chinese Popular Religion: meditation, prayer, ancestor veneration, and *fengshui*.

Race and Gender

Beyond the class factors identified in chapter 3 that led some second-generation Chinese Americans to identify as atheists and others as spiritual but not religious, race and gender also influenced their affiliations. While they are not causal factors, they shaped the second generation's experience such that they were either more likely to adopt or to reject identifying with a minority religion in the U.S., that of Chinese Popular Religion. Strong and negative racialized experiences oriented the second generation to avoid appearing too Chinese, while positive gendered expectations encouraged them to maintain their family's traditions.

When specifically asked, "What was it like for you growing up Chinese?," many in our sample answered that they experienced racial taunting and stereotyping. These individuals generally grew up in white suburbs. The young adults who lived in Chinese ethnic enclaves tended to first cite their family's cultural practices as being significant. For example, when posed this question, Scott Lai, who grew up in the Midwest, responded:

> Fighting. That's definitely the most distinctive. Racism, being made fun of at school, fighting on a regular basis. There are innumerable memories of mock-Chinese language and, you know, half-joking, half-making fun of kung fu. I mean pretty much every generic Chinese and/or other Asian ethnic stereotype you could exploit, it was exploited.
>
> And so, at least publicly, the thing that I think about most—being Chinese being raised in the Midwest—is hostility.

Many of the men in our sample discussed the fights they had because of racial taunting and felt alienated from their peers. Beyond their childhood experiences, these men recognized the continued impact of race in their workplace.

Another example of the institutional racism that the respondents reported was the glass ceiling, an invisible barrier to promotion because of their racial background and stereotypes. Irving Shue, an entrepreneur from Scarsdale, New York, who now works in Boston, detailed his own experience:

> As an Asian, I'm definitely stereotyped. People just looking at you are going to judge you differently. That's how I felt. Sometimes we go to these meetings, where they brought in all these executives. We were an Asian management team and we hired a white vice president of operations. We didn't introduce ourselves. But the others automatically assumed that he's the CEO. That's how it is in a lot of meetings.

Whereas men described physical altercations in their childhoods, women complained of teasing. Danielle Hsu, who grew up in a few suburbs of the San Francisco East Bay, recalled being teased and bullied each year of elementary school:

> When I was five, I got teased and my mom explained that I should ignore it. Of course, it didn't stop the teasing. You know how when you're in elementary school, when you go get milk? I went to get the milk and these kids stopped me and harassed me. I remember more stuff in second grade: being told I was different and other types of racial teasing.

Peers also made Serena Zhang of Cleveland, Ohio, feel badly about her ethnic and racial background: "I definitely thought that I didn't have good feelings about [being Chinese]. I thought they were nerdy, and it felt stressful. The community didn't seem fun. . . . Once I hit high school, I could turn [being Chinese] into something a little interesting, but still not necessary cool." Boxed in by the stereotype of the model minority, in which Asian American students are seen to be overachieving, Serena felt that she could not be "cool," even though she felt proud of her ethnic heritage.

Given these negative dealings with race and stereotypes, the second generation attempted to distance themselves from stereotypical characteristics or traits perceived as foreign and strange. In the past, Chinese Americans were stereotyped and politically disenfranchised as unassimilable pagans, and such caricatures discouraged post-1965, second-generation Chinese Americans from being seen as too "Orientalized," that is, exotic and different. They certainly did not explore Chinese popular religion as a plausible worldview to adopt or to practice.

Just as their racialized experiences were gendered, the religious experiences of the second generation were also gendered. Over 66% of the atheists in the sample were men, and 80% who were spiritual but not religious were women. This pattern corresponds to a general American trend.[6]

The atheists in this sample were scientists or, interestingly, attorneys. The spiritual but not religious were in the health or education fields.

These women were more open than others to spiritual forces that intervene in this world and were also more likely to maintain aspects of Chinese popular religion. Erica Tseng, whose quote introduced this chapter, grew up in an extended family household in Boston's Chinatown. Daily she witnessed her grandmother and mother light incense at two home altars. Her father, who taught martial arts, always wore a Buddha pendant for protection and hung a religious medallion on his car's rearview mirror, which he swore saved his life once. Given this environment, she continues to maintain family altars and believes in karma and fate:

> I believe in fate, but I believe in free will, too. You're destined to a specific path or for a specific person. I got it from my family, my dad and my mom. They didn't have a serious talk about it, but they'd say it in passing. They say "It wasn't meant to be," or "That's not just the type of luck I have."

Her parents integrated such comments into family conversations, especially when gambling:

> A funny example would be at the casino, and they never won big money there. They would win sometimes; my dad was really good at cards but he would never really win. So my dad would say, "Yeah, I have bad luck. I'm not meant to win big money." And my mom would win, and she would say that she has a small part of her destiny or fate where she does win small money.

Since Erica had been raised in this spiritual tradition at home, and also participated at Christian church services with friends, she lived in an environment where spirits and supernatural forces were seen to be at work. Since she was not in the science or engineering field, she was not as exposed to secular worldviews. Subsequently, keeping the traditions of Chinese Popular Religion posed no conflicts, and "it doesn't hurt," as she practically points out.

Wendy Tong's mother was a faithful adherent at a Buddhist temple who brought Wendy weekly. That influence, along with her grandfather's love for Chinese martial arts, led her to explore Buddhism and Daoism. She has since become an acupuncturist and admits, "I believe in a qi. It makes sense to me that something makes us alive and I think it does flow through our bodies while we are alive. I didn't grow up with it. Well, I guess it was in kung fu movies!" She recognized that her perspective, as a spiritual but not religious individual, differed from most people:

> I don't really believe in science as my guiding in life, because people can really take science as their belief structure. It is their religion pretty much, because that's how everything works for them. I don't think that's the way it is. I think science is what a lot of people are comfortable using to engage life. And that's okay for them, but I don't think it explains everything or even most things.

Instead, Wendy practices many of the Buddhist principles she was raised with and believes in "souls for both people and animals."

Both Erica and Wendy hold different beliefs and practices than their immigrant mothers, but they have chosen to continue practicing aspects of Chinese Popular Religion. They have selectively maintained certain traditions and beliefs because of the strong influence of their family. In their case, as with other Americans, ethnicity, gender, and mother's religiosity predicted their own religiosity.[7] They also had extended family members who reinforced Chinese Popular Religion, and local temples where they could practice. Residing near San Francisco, they did not mention experiences of being racialized outsiders or of being taunted for cultural or religious differences. Being Chinese and being practitioners of Chinese Popular Religion were acceptable identities in the San Francisco Bay Area.

CONCLUSION

Chinese Popular Religion, as well as Confucianism, translates poorly into the American context for four main, interrelated reasons. First, Chinese immigrant parents do not explain or explicitly teach the rituals and traditions to their children. In the situations where they do demand adherence to rules of luck or taboo, they do not offer reasons as to why. We speculate that these parents were not trained in the meanings of the traditions or the mechanisms of rituals, but relied on specialists to guide them, if needed. Second, the second generation adapted to the United States quicker than their parents did, leading to dissonant acculturation. Although the parents may have wanted to maintain values and customs from the homeland, their children preferred to use the English language and could not understand the Chinese terminology or fully participate in the practices of Chinese Popular Religion. Instead, they saw American ways as modern and progressive, while Chinese customs and beliefs were outdated and foreign. Thus, within the Chinese American household, immigrant parents had difficulty passing on the traditions as their children often sought to acculturate to the mainstream, American context.

Third, the American religious landscape privileges established religions with strong institutions, such as Christianity. The Christian church and its modalities of doctrinal belief, voluntary congregationalism, and evangelism are standards for authentic religious experience. In contrast, the key institutions of Chinese Popular Religion—the extended family and temples—are often not available for the Chinese American community. So Chinese Americans are at a loss to learn about their spiritual heritage.

Fourth, just as the religious context of the United States hinders the preservation of a minority religion such as Chinese Popular Religion, race relations also discourage its retention. Almost every Chinese American in this sample, especially those who grew up outside of Chinese ethnic enclaves, reported incidents of racial teasing, harassment, or stereotyping. These events in their formative years had a chilling effect, such that the second generation reported wanting to fit in with their peers and to avoid looking different or weird. One clear consequence of the religious and racial context is how Chinese Americans discussed the practices of luck and *fengshui*. Whereas in Asia these taboos and customs might be norms, in the United States they are considered "superstitions" that are "silly" and "weird." With such negative connotations, very few of these traditions were continued.

These obstacles to the translation of Chinese Popular Religion clearly hampered its retention in the United States. However, second-generation Chinese Americans reported that they do prize and retain some key values and rituals. Just as Chinese have for centuries, they continue certain moral rituals and righteous relationships centered around the family, albeit in a hybridized manner. These rituals and relationships are the subject of the next chapter, in which we investigate the highest values and most important social bonds of Chinese Americans today.

CHAPTER 5

✦

The *Yi* of Family Sacrifice

Chinese Americans' Highest Values

After Jodi Shieh, who grew up in Minnesota, worked a few years in information technology for Target's corporate headquarters, she decided to return to graduate school with the goal of maximizing her skills and talents. Following the aims of most Chinese Americans from where she was raised, she did not want to merely succeed; she wanted to follow the "Silicon Valley narrative" of getting rich and making a difference in the world: "I went to get a MBA for money and prestige. I wanted my cake and to eat it too. I had bought into the Silicon Valley narrative of changing the world—Google-fying the world and bringing education online, but also the gaining of extreme wealth." While at U.C. Berkeley's Haas School of Business, she underwent a quarter-life crisis and reevaluated her main goals for her life. She originally went to business school because she wanted to work with social enterprises that could provide her with a "corporate lifestyle." She bluntly commented, however, "Now I realize that I was mistaken!" She could not do it all—both become materially successful and serve the underrepresented, change the world and have a fulfilling personal life. So she developed a more chastened view of her dreams. Seeing herself as progressive, she wanted to live authentically. Given her political values and her ethnic background, Jodi is in search of how best to make a difference: "I'm trying to figure out where I could be an authentic leader based on where I am, and in contrast to what the business world thinks is a business leader." At the same time, Jodi acknowledges that her aim in life is no longer about becoming self-fulfilled through accumulating experiences. Rather, she seeks to be mindful of these experiences:

> I'm trying to work on that, let go of life as the consumption of experiences. The best thing I've found is yoga, which is leading me to meditation. I'm trying to explore that the purpose of life is to be present; fight or flight is not our only options. We can just experience.

Similar to most of our respondents who were under 30 years old, she reflected the three primary values of American millennials: (1) maximizing their skills to make the most use of them, (2) making a difference in the world, and (3) having authenticity in their lives.

Although Jodi held high ambitions for herself, her devotion to family counterbalanced her individualism. She highlighted her parents' efforts on behalf of her and her brother, who is autistic, such as when she was in the sixth grade and they moved to a new school district for her brother's special education classes. At that time Jodi complained about leaving her school, and her parents were indignant about her selfishness. She spoke repentantly about her attitude then: "The fact that I was thinking about me, my parents were 'What?! We do everything for you! We sacrifice for you!' [My attitude] was a rejection of that." Despite their exasperation, her parents acceded to Jodi's demands and did not transfer her to a different school. In fact, they drove 45 minutes every day so that she could stay at her original school. That sacrifice continues to astound her, as she remarked: "In retrospect, it was very kind, but ridiculous for them. In traffic, it was forty-five minutes. That's a big thing to do."

Jodi reflected that her highest responsibility is to care for her brother. Self-identified as a queer woman who questions traditional marriage and monogamy, she retains her Chinese American value for family:

> I just think it would be unconscionable not to [take care of my brother]. He's not my only family, but he's the only family I know. Once my family are gone, that's it. I know there are people who don't take care of their family, but I don't understand it.

Her concern for her brother dictates her future career plans, choice of residence, and even her relationships.

A bit older than Jodi, David Jong developed a different set of values. A therapist who was raised in Texas, he followed his girlfriend to Philadelphia. While Chinese Americans under 30 tended to focus on maximizing their careers or talents, those over 30, like David, were more likely to be expressive individualists who sought individual happiness, fulfillment, and relationships.[1] He observed that he became self-introspective through his graduate training:

> I value my quality of life; it's a selfish statement. In graduate school, there's a huge emphasis on the self. When you go through all these theories and how they work, you learn them, turn them inward and review your own experiences. A lot of coursework is around self-reflection and processing your own stuff.

Through "self-reflection and processing" he came to a clear understanding of his own values and desires. His primary goal is to have a strong relationship with his partner:

> With a background in therapy, we have ideas of who we are and there's the reality of who you are, and the values you have of certain things; an awareness of who you are and working towards what you want to become. I want a relationship where you can be open about who you are, and where you're trying to go, and have someone supportive of that.

David also shared his desire to pursue his passion, which involves identifying as an ally to the LGBQT community and as a feminist. He continued discussing his values:

> A lot of folks want to reward themselves with financial things, but I want to do things that I'm *passionate* about—around my values working on inequality and the social justice issues in today's news. Trying to find ways to be more proactive and have a hand in those things or doing things that make a way better for what I feel are not right.

Unlike world-changing millennials who maximize their efforts to make a concrete difference, his aim was simply to be an ally.

David derived his ultimate values from his Chinese American family. Like Jodi, he had an emotionally ambivalent relationship with his parents, but he continued to value their priorities: "I definitely internalized the 'You take care of your family no matter what.' Even though I don't have a good emotional relationship with my family, I value my family. Family is important because that's how I was brought up." Employing the language of family sacrifice, David noted his parents' offerings of care and his attempt to repay them:

> I've been reflective of my life and I'm very grateful for the things that were afforded to me and I'm grateful for the *sacrifices* they made. And I'm trying to pay it back—also, knowing they put on all this emphasis on my siblings and me. I'm trying to build that relationship on a more emotional level and less on a caregiver, nurturer, dependent level.

Interestingly, his hybridized way of relating to family included caring on an emotional level, besides providing physical care.

Just as David's parents modeled for him how to live righteously and sac-rificially, he plans to pass those same values and ethic to his own children someday: "I hope to have a family, too. I hope to pass on the good—the values that I got from my parents that I connect with and agree with. And pass on the opportunities that were given to me." As illustrated, this se-lective, hybridized value system includes multigenerational relationships, whereby each generation takes mutual responsibility to care for one an-other: "I want to pass down the good parts of their background. I want [my children] to have a connection to their culture for the sake of my parents, and staying connected—a connection to the family. Mainly, the family is, above all, important."

David's statement neatly encapsulates the focus of this chapter. Even though all the second-generation Chinese Americans we interviewed claimed that they were nonreligious, they did hold to an ultimate value and meaning system that we term "Chinese American familism." Their families offered them both their purpose in life and the deepest meaning for their ex-istence, both their primary identity and their greatest source of belonging. In fact, family became the central narrative by which they understood the course of their lives—past, present, and future.

Chinese American familism, thus, acts as a framework for living out right relations, or *yi*. *Yi* translates roughly as "righteousness" in two senses. First, *yi* is a moral disposition toward doing good that can be cultivated. Second, *yi* governs the proper responsibilities by which one relates to others, in particular, five main relationships. These relationships are fa-milial (parent-child, elder sibling–younger sibling, spouse-spouse), as well as societal (friend-friend, subject-ruler). Chinese American fami-lism is a way of relating to others by which family becomes the sym-bolic boundary that dictate how one loves, assumes responsibility, and interacts ethically.

A theory of *liyi* examines *yi* by articulating a group's highest values and key relationships. By identifying Chinese Americans' top goals, their self-stated priorities, and their ultimate responsibilities, this chapter details how familism operates as the *yi* of Chinese Americans. Along with specifying familism, a theory of *liyi* helps to explain the formation of these values. In the Chinese American case, key factors establishing and maintaining the *yi* of familism are (1) traditions of Chinese Popular Religion and Confucianism, (2) migration reinforcing group boundaries for survival, (3) educational attainment supporting certain family patterns, and (4) a racialized multicultural discourse that privileges family, food, and fun as hallmarks of ethnic culture.

Data from the Pew Research Center national survey of Asian Americans substantiates Chinese American familism. When asked about their top goals in life, Chinese Americans ranked "being a good parent" more often than having a good marriage or a successful career. The emphasis on being a good parent to have a strong family and raise children well indicates the priority this ethnic group gives the family unit—even those under 30 who do not have children of their own.

After reviewing the Pew survey data, this chapter compares Chinese Americans under 30 with those over 30. As exemplified by Jodi and David, those under 30 tend to be "maximizing world-changers," and those over 30 generally aim to be "expressive balancers." Even with this age variation, however, Chinese Americans of both groups are overwhelmingly consistent in their familism. This familism consists of three aspects that make Chinese American immigrant lives meaningful: (1) deep appreciation and respect for their ancestors' and immigrant parents' sacrifices, (2) a felt obligation to give back to and take care of their parents and grandparents, and (3) responsibility to love, nurture, and provide for one's own generation—siblings and cousins—as well as the next generation. Even the outliers in our sample prove the rule of Chinese American familism.

THE TOP GOALS OF CHINESE AMERICANS

A national survey of Chinese Americans best demonstrates familism in terms of their top goals and the role of parents in major decisions. This study analyzes survey data made available by the Pew Research Center. Phone interviews were conducted with 728 Chinese Americans in early 2012. In our sample, 157 (21.5%) were under 30 years old. Among the largest religious affiliations of Chinese Americans, atheists made up 13.3%, and "nothing in particulars" 36.3%. We compare these groups of young Chinese American atheists and nothing in particulars with the Chinese American population overall.

The Pew Research Center asked respondents about their most important goals and allowed them to give more than one answer. Chinese American young adults valued being good parents slightly higher than did other Americans. Among Chinese Americans, 57.1% of atheists and 49.1% nothing in particulars rated this as their top life goal, as compared to 56.7% of Chinese American overall. About half (52.0%) of millennials rated being a good parent as a top goal.[2]

Having a successful marriage is the next highest rated goal, with 23.8% of Chinese American atheists and 43.9% of nothing in particulars citing this

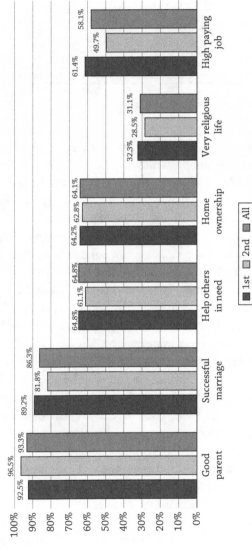

Top Goals by Generation

Figure 5.1 Top Goals by Generation

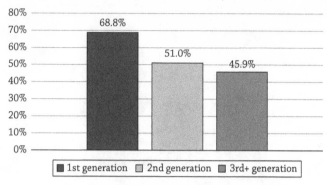

Figure 5.2 Parental Influence on Career by Generation

value. About half of Chinese Americans in general (45.7%) prioritized marriage. Only 30.0% of American millennials rated marriage this high.

While young adults are at a stage in life to focus on their careers, doing so was not as important for Asian Americans as being a good parent. Only 9.5% of Chinese American atheists and 19.3% of nothing in particulars identified having a good career as one of their top goals, as compared to 16.8% for all Chinese Americans. These rates are comparable to other American young adults, of whom 15.0% wanted a successful, high-paying career.

The American millennial generation is more likely to value social justice and activism than previous generations. Similarly, 9.5% of Chinese American atheists and 19.3% of nothing in particulars listed helping others in need as one of their most important goals. Overall 21.0% of all Chinese Americans and 21% of American millennials rated this value highly.

In sum, even though Chinese Americans under 30 tend to be much more highly educated than other Americans and have not yet married or started families, they still value being good parents and having a family more than the general population.[3]

Another way to demonstrate Chinese American familism is by looking at the weight of parental influence in major decisions. Chinese American young adults state that their parents should have some or a lot of influence in their careers and even marriage choice. In fact, 38.1% of atheists and 64.9% of nothing in particulars believe their parents should have some or a lot of say in their career choices. Overall, 62.9% of Chinese Americans feel parents should have such career influence.

Similarly, 42.9% of atheists and 65.0% of nothing in particulars believe their parents deserve some influence in their choice of spouse, as compared to 56.8% of Chinese Americans overall. Instead of viewing marriage simply as a relationship between two individuals, Chinese Americans seem

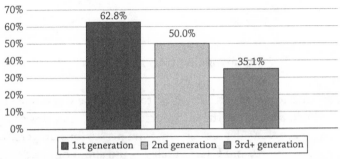

Parents Should Influence Spousal Choice by Generation

62.8%

50.0%

35.1%

■ 1st generation   □ 2nd generation   ■ 3rd+ generation

Figure 5.3 Parental Influence on Spousal Choice by Generation

to acknowledge that marriage involves a relationship between two families and that their parents' wishes and concerns are important to them.

Even though familism is not exclusive to Chinese Americans, the traditions of Confucianism and Chinese Popular Religions provide certain group boundaries, values, and rituals to reinforce it. They include the strength of extended family ties, reciprocity and loyalty, and ancestral veneration. The processes of migration and resettlement reinforce the family as an institution necessary for group survival and mobility. Subsequent educational attainment by the second generation then offers them the financial capacity to maintain a certain family-oriented lifestyle and to care for the elderly. Furthermore, America's racialized context privileges specific multicultural practices, especially regarding food. Consequently, Chinese American familism takes specific contours.

DREAMS OF THE AGE: CHINESE AMERICAN YOUNG ADULTS

Chinese Americans in this sample were 21 to 45. When asked about their purpose in life or what gave them their greatest meaning, their answers tended to diverge depending on whether they were under 30 or over 30, as they had different life concerns upon graduating, becoming settled in their careers, and marrying. We term those under 30 "maximizing world-changers" for their orientation toward utilizing their time, skills, and abilities to make a difference in their careers and in the world. In contrast, those over 30 we describe as "expressive balancers," for their desire to gain individual happiness while juggling career, relationships, and personal interests. Despite this age-based variation, Chinese Americans were decidedly not as individualistic as other Americans. Both groups of Chinese Americans widely adhered to familism, which shaped their top priorities and deepest held values.

Maximizing World-Changers

Chinese Americans under 30 tended to utilize the discourse espoused by Jodi Shieh, profiled in the introduction. Since all in this sample had obtained a bachelor's degree—many from prestigious universities such as Harvard, Stanford, and U.C. Berkeley—and about one out of four had obtained graduate degrees, they developed a sense of entitlement to accomplish much, as well as a sense of efficacy that they *could* attain their goals.[4] Whatever the arena—whether their careers, their civic engagement, or their personal interests—they valued making the most of their time and abilities.

A high percentage of those under 30 (44.0%) discussed maximizing their resources in a utilitarian fashion to further their own individual interests, especially in their careers. For example, individuals under 30 shared this maximizing, rationalizing approach toward being as productive and impactful as one can be:

> In technology, on the product side, I want to build something that people use. *Useful* is the key.—Daniel Lui, project manager from Cupertino, California
>
> It's important to do something with your life. So I'm definitely driven by that: *wanting to contribute* and improve myself.—Marilyn Hong, medical student from Milwaukee, Wisconsin
>
> Everyone wants the bigger impact. Earlier in your career, you want to *make a big impact* but it's just preparing you for the things to come.—Derek Qian, electrical engineer from Fremont, California

Two other interviewees, Ken Li and Irving Shue, illustrate this value system. Ken Li grew up in San Jose, California, in a large extended family. His father, who was a refugee from Vietnam, did not graduate from high school but made his way from being a produce seller to owning his own jewelry store. His mother, also a Chinese Vietnamese refugee, obtained some adult school training to become a production planner for a Silicon Valley manufacturer. Ken explained how his grandparents primarily raised him:

> When I woke at seven or eight a.m., [my father] was already gone. I'd stay up late to see my dad, until ten p.m., but still I wouldn't see him. We had our grandma and grandpa

on my dad's side and they took care of us. My grandpa walked me to preschool, and my grandma cooked dinner.

Seeing his parents work so hard, he wanted a different life for himself. Like Jodi, he spoke of "maximizing" his resources and "making the most" of life. When asked about his current purpose in life, he recalled the hardships of his parents:

> I want to be rich, so I'm trying to *maximize* my finances. I'll try to look at different paths. I tried to go through being an actuary, but I got to be a financial analyst instead. Different routes will help me get to where I want to be. [Working and making money] is how I make the most out of my life. My life is a playground, and I'm just trying to enjoy my time here.

As he explained, Ken and other Chinese Americans act in a pragmatic fashion, trying out "different routes" that best get them to their ultimate aims. He works now as a financial analyst but still thinks about becoming an actuary so that he can earn more. His Silicon Valley roots clearly shaped him, just as the mythic land of the Information Age even influenced those outside of California.

The "Silicon Valley narrative" that impacts so many maximizing world-changers not only sets the economic context for wealth production and globalized impact; it also provides role models for Chinese Americans. Irving Shue, who has established a thriving food truck business in Boston, summarizes the rationalizing, goal-oriented approach of these younger Chinese Americans:

> This [entrepreneurship] is a means-to-an-end kind of thing. I'm still trying to figure it out. Whatever I do, I want to have a positive impact on the world. In what format? I have a nonprofit now. But something what Bill Gates does. That's what I would love to do. I think he makes a big impact on the world. The person I look up to the most now is Elon Musk, who's using business to change the world. I want to figure out what I'm best at, and if maybe I'm a really good businessman, that's how I can change the world, through business.

Irving is not necessarily oriented toward being a successful entrepreneur as an end in itself. Rather, he and other Chinese Americans look to models like Bill Gates and Elon Musk, who are not only financially successful but also use their wealth to "change the world."

Along with prioritizing their individual career success, another large proportion of Chinese Americans under 30 (29.0%) spoke about wanting to "make a difference" in the world, believing they can have an impact on social ills. American millennials are much more likely than Gen X to say it is important for them to "give back" in their work.[5] Lila Song, a software engineer who grew up in Fremont, California, used the language of maximizing impact and making rational decisions in order to change the world. When asked about her goals in life, she ruminated about her contribution to alleviate suffering: "[I have] a mini-crisis about what I want in life. I want to have an impact while I'm here. I can help [alleviate] people's suffering. There's something I could contribute, and improve some kind of life somewhere." Like Ken, she's still trying to discern which career path to take in order to be of greatest use. She, too, spoke of economic, rational decision-making guiding her use of time:

> It's hard to figure out which course will maximize my impact. While I'm doing something, I can try out new things. The goal is to maximize. As an economist, I make a rational decision on what is worth the trade-offs of my time right now. If I have difficulty making decisions, I'll default to economics.

She is looking to work with a corporation that provides public health goods.

Another individual wanting to effect social change through his career is Craig Quan, a medical student who was formerly a software engineer. He identified three main values that motivate him and that he integrates through his medical work:

> Fundamentally, I like the idea of a few noble things in life. [First is] improving the lives of others, reducing suffering. [Second,] expanding the collective knowledge of mankind. [And third,] creating things—products or organizations—that make lives better. With medicine, I can participate in all three. The core of that is *maximizing happiness* and diminishing suffering—I obtain motivation and purpose by doing this for others.

Given that these Chinese Americans are highly educated, they have more options in their careers and were more financially stable to be able to give back with time and money.

Offering a contrast is Rhonda Woo, the only Chinese American under 30 in our sample who is a single mother. Her father never attended high school, and her parents were both working class. Two years after obtaining a B.S. degree from UCLA in environmental sciences, Rhonda had her daughter. As a result of her limited options and lack of parental support, she could not pursue the field of her major and instead obtained a job as a paralegal because it provided benefits. Her aims differed greatly from the maximizing world-changers. Even though she dreams of the future, she does not expect to make an impact or utilize her education: "I think about [the future] all the time. I just have to work with what I have right now. I'm happy when my daughter is happy and that I am healthy and I am able to support my family." When asked what gives her the greatest meaning in her life, she mentions being able to support her daughter on her own: "As long as I could support myself and my family, then I have a lot of meaning to live because I'm able to do such a thing."

Expressive Balancers

In contrast to Chinese Americans under 30 who were more likely to want to go out and change the world, those over 30 sought fulfillment in balancing family, career, and personal interests. Just as David in the introduction stated that he wanted to do what he was "passionate" about, many of those over 30 also employed the language of emotions—passion, fulfillment, and individual happiness—when discussing their top goals. These comments are indicative of this expressive individualism, which privileges the search for personal autonomy, fulfillment, and creativity. For example, these individuals discussed their main goals of balancing responsibilities and pursuing interests for fulfillment:

> What is meaningful to me? Simple things. Being sure I call my parents. It makes me happy and makes them happy, too. Career success—being able to share it with them. Knowing that the ties of my sisters make me a stronger person.—Wendy Foo, astronomer from Rochester, New York

> I think I want my children to be happy and in a stable place. That, for me, that's important. For most of my adult life after college, I've felt I don't want to be too close to my parents. Now as I get older, I want to see them more. I'd like to work on these connections with friends and family. Personally, I'd like to see more of the world myself.—Edward Song, software engineer from Boston

> I'm very much more in general a "work-just-to-play" person. I thought about that, and I think work-life balance is really important, very important. I want my career and my work to be enjoyable and something that I'm proud to do, but in all honesty that's mostly so that I can afford to do all the other things that I want to do.—Teresa Owyang, nurse from Los Gatos, California

Scott Lai articulated a highly developed philosophy of life and personal meaning system, as first described in the introduction. Because of the abuse in his home, he ran away at the age of 16, was briefly homeless, and has been independent since then. When he made his way to the San Francisco Bay Area he explored a variety of philosophies and religions and experimented with hallucinogenic drugs. Scott discussed his insatiable curiosity:

> I think my intellectual curiosity was driven by a need of personal fulfillment. Whether or not I saw it at the time, I think that's true now, in retrospect. Because I'm still as intellectually curious about it, but I have a lot less of that personal drive, so I seek out these experiences a lot less often.

After a time working in IT consulting, Scott became a public interest attorney. Having gone through therapy and feeling more settled, he now finds purpose in a variety of ways:

> I don't suppose there is a single ultimate purpose; there are multiple nodes and a lot of connections between them. It's kind of a web of purpose. First of all, I am tied to this carbon-based body. So, one of the purposes of my existence is going to be to try to extend the life of the body so that I can have more experience or enjoyment.
>
> But then, one of the other ones is the people that I have genuine connections with and care about the well-being for. I would want them to have the same thing. So that is another major purpose in my life.

His expressive individualism finds itself seeking experience, enjoyment, genuine connection, and support of others.

Like Scott, Teresa Owyang spoke of her search for meaning and her desire to change the world when she was in her 20s. In her 30s, however, she noted that her own limited impact shifted her perspective of herself and her role:

> I struggle in working with the frustrations of working in nonprofits and communities, and of watching the wheel get reinvented all the time, and seeing how little effect you have. So I think I backed away, in the sense that I feel a little bit helpless . . . like I don't feel that I could have that much influence on a larger picture.

Instead, she balances her own agenda with doing some limited good. She no longer tries to be "most effective" or "most happy."

> I struggle wanting to get involved [with the community] because I know it becomes frustrating and I know there's going be a lot of failures. I don't know how to get involved to where I would be most effective and also most happy. So I'm going to do what's personally best for me, and hopefully do some good also.

Having traveled and worked throughout the United States in public health, Teresa now aims to settle down where she grew up, where she finds fulfillment in relating to friends and family in regular obligations, such as family meals:

> [Purpose] in life? I think for me I find a lot of fulfillment and I gain a lot from my friends, from family. I'm in an odd transition. I've been away from home for eight years, so family obligations—like dinners and events and things like that—have not been a big part of my life and I've been able to avoid such things. Coming back, I'm realizing how much it's going to have to become part of my life. It's going to be fulfilling.

Growing up in the United States socializes second-generation Chinese Americans to be concerned with their personal happiness and individual goals. At the same time, their Chinese upbringing inculcates a value for family caretaking that becomes paramount.

Teresa observed how her parents took care of her grandparents, which provided a model for her to follow as she settles down:

> My grandfather on my mom's side is still here. He lived here, and I watch my mom, her brother, and her younger sister take care of their father. That comes from respect for their dad. You know how much my grandfather has given to his children, and now they're setting an example for me.

Although she doesn't plan to have children, her purpose in life continues to include family caregiving:

> I know the expectation for me later is for me to take care of my mom in such a way. Financially, weekly visits, taking them out to dinner, and supporting them in a lot of decisions. It's going be good for me to be here, to be a part of that now, I hope.

Financial support, regular visits, and help in decision-making for her divorced mother exemplify three primary ways that Chinese American familism is expressed. Almost all Chinese Americans who were interviewed utilize family sacrifice as a narrative that provides meaning for their own lives, include their past, present, and future.

VENERATING THE PAST: RESPECTING
THE SACRIFICES OF GRANDPARENTS AND PARENTS

The first key element of Chinese American familism is respect and honor for one's grandparents and parents, especially for their sacrificial love. Chinese Americans did not hearken back to their older ancestors but tended to remember those whom they personally knew. Several respondents made the comment "I wouldn't be here if it weren't for them," explicitly stating that they owe their entire lives to their parents and grandparents. As explained in the introduction, second-generation Chinese Americans tended to highlight the suffering of their grandparents in Asia, the migration experience of their parents, and the hard work of their parents on behalf of their children as their models for Chinese family sacrifice.

Even if their parents were voluntary migrants to the United States, Chinese Americans often reflected on the hardships that their grandparents and parents went through in Asia: war, poverty, and political unrest. For example, Henry Zhou, an IT professional who grew up in Kent, Ohio, shared how his parents and relatives suffered during China's Cultural Revolution in the 1960s, when millions were persecuted and forced into labor camps in the countryside. Henry reported that one of his older relatives tried to commit suicide to avoid Communist arrest, but survived and suffered greatly. His own grandfather had a successful business in Shanghai, but the government confiscated the company. When Henry's father was five, the government sent the family to the countryside. Henry elaborated about his father's hardships during this time:

> They kept sending my dad back to the farm. [My parents] told me the hard stuff they had to do in the rural area—they'd fight just for a bowl of rice. The struggles that they had to go through during Communism and the Cultural Revolution, that made me respect them that much more.

In recounting stories related to family photos, Henry repeatedly expressed his deep appreciation for his privilege and opportunities in comparison to the government oppression that his family faced:

> I appreciate what I have, that I don't have to starve or worry about being arrested or being beaten up. I don't have to be judged. I live in a society that's pretty free. They keep reminding me how good I have it here. I really appreciated what they did to bring me to the U.S. I understand what they went through. By them telling me the story, I can feel it.

Along with appreciating the hardships their family endured in Asia, the second generation revered their grandparents and parents who migrated for the sake of their families.

Sharon Chung, a nonprofit director who grew up in Boston, teared up when she rehearsed the journeys and hard labor of her grandparents and parents, who had migrated first to Zimbabwe and Mozambique: "I don't know why I'm getting so emotional about it, but I can remember being at the cemetery with my grandparents and feeling that in this small plot of land, there's about fifty Chinese people buried in the middle of Harare, Zimbabwe." She marveled at the resilience of this small overseas Chinese community, who traveled so far to become peddlers to destitute locals. Both her mother's and father's families ran grocery stores; her mother, living in Mozambique, met her father in Zimbabwe at a Chinese basketball tournament.

When Sharon's father left Zimbabwe to move to the United States, her grandfather made just one request of him:

> My dad said when he left Africa, his father told him, "Make sure she gets to go to school." That was his one thing that he requested of my dad—for me to go to school. I feel that was, in some ways, so much of the sacrifice that my parents put themselves through was so that the wish could become possible.

Without much education and English-language skills, Sharon's parents had to work within the Chinese American ethnic economy in a restaurant and in a garment factory. Nevertheless, her father fulfilled her grandfather's last wish by sending her to the best public school system near Boston and, later, to an expensive, private university. She expected to have to take out personal school loans, but her father spent his entire retirement savings on his daughter.

In response, Sharon feels that her calling in life is to share the story of the Chinese diaspora in Africa and to pay back her parents. She summarized her primary responsibility: "I feel responsibility to my parents. They've given me so much! They've spent so much time investing in me, through driving me around, making sure I had a meal cooked for me, always having breakfast. Things they're supposed to do, but I feel very fortunate." As she elaborated on her sense of calling, she spoke of family respect and honoring her elders. Like Henry, she eulogized her family for their sacrifices, both in migrating and working:

> This calling thing is that I wanted to honor my ancestors who made that journey. It's about family respect. Respecting their effort—like my mother-in-law, she works, she has a family business growing bean sprouts, she works in a mailroom, but she continues to cook every day. She takes care of the grandparents along with her sister-in-law. She always makes soup for us; whenever she thinks the kids are sick she'll make this special soup. They still try to take care of basic needs.

Sharon dedicates her work and her family life to honor her ancestors, parents, and in-laws.

As mentioned in the opening vignette, David is "trying to pay it back" to his parents. His father was a doctor, but David highlighted the physical labor that his father did when he was younger on behalf of the family. That hard work and diligence make up the ethic by which Chinese Americans sacrifice for their family. As David explains, both immigration and hard labor are two exemplars of Chinese American familism, in which the family takes precedence over the self:

> [My parents] didn't have the opportunity to live as selfishly as . . . I have lived. My dad sacrificed his childhood. He worked his whole life. When he moved to the U.S., he worked in the restaurant his whole childhood. He helped my grandparents run the restaurant. He'd go to school, and then he'd go to work, and then he'd go do his homework. And then he'd go to sleep and the next day he'd do it over again.

These parental sacrifices aimed to improve the lot of the second generation:

> I would say the sacrifices of my family—and also the sacrifices of my grandparents— the immigration piece is big to me. Chinese culture puts much emphasis on family and community, and to uproot yourself and leave that community and leave that family felt like a very big sacrifice just to secure more opportunities for their children.

In particular, Chinese Americans recognize immigration as a paradoxical act of sacrifice: immigrants must leave behind cherished family and community for the sake of their future family and community.

In return for his parents' and grandparents' sacrifices, David offers his form of respect. He acknowledges their efforts and struggles on behalf of the family, he works hard to honor the opportunities they have granted him, and he spends time with them and eats with them.

> I try to be respectful to the elders. When we spend time with my grandparents, we definitely try to talk about the old times—knowing what the older generation sacrificed, and that they want us to appreciate the opportunity. Showing that their sacrifices are not in vain is a way of giving back. Also, my grandparents are frail and brittle, so we spend a lot of time taking them out to eat.

David's acts of honor reflect a common pattern among second-generation Chinese Americans regarding how they love their family in culturally appropriate ways.

RELATING IN THE PRESENT: LOVING ONE'S
FAMILY, CHINESE AMERICAN–STYLE

Caring for their parents is a primary element of Chinese American familism, and our respondents love and honor the older generation in cultural ways that the elders can appreciate. First, Chinese Americans repay the hard work of their parents with their own hard work, both in school and in their careers. This ethic acknowledges the diligence of the parents and demonstrates that the children have learned from their parents. Second, Chinese Americans strive to maintain good communication with their parents. Many made a point of speaking to their parents more than once a week just to check in. Third, they expressed love through food, by going out to eat, by sharing recipes, and by treating each other. Fourth, they considered their parents in major decisions, especially where to reside. Knowing that they might have to become caregivers, they often chose to live near their parents.

Immigrant children work harder than other, similarly aged Americans, and for Chinese Americans this primary ethic finds its source in family obligation and indebtedness. Recognizing the time and effort that their parents made, the second generation want to give back. Observing them work so diligently provided role models and a norm to which they aspired. Thus, the work ethic of Chinese Americans derives from familism, where the source and the end of one's efforts is the family.

Computer designer Peter Hsieh, from Napierville, Illinois, works full time at Apple. Yet he also has competed nationally as a pianist and presented his own art pieces at multiple galleries. As someone who is a nonreligious expressive balancer, he seeks to enjoy "things that make [him] happy":

> I think our most important time is the time that we have here. So there's no point in saving up karma. Or there's no point in saying, "Oh no, I'll do that when I'm in my afterlife," because this is all we have. So the things that make me happy, give me contentment like—painting, being with my girlfriend, being with family—I try to enjoy that stuff as much as I can, and not get caught up in money, or in just being overly competitive and ambitious for not sincere reasons.

Like other Chinese Americans, he attributes his diligence, competitiveness, and widespread accomplishments to "respect" for his parents:

> Me and my sister . . . we both excelled academically. We both got the National Merit Scholarship. That kind of drive—a lot of that is out of competition, and a lot of that is respect for myself, respect for my parents. I think [seeing the sacrifice of my parents] is

why I wanted to do computer science, too. Well, my dad did it, and he struggled, but he made money to put food on the table. But they pushed me and said, "We did this so that you'd have a chance. Now you should take this chance."

With his salary from Apple and income from his art, he has become financially successful enough to purchase an expensive home in San Francisco or even retire. Given his financial freedom, Peter does not seek to accumulate more but asserts that one of his primary reasons for living is to care for his parents, who gave up what they wanted to do for his sister and him:

> But I think what might have been a big contributor to how me and my sister grew up is that my mom and my dad both sacrificed a lot of what they originally wanted to do so that my sister and I had a better chance. That's part of why I want to help take care of them. Me and my sister keep offering to give them money, but they always push it away. We just want to be the good Chinese kids and take care of them.

Even though most of our interviewees lived up to the model minority stereotype in that they did well academically and worked hard, they did not necessarily have Tiger Moms or Tiger Dads who were emotionally distant and noncommunicative. Instead, the second major way that Chinese Americans enacted familism was to visit with and communicate regularly with their elderly parents or grandparents.[6] For example, when Craig Quan, the medical student who wants to maximize happiness for himself and others, was about to graduate with his M.D., he reported that he did not expect to celebrate with a major vacation but planned to go to Seattle to spend time with his grandmother. He explained his reasoning:

> I have a duty to honor the people for me. For example, my grandparents were in the Cultural Revolution, suffered a lot. I know that my life is a lot easier than my parents' life. I still feel like I should work hard and honor the life they've given me. That's one of my core elements—to honor my grandparents.

As others have shared, working hard is a way to honor parents and grandparents. Spending time with them is also motivating for Craig as he prepares for his medical boards: "I've decided to go back and live with my grandmother for six weeks. It'll be very motivating. It'll be honoring to study hard for her legacy. That, and she's going to cook great food for me!"

Similar to Craig, a high proportion of Chinese Americans reported that they spoke with their parents on a regular basis when visiting was not an option. Two women provide extreme examples of constant communication between immigrant parents and their Chinese American children.

Susan Lau, a museum employee, grew up with her single-parent mother in Providence, Rhode Island, on a limited income. Her main goals for her own life crystallized when her close friend became very ill during her freshman year in college:

> I began thinking about my own life after Elizabeth got sick. She was a very, very smart and beautiful person. I met her in seventh grade and she said, "I want to be a neurosurgeon and go to Stanford." She got into Stanford, but then she got sick, and it was ironic because she got brain cancer.

From the East Coast, Susan flew out and spent two weeks with Elizabeth. Desperate, the two began to pray together: "We began praying to every god. I would also pray, 'Please God, don't make her die.' I was praying to God, who was supposed to do something." Susan had to return to school, and just two days later, Elizabeth passed away. Susan somberly reported her own grief:

> I was angry. And I lost any inkling of faith that I could have had. I convinced myself that she was going to live and cure herself, but I lost any sense of faith. I can't blame God, because now I don't believe in God. I don't blame anyone. I accept that things aren't perfect.

In honor of Elizabeth, Susan pledged to be happy and make the most of her own life:

> This person who had so much ambition in her life—I wanted to fulfill her ambitions to be happy and do things. She didn't have the privilege to do that. So I'm going to do whatever makes me happy. One of the things Elizabeth said to me before she died was, "I hope you will have a happy and wonderful life." That's what she said when she knew she was going to die soon. So I try to live up to that command.

When asked what makes life happy, Susan spoke about her own joys, her friends, and her mother, who raised her by herself. She reflected on her mother's care:

> I think having fun, having my family and friends healthy and happy. I know that's cheesy, but I'm hoping my mother is happy. I want to provide for her and make her life is easy. She raised me. She made me into a person. She sacrificed things for me. She fought for me. She paid for my piano lessons. She really, really cared for me. She's my mother, my best friend. If I could buy all the stuff in the world, I would do that for her. I want to shower her with presents.

While in college, Susan spoke face to face with her mother daily via Skype. Since she graduated and moved to New York City, she reported that she texted her mother every one or two days and speaks on the phone one to three times a week. She concluded that regular communication with her mother is how she lives up to Elizabeth's dying wish and how she respects her elders: "We're just so close. She's just so supportive. I see that [constant communication] happening for the rest of her life."

Tracy Lee exemplifies not only the constant communication that Chinese Americans maintain with their parents but also the way they relate to their parents through food. She chats on a daily basis with her parents, even though she works in Maryland in public health and they are in Houston, Texas. When asked "What's most important to you?," she immediately responded:

> Family is most important to me, followed by my career. My parents, my brother, my niece—I make sure I keep in touch. I'm the only one in Maryland, so I keep in touch daily by phone. If I didn't call to check in everyday, they would call the police! We chat fifteen to twenty minutes every day.

Tracy's phone calls alleviated her parents' anxieties, since they worried about their single daughter living far from home. As refugees from Vietnam, they had grown up in the same hometown and then remained rooted within the Chinese Vietnamese ethnic community in Houston. She understood their heightened worries stemmed from their traumatic migration experience, their unfamiliarity with mainstream American society, and her gender: "I think [their great concern] comes from being really close to their kids, and me being a girl. If my brother were here, they'd worry but not so much. Me being single, there's no one to take care of me." Yet Tracy called regularly not only to allay her parents' fears but also to demonstrate her respect for them, to inquire about their well-being, and to discuss their common love for food:

> I ask them how their day was, what they had for dinner, and I'd tell them about work. The dinner is something I ask about—I personally enjoy food and my mom cooks a lot. One of the things I really miss is my mom's cooking. Since I've been here in Maryland, I've been trying recipes my mom makes.

Tracy is the fourth person in this chapter to have mentioned food in relation to parents. David spoke of food as physical care, as what parents are supposed to provide. Craig said it is the way he spends time with his family, and Peter explained it is the means by which the second generation give back to their parents. Tracy uses food as a way to connect with her family while apart from them.

Cary Yu, a freelance communications director and environmental consultant based in Washington, D.C., employs food in another way, as a means of communication with his parents. He stated that it's ironic that he works "in communications and my family is crap in communication." That poor communication, Cary explained, is a result of his father's own issues with his grandfather, negative family experiences and dynamics, and Cary's gender and sexuality identity as a transgender person. Consequently, he summarizes that he is personally "crap at filiality." He had not visited his father in Oregon for six years before returning recently for a conference in Portland.

In spite of his estranged relationship with his father, Cary fondly reminisced about when he returned for that reunion and his father taking him to a new Taiwanese restaurant. Food became the vehicle by which they reconnected:

> Bonding over food still works perfectly. He's a chemical engineer and he raised me. In his engineering mindset, we both approach food from a scientific method in terms of what works and doesn't in the food. We're both food snobs. So I can nerd out about the molecular gastronomy and he can tell me stories about Taiwan and what food was like.

They then talked about traveling to Taiwan again, as they did when Cary was younger. Cary, noting that Chinese are verbally expressive, recognized that his father was demonstrating his love for him:

> We bonded over the street foods and bonded over the snacks we'd get [if we returned to Taiwan]. We let food be the thing to share. Chinese have a hard time talking about love in general. Culturally, we just don't know how to do it. So we let bonding over food do it for us.

Even though he has come out to his sister and his mother, who had divorced his father, Cary has yet to discuss his gender and sexual identities with his father, and he choked up when he considered his relationship with his father and his own desire to improve upon his "crappy filiality." One of his issues is that he wants a new job before he comes out, so that his father has one less thing to worry about. The other barrier is language; Cary does not know the correct terminology in Chinese to explain his gender identity and sexuality. So for the time being, food is the means by which he expresses filial devotion and love.

The fourth culturally appropriate means by which Chinese Americans love and honor their parents is to be physically available and living near them.

Although her work at the National Institutes of Health offers her great career advancement opportunities and she wants to pursue a Ph.D., Tracy is leaning toward returning to Houston to be geographically closer to support her parents. Despite the fact that her parents do not necessarily need her help and her brother is already close at hand to assist them, she still wants to be with them: "I feel guilty being here because my brother is a physician and he's not available to help them as much. If I'm not here, I would be more available. They're in good health and working, but I worry about their future." Her prioritization of her parents over her career, even though she has quickly advanced to a high rank as regional manager, once again illustrates Chinese American familism in action. Her regular communication with her parents and her plans to live in proximity to them both reflect what Tracy values the most in life.

In fact, the great majority of our respondents who lived far from their parents agreed that they would relocate should their parents need their assistance.[7] Craig Quan explained that he realized being a mature adult as a Chinese American did not entail moving out of one's home, but actually involves returning to one's home to become responsible for another. He defined maturity as growing from independence to interdependence:

> Growing up, I thought it was a sign of maturity to move away from family. Both [my sister and I] wanted to go to college wherever college was good, we didn't care about staying close to home. I thought I wanted to be in a major city. Now, both my sister and I want to be home, live in Seattle, so we can be close to [our] parents.

This shift in perspective came about after he had a talk with his grandmother when he visited her in China: "When [I was] in China, my grandma sat me down and said it's important to stay close to family. Now, I find that when I visit home, I enjoy it." For Craig, being nearby and with family transformed from being an obligation to an enjoyable way of caring for his parents and grandparents.

PAYING IT BACK, PAYING IT FORWARD: GENERATIONS OF FAMILISM

Familism provides a meaningful, coherent narrative for the life course of Chinese Americans, their past, present, and future. It offers an interpretation of their family's history, as they view both their Asian roots and their parents' migration to the United States as exemplars of family sacrifice. The second generation understood their grandparents' and parents' lives, especially their hardships, as oriented toward giving them better lives and opportunities. Familism also provides a counterbalance to American individualism, which is based on maximizing one's own interests or fulfilling one's own desires. It helps Chinese Americans think beyond themselves and establish relationships where they can direct their love and focus their attentions. In these parent-child relationships, they have culturally specific ways to demonstrate that love. By working hard and communicating regularly, by being physically present and sharing a love of food, Chinese Americans express their deepest love and affection. Familism guides Chinese Americans in how they dream about the future: what major responsibilities they would handle, what hopes they have, and what ideals they would like to see accomplished in their lifetime. Their plans for their lives included being able (1) to care for their parents, (2) to support their siblings and cousins, and (3) to love their own children by offering them the best opportunities. They planned to pass down to their children their most deeply held values.

When looking toward the future, most Chinese Americans expect to assume financial responsibility for extended family, not just their nuclear family. Repeatedly, our respondents asserted that providing for elderly, frail, and dependent relatives was their major concern and one of their primary roles in life. This filiality, in which parents raise their children and then adult children care for their parents, is the cornerstone of familism. A high percentage of our sample of first-generation immigrants, 20.9%, had grandparents reside with them and 30.2% lived in close proximity while they were growing up. Thus, they observed how their parents respected and treated the elderly. Comments about parental role modeling were commonplace:

> My mom took care of my [paternal] grandma and my grandpa, even though that wasn't her own parents. You respect your elders and you care for them. I think it was a tough thing to do; not every family would be able to let your in-laws live with you.—Julia Tom, advertising executive from San Mateo, California

> I recognize in the back of my mind that my parents are eventually going to need my support, financially, with time, everything. I'm going to come back and start taking on some of those family obligations now and start building myself as that support person for my family. That [assumption] was from watching my parents take care of their parents, watching my friends taking care of their parents.—Teresa Owyang, nurse from Los Gatos, California

In a similar manner, Craig Quan reflected on how he and his sister share the same sense of responsibility for their parents, even though they do not need their children's financial support. His rationale not to put his parents in a nursing home reflects this ethic of reciprocity, a Confucian value:

> I would take care of my parents in old age. I would never put my parents in a nursing home. I'd have them live with me. My sister is on the same page. [This is important because] they take care of me, and I take care of them. Nursing homes don't feel that great. My parents never put their parents in a nursing home. My grandma lives with [my] uncle. It's a sacrifice, but a meaningful sacrifice.

His uncle and parents modeled for him how to care for his elders, and Craig recognized how the burden of caregiving can be meaningful, not just an obligation.

Michael Chen, a community organizer in San Francisco, best demonstrates the extent of filiality among our sample. His father, a cook at a Chinese restaurant, abandoned his wife and four children when Michael was 13. Michael bitterly recounted his father's neglect and his own response:

> He rented a room at the family association building. He gambled, he womanized, and he spent a lot of money trying to impress other people. It was very important for him to appear to be a big shot. So I shut down. I put walls up around my mind, my heart, everything. I started to pretend like I didn't care about anything or anyone.

For over a decade the family remained estranged from the father. He returned only when he had run out of resources and could no longer borrow money from fellow association members. Initially, Michael and his siblings did not want to have anything to do with their father. However, their mother, who thought of her family responsibilities as very "noble," pleaded to them to receive their father back—out of loyalty to her and not necessarily to him. So the children complied grudgingly; Michael recalled that they told their mother, "Okay, but you need to understand something: we're only doing it for you."

After an awkward homecoming for the father, he returned to his gambler lifestyle. He incurred such a severe debt that he secretly took out a second mortgage on the family home. That act was the straw that broke the camel's back and led his mother to divorce his father. Nonetheless, Michael's mother still requested that her sons continue to take care of their father. Again, they complied and took over making the mortgage payments. In fact, they continued to house and live with their father, who had become disabled by this time. Michael explained why he and his siblings continue to care for their father, even when he has gambled away their household assets twice: "We're thinking about our family over ourselves by basically saying, 'You know what, we're taking care of you, Dad, only because Mom wants us to.'" Michael's extraordinary filiality toward his father stemmed from his loyalty and respect for his mother, whom he sees as a "martyr."

Chinese Americans were socialized to provide care not only for their elderly parents and grandparents but also for their siblings, even when all are adults.[8] Laura Chan from Boston complained of how her father showed favoritism to her brother. The father eventually ended this double standard when Laura's mother argued that his mistreatment of his daughter might disrupt family unity, not necessarily because it was unfair or mean: "My mom would tell my dad, 'Stop being so hard on her. Do you want them to hate each other? They're family, their brother and sister, and you're going to tear this family apart.'" Even though her children are college-educated and financially independent adults, Laura's mother remains concerned about family unity among the siblings:

> Now that I'm older, my mother would pull me aside and say things like, "You and your brother and sister promise me that you'll always look out for each other. You'll take care of each other." That's how she is with her siblings and I know that is really important to her.

Consequently, the siblings did draw close and remain so. Laura appreciated that her older brother supported her desire to play sports in high school and advocated on her behalf to their parents. He has since taken their retired parents into his home, and the sisters support him when they can.

Other Chinese Americans also spoke of their sense of obligation to their siblings. A postdoctoral researcher in New Mexico, Wendy Foo grew up in Rochester, New York, with two older sisters. Whereas she was quite career-oriented while pursuing a doctorate, she now most values her relationships with her parents, her boyfriend, and her sisters. Since they all now live in different states, they maintain a family discussion thread to share texts and photographs. Wendy notes that one of them will eventually have their parents move in with them:

> If they were sick, I don't think I would want to put them in a nursing home. That's a non-option. Out of my sisters, we all value family. When I was little, my parents instilled in me to respect your elders . . . and that shaped what made me try to keep ties with my family.

This shared agreement and mutual sibling support for one another derived from what her parents taught Wendy and her sisters when they were young:

When we were little, my parents would get upset if I got into fights with my sisters. That taught me to get along and be close. We were taught to be close. My dad always explained, "These are your sisters. You have to know how to get along." They wanted to make sure that we care for each other and [are] getting along. After they pass away, they could be happy that we could take care of each other. More recently, he told us to get along. It worked and I prioritize my relationships with my sisters.

One respondent, Ben Hao, an attorney from Seattle, said that he would sacrifice his life for his sister.

In contrast, Jane Man, a healthcare consultant who was raised in St. Louis, Missouri, said that her family is not that close or communicative. In fact she confided, "I've never gotten along with my mother. My mother and I were never close because she was constantly yelling and scolding me." Nevertheless, like Wendy, she accepted her responsibility to her parents and her brother because of her parents' care of them. Her parents even flew in a piano teacher from Kansas City so that she could compete nationally. She then affirmed the oft-repeated refrain about owing one's parents:

Definitely, I'll support my parents. I owe it to them. To a certain extent, if they did nothing for me, I'd be less likely to support them. I'll also support my brother. He's my brother and he would do the same for me. In his mind, he would do the same thing. I would definitely give physically or financially. If my brother came to ask me for anything, I would do it.

She concluded about her unconditional love for her brother, "I would definitely support my brother even if he's a drunk."

Michael Chen, who had to take in his negligent father, described the key values that his mother instilled in him: "Work hard. Be honest. Don't ever hurt anybody. Study. Be loyal." He then elaborated on how loyalty—a Confucian dimension of a virtuous life, along with reciprocity—was to be applied to his extended family, who assisted them when his gambling father was absent:

The loyalty thing meant being there for our cousins. It was kind of like that extended family thing, that we would have to help each other out when the time came. My mom would always tell us that, "Look, they're your family members, they're your blood, you know. You should expect to help them out when they need it and likewise they will be there when you need it."

The norms of Chinese American familism thus included an assumption of future responsibility not only for one's parents and children but also one's siblings and even cousins.

Most important, Chinese Americans aim to be good parents, and almost all our respondents discussed how this top goal guides their future plans. Like most Americans, their career objectives, residential decisions, and time allocation focused on their family. In particular, when discussing their child-rearing style, our interviewees revealed that they wanted to transmit to their children their most deeply held values, those belonging to Chinese American familism.

Sharon Chung, whose family migrated from Africa, clearly stated her main purpose in life, which was her own parents' purpose as well:

> First, to the next generation—to contribute, provide. I'm [my parents'] only child, and they would do anything so that I would succeed, in terms of whether it be helping me prepare for tests, or calling me every day now, to see what I'm up to, what I'm doing.
>
> So part of me is probably going to take that on in terms of the next generation. I will have a certain "Do everything that you can for your kid" mentality.

Doing everything for your children involves getting them the best education, providing them with extracurricular activities, and creating a nurturing, loving home life, according to Sharon.

Even single persons who did not have children thought about ensuring opportunities for the next generation. Karen Lai, a design student from Alhambra, California, who had not even started her own career, reflected, "I would just want [my children] to be better or at the next level. I know how I got to X, but I know that there were so many people better than me at everything that I did, that I'd want them to be even better. That kinda thing." In the same way, Henry Zhou, an IT consultant from Kent, Ohio, discussed his aims:

> I think I want my children to be happy and in a stable place. That, for me, that's important. For most of my adult life after college, I've felt I don't want to be too close to my parents. Now as I get older, I want to see them more. Family is important to me—to know that my children are in a good place.

Interestingly, few of the interviewees named their relationship with their partner as being their main focus in life.

Larry So, a medical researcher from Sacramento, California, is engaged to be married and does not yet have children. He confided that his fiancée, who is European American, does not fully understand or agree with his close familial relationships. She objected to his lending money to his cousin, who then purchased a car rack. She complained even more when this car rack was promptly stolen. Larry shrugged and rationalized his commitment to his extended family: "We're still family oriented. We always do stuff together, got each other's back. If they need help, you need to sacrifice your time. She is not too agreeable. But I just do it." Besides loaning money to his cousins, Larry was making preparation for his future family. He explained, "I'm already saving for my kid's college education and future education plans." In the event that he and his partner do not have children, Larry still planned for the future:

> Even if we didn't have a kid, I want to have [the money I've saved] in case possibly another cousin's kid needs it. All of us have helped one another. I don't see it, but it's good to have a backup plan for the family or someone who has helped the family.

His plans reveal the depth and extent of Chinese American familism: they think of and prepare for the future generation, even at the expense of their own immediate gratification. And they think not only of their nuclear family but also the children of their cousins.

Another example of how Chinese American familism operates as an ultimate moral boundary system is how the second generation raises their own children with specific morals and ethics:

> I would want my child to understand what Chinese New Year is and why food is important. I feel like food in general—to eat together—is to be a part of your family. So regardless of your differences, to eat together is how I embrace my family.—Karen Lai, design student from Alhambra, California

> I hope to pass on the good values that I got from my parents that I connect with and agree with, and pass on the opportunities that were given to me. I want them to have a connection to their culture for the sake of my parents, and staying connected.—David Jong, therapist from Amarillo, Texas

> I think with the Chinese culture, for my family, it's very family oriented. You want to respect your grandparents, and you want to help them out as much as you can. Of course studies are important. Learn to use those skills for adults. These are some of the things I would like to teach my children.—Julia Tom, advertising executive from San Mateo, California

Sharing meals to connect with family, providing opportunity for the children, and respecting one's elders—these values that the second generation aim to inculcate in their own children are the hallmarks of Chinese American familism.

CONCLUSION

Familism provides a meaningful, coherent narrative for the life course of Chinese Americans, their past, present, and future. It offers an interpretation of their family's history, as they view both their Asian roots and their parents' migration to the United States as exemplars of family sacrifice. The second generation understood their grandparents' and parents' lives, especially their hardships, as oriented toward giving them better lives and opportunities. Familism also provides a counterbalance to American individualism. It helps Chinese Americans think beyond themselves and establish relationships where they can direct their love and focus their attention. In these parent-child relationships, they have culturally specific ways to demonstrate that love: working hard and communicating regularly, being physically present, and sharing their love for food. Familism guides the future dreams and hopes of Chinese Americans. They plan to take care of their elderly parents, support their siblings and cousins, and, most significant, love and nurture the next generation. Their own parental love includes establishing opportunities for their offspring and inculcating their own deeply held values of familism.

Thus, Chinese American familism is a moral boundary system of *yi*: an ethic of how to rightly relate to key individuals one considers family. Certainly not every individual in our sample adheres to familism, and a few did not plan to have their own children. Nonetheless, the shame and guilt that Chinese Americans have reflect that familism remains an ethical standard by which they evaluate themselves. Selectively translating elements of Confucianism and Chinese Popular Religion, the second generation of this ethnic group hold a remarkably uniform set of values and morals.

Many of the interviewees recognized the influence of Confucianism on their family lives, but they also made the point that they disliked the hierarchy and sexism of that tradition. When Cary Yu majored in philosophy and political science, his father recommended that he study Confucianism. He learned to integrate Western and Eastern ideals:

> I internalized the round and squareness of Western individualism and Confucian responsibility. I'm constantly thinking of my place in society or the role of communal health—rather than only individual health, I consider the collective consciousness and put those together as one.

At the same time, he recognized that his father, and subsequently he, were afflicted with a "toxic masculinity" that hampered their emotional life and communication skills.

In several ways, Cary is an outlier to Chinese American familism, in that he has physically distanced himself from his family and does not communicate with them. He also does not plan to have children, due to his own sexuality and environmentalist concerns: "I'm polyamorous, so the two-parent, two-point-one children relationship is not a thing I take as a norm. As a person living in the developed world, I don't think I can have children. That's way too much carbon." As a progressive, queer trans person, he sees himself as active in the movement for the recognition of intersectionality—the mutual oppressions of race, class, and sexuality—and an inclusive approach toward sustainability.

Yet even with his American millennial progressive outlook, Cary rues his failure to live up to his Confucian filial duties and quickly itemized the behaviors he is ashamed of: "I should be talking to my parents more. I should be responding to their texts more often. I should be consulting them more on personal life decisions. I should tell my dad I'm trans." And when he addressed his future plans, he still thought in terms of family: "I really don't know what family looks like in the future. Regardless if I don't have children, I'm going to put my wealth in securing my friends' children. That's where I'm putting my energies."

From the outside, Cary Yu might not appear to be a model of Chinese American familism. However, in his Confucian collective sensibility, his concern over his poor filiality, and his future orientation to secure the opportunities of children, he is indeed.

CHAPTER 6

⚬✧⚬

The *Li* of Chinese American Familism

Ritualizing Family, Food, and Fun

My parents do [ancestor veneration] at our kitchen table. They lay out all the food that they cook, light incense, and let the incense burn out before we eat the food.

I don't know if I necessarily believe in it, but I do [light incense] to pay respects to my grandparents and to my parents. For example, I moved to Maryland by myself and I still did something for my grandparents' death anniversary.

—Tracy Lee, public health manager from Houston, Texas

We would have a lot of house parties, like family parties. And it'd be a lot of people coming, and I would always help around the kitchen and I would clean up or set up the table or things like that. I remember the other parents always saying, "Look at your daughter! She's so good, she's helping."

And my mom, that would be a sense of pride for her, would nod, "Yeah, she's a really good daughter."

That's the model, that's the behavior that we're expecting that we're going to reward with verbal praise. Not even directly to me, just with each other. That's really the only direct reinforcement I could even get from them: in the way you talk about kids. You just see other kids or other families operate.

—Teresa Owyang, nurse from Los Gatos, California

Tracy's and Teresa's comments illustrate the *li* of Chinese American familism. In their ritualized practices, Chinese Americans regularly learn and rehearse their *yi* values for relating to others in a righteous manner. Through formal rituals, such as ancestor veneration, and informal common events, including regular get-togethers, they embody respect for ancestors and elders, support and presence for siblings and cousins, and care and concern for younger family members. By committing themselves to these social practices, they demonstrate their highest priorities and most valued relationships, which satisfy their self-identified needs for meaning, identity, and belonging. Tracy, even though she lives alone in Maryland, continues to honor her grandparents by commemorating their death anniversaries in a manner similar to what her parents modeled. She lights incense not only to pay respect to her grandparents but also to please her parents, who are still living. Teresa recalled how the oft-held parties her family had with other Chinese American families were more than events to socialize. They were recurring times and places to develop proper behavior and to earn status, to behave with propriety and to relate appropriately. At these events the community displayed correct behaviors that were not directly taught, but observed and indirectly reinforced.

Li, for Confucians, are ritual proprieties that are proper ways of behaving and relating on a regular basis. They are not just religious rites, as in the Western religion paradigm; they encompass the entire range of human interactions by which one can live out internalized, key virtues such as filiality, loyalty, and righteousness. In fact, to act with *li* is to relate in accordance with the natural order of things. As a theoretical concept, *liyi* focuses attention on a group's most cherished, recurrent practices and interactions. They reveal the deepest values that members have internalized, their highest commitments to which they give precedence, and the most significant relationships that they prioritize. A frame on ritual proprieties, in our case, highlights how Chinese Americans inculcate, reproduce, and continually reconstruct familism.

This chapter details the most significant rituals that Chinese Americans report doing and maintaining. The first are institutionalized, traditional Chinese ceremonies for the human life cycle, including marriage and death rites. Second, Chinese Americans repeatedly discussed ethnic American routines that their families developed while living in the United States: (1) family dinners, (2) visits to family in Asia, and (3) family reunions and vacations. They work hard to continue these activities and the lessons learned from them, despite their acculturation to the American lifestyle. Third, those living away from extended family described hosting rotating house parties with other Chinese American families. These parties, as well as Chinese schools, utilized shame to help the second generation internalize expected roles and norms. In other contexts, Chinese Americans continue to maintain and display values of hospitality and reciprocity. Fourth, even daily rituals, which we call "table tradition," are means by which Chinese Americans demonstrate core values of familism. The chapter concludes by discussing the ways that the second generation passes on Chinese American familism to the third generation and extends it into their communities and broader society.

RITES OF PASSAGE: MARRIAGE AND DEATH

Rites of passage mark transitions from one stage of life to another, and the objects, rituals, and roles of these rites represent what a community considers important about these transitions. Second-generation Chinese in the United States who conduct traditional rites are doing so out of their own conscious volition; these are not necessarily obligatory customs required by the norms of one's environment, as they might be in China or other parts of Asia. The fact that our respondents chose to continue ethnic traditions meant that they were imputing these rituals with their own meanings and interpreting them with their own understandings. Both marriage and death rituals continue to be a means to demonstrate honor and respect to one's elders, as well as to celebrate family unity and harmony.

The tea ceremony at Chinese weddings is a ritual joining the two families of the couple.[1] In serving tea, the couple convey respect and appreciation to their parents and family elders in descending order of status: from grandparents to eldest uncles/aunts; then, onto the next eldest family member, and so on. In receiving the tea and giving gifts, the elders bless the wedding couple. With the parents seated, the wedding couple kneels and serves a cup of tea, both hands holding the cup. The elders may present gifts of jewelry or of red envelopes containing money. The tea itself represents the purity of love, the stability of the marriage, and the fertility of the family. Since it is not part of the typical American wedding ceremony, couples usually choose to conduct this family ritual at other times and at another site during the wedding day.

Sharon Chung, who closely adheres to Chinese customs passed down from her family residing in Mozambique and Zimbabwe, explained why she elected to do the ceremony and serve both her husband's side and her own:

> We did the tea ceremony at my husband's side of the family after the wedding. Two or three days later, we went to my mom's house and did the tea ceremony. For me, it meant paying respect to my parents for everything they've done—life and opportunity. Recognizing that they had done so much.

She wanted to take the time and space to acknowledge how much her parents—a working-class couple without much status or opportunities of their own—had done to give her greater prospects. Not only was the ceremony meaningful for her, but her parents also appreciated her attempt to maintain the Chinese tradition. She began to tear up when recalling how pleased her parents were with the ceremony: "They appreciated the fact that [the ceremony] was respecting tradition and the fact that they were able to raise a Chinese daughter that was respectful of the culture." For Sharon, the tea ceremony was a symbol not only of respect and unity but also of ethnic pride. Conducted in the United States, where Chinese are a minority, the ritual gained even greater significance for Sharon's family because of the effort it takes to maintain ethnic roles and traditions.

In contrast to Sharon's working-class childhood, Diana Ngai grew up with Danish au pairs and was one of the few Chinese Americans in her elementary school. She, too, did a tea ceremony at her wedding and did so as a way of honoring her elders. A product manager from Palo Alto, California, she recalled that her Hong Kong–born mother was insistent about maintaining traditions, such as holding the wedding on a lucky numbered date. Conflict over this custom, and the tea ceremony, led to much strife:

> We did not have an auspicious day for our wedding, so neither of our parents were going to do it. [My mother] got more superstitious around my wedding, which was really funny. She knew a surprising amount of the tea ceremony—the customs and how they were done. For major occasions, she said that we should throw in the customs: "Oh, it's my wedding; therefore, we're going to do all this stuff."

Her parents and grandparents were upset that the wedding was small by Chinese standards, for only 150 guests were invited. Just as her parents wanted to withdraw their support over the wedding date, her grandparents threatened not to attend because they could not invite their own guests. Diana spoke about that strain in her wedding planning: "[Inviting my grandparents' friends] was not in our budget and it got really complicated, which was stressful. It would have been sad if my only living grandparents did not show up to the wedding. But it was fine in the end, since they came." To appease her family, Diana made some concessions to honor their role in her life. She concluded, "We had a Chinese banquet, and it was important to have that—and, very important that we have the tea ceremony!"

She later explained why she included the Chinese tea ceremony even though she was adamant about organizing her wedding in her own way, including having it at a Unitarian church. Her family does not show love in an emotional way, she said, by speaking of their care or demonstrating physical affection. Instead, they demonstrate care by serving food and drink: "My grandparents, aunts, and uncles, no one gets super emotive, and you miss them from college. So you would pour them tea." Serving tea is her Chinese way of pouring out love.

Just as the tea ceremony during a wedding was a means by which Chinese Americans paid respect to their living elders, funeral services and death memorials are opportunities for them to honor deceased relatives. And similar to how second-generation Chinese Americans are unsure of the specific meanings of each element in their marriage rituals, they are unclear about different aspects of a funeral or proper ancestral veneration. Nonetheless, they maintain these traditions out of a desire to commemorate the lives of their parents and grandparents and to rehearse family unity.

Chinese funeral services contain some common practices as the deceased pass from this life to the next.[2] Services do vary by region and tradition, just as Buddhist and Daoist funeral practices differ, but second-generation Chinese Americans in our sample observed the following rituals most often. Commonly, family members make food offerings to the deceased so that they might be well nourished for their journey to heaven. Chopsticks are placed standing up in bowls of rice so that they have utensils with which to eat, and three cups of drinks are also provided.[3] Mourners burn paper replicas of objects, such as homes and cars, for the deceased to use in the afterlife, and they also provide blankets to keep them warm and secure. An important tradition is lighting incense and candles to guide the deceased on their way. Family and guests, in addition, bow three times before the coffin.

Confucius suggests that rites honoring the dead teach children how to obey and respect their parents in life. Beyond their function of teaching moral virtue, rites are also embodied acts of virtuous manners. For Cary Yu, the transgender activist based in Washington, D.C., the rites served both functions. He detailed the huge, elaborate funeral held for his grandmother in Taiwan. His family bowed three times before her body, and they held up food with chopsticks to her face. Since he is the eldest son of the eldest son, he carried her cremated remains to the burial ground. He explained the significance of these rituals for his father and uncle. While his uncle believed that he was helping his grandmother into an actual afterlife, his father and cousins did it to respect her: "My dad did it out of respect; my uncle did it out of belief. My cousins bring values of respect." For Cary, the funeral service was a sign of veneration and a social grieving process that carried great import on an emotional and ethnic level: "For me, it was partially respect, and a lot of participating in a cultural practice because of the communal healing value. Regardless of whether the belief [in ancestral spirits] is metaphysically real, they have emotional and cultural power. Those have real effect on me." The funeral was an alternative means for him to express what it is to be family and love one's family. He concluded, "I understood my family more, and this was one of the places where language breaks down for me. It was an embodied understanding of what it means to be a family." Bowing, offering food, carrying the remains, and being with extended family whom he had never met were each modes of enacting his highest value—being family—without words or tenets.

Although they have observed these rituals practiced by their parents, second-generation Chinese Americans do not fully understand the meanings and specific requirements of each death ritual, as described in chapter 4. Instead, they impute their own meanings onto the acts. For example, Ken Li's parents devoutly prayed to their parents and deities. They taught Ken to pray as well, but he did not know to whom he was praying:

> [My parents] say to pray to the grandpa and to someone else. I always assumed it was to a deity, in a picture frame.
>
> When we pray for our grandma and grandpa, they put out a statue on a coffee table. They put one for our grandparents and this other altar for whom I've no idea. They tell us to pray.

Ken did not know how to pray, so he simply obeyed his parents' instructions, and then prayed as he learned in his private Christian school:

> At first, they'd say to put your hands together and bow three times. Later, they told me to ask your grandfather for good fortune, good health and good job. Now I talk to him as usual. I think it's from Christianity, actually. I associate them as similar, since my mom tells me to ask him for fortune and luck. So I thought, maybe I could talk to him normally like I learned in Christian school.

For Ken, ancestor veneration is a practice of commemoration and a means to maintain his Chinese heritage. When asked what he plans to pass on to his own children someday, he replied, "The incense thing for those who've passed away. I'm going to tell them, 'When I die, pray to me so you remember me.' I've done it, so I'll keep that culture part. I liked the tradition, so I'm going to pass that down." He, too, wanted to be honored and remembered by his children just as his parents expect to be remembered by him. "The incense thing" is part of their "culture" and "tradition."

Similarly, Serena Zhang, a Ph.D. student from Cleveland, Ohio, vividly recalled her grandmother's death memorials as one of the most emotional experiences of her childhood, as well as "the most traditional thing we would do." She described the bowing, incense lighting, and food offering;

> When my grandma died—by that time I was ten—she was a devout Buddhist. My mom would cook a meal on the anniversary as an offering and we would read a favorite passage of a Buddhist text. That was the most traditional thing we would do: we would read

the passage, do the three bows, and let the incense burn and have a bunch of vegetarian food. All the food was an offering to her, but we always ate it afterwards.

For her father, the ritual was a way to remember, and to make amends for past mistakes: "[My father] saw it as tradition and trying to pay respect to my grandma because he had a ton of guilt that he didn't take care of her enough. It was a really sensitive topic. Whenever he would talk about her, he would cry, and he never cries!" Although she claims that her parents are both atheists, her father continues to make offerings to his mother. She explains that she does not know the exact reasons why he keeps fresh flowers for her grandmother, but that he is devout in doing so:

They do the grandma [veneration] in the living room. My dad has a vase of flowers that he always makes sure there are fresh flowers, but that is it. I don't know if he believes her spirit is somewhere out there or if that is more of a remembrance. He feels so guilty and sad about her life.

Learning from these memories and observances, Serena shared that her own highest value was to be responsible for her parents. She explained the different ways she would assume this responsibility:

My dad used to do this thing where he told me to give my mom a hug or to make her feel better so if, over time, it was my responsibility [to care for her I would know how to do so.]

They always said you are supposed to take care of your elders and respect them. I think it's the way they always took care of me and I felt really loved. I just feel like I have to make sure [my mother] is happy. My dad, it's more about finances. He's always supported me and I want to make sure he's supported too.

Her filial duty was to be concerned about her mother's happiness and her father's finances. She, like Ken, plans to keep a shrine for her parents when they pass away and to teach her children the same lessons she was taught. She wants them to take pride in their Chinese background: "I really want [my future children] to have a really positive feeling about who they are and where they're from."

When asked about the Chinese culture that his family maintained, medical student Craig Quan immediately described his first experience of a Chinese funeral:

One grandfather passed away and I went to his funeral in China, in a place that was a little more remote, not in the city. I remember a lot of fire, a lot of burning of symbolic items. Going through the motions of kneeling and bowing with incense. Saying a few words to my grandfather. We spoke to them as if they were in front of us. Like, "We miss you. Thank you for our life. We love you."

He reported that he often had to look to his father about what to do during this "elaborate process" of "role-playing," as he termed his actions. After two more funerals for his other grandparents, Craig said that he became familiar and comfortable with the memorials. He noted that he continues the practice of lighting incense before a shrine:

> I didn't really believe my words were getting through, but it was therapeutic. Now, every year on the anniversary, I'd say a few words for them. We'd set up the altar and the table. We'd kneel with incense. I say a few things at home in general. It's a nice way to think about them.

Craig, like the others, saw the ritual as "a way to think about" his grandparents and the role they played in his parents' lives and his own.

Craig plans to continue honoring his grandparents and his parents to "keep his Chinese culture" and to "remember them and memorialize them." However, by tailoring the ritual for himself, he believes he will create a distinct practice that is more authentic for himself and his own beliefs:

> These memorial practices, I probably will continue. I appreciate my culture. When my parents pass away, I'll probably do something for them. Maybe I won't do it right—maybe, a bastardized version. The purpose for me is to remember them and memorialize them.
>
> I've not experienced how to organize these things. It'd be my own version of it. There's no point in getting it right. It wouldn't be aligned with my experience—it's my way of commemorating.

As a Chinese American, Craig is less concerned about memorializing his parents in the right way and more desirous of doing so in an authentic manner that is "aligned with" his experience.

To summarize, continuing ancestor veneration rituals serve multiple functions for second-generation Chinese Americans like Cary, Ken, Serena, and Craig. Setting up a shrine and lighting incense, or going to the gravesite and cleaning it, are primarily ways to remember the roles their elders played in their lives. These practices also provide the participants with roles to play as loving and dutiful grandchildren. Furthermore, they are visible reminders, especially for the children, to teach family members how they are supposed to relate to one another. Finally, for Chinese in the United States, these rituals represent ties to their heritage and are the outward signs by which they can express their ethnic pride, even if they are their "own version."

FAMILY REUNIONS: RITUALS OF BELONGING

Rites of passage and death memorials are formalized activities not often conducted, yet these milestones hold great significance for Chinese Americans. The informal practices and interactions of Chinese Americans reveal what they prize and prioritize more regularly. As we suggest, the *li* of Chinese Americans includes the entire range of human experiences, from life milestones to informal parties, from formal, prescribed behaviors to table tradition. In discussing their familism, second-generation Chinese Americans identified three rituals that meant the most to them: regular meals with extended family, transnational visits to Asia, and reunion vacations. The reunions are the spaces that give them their deepest joy and the times that they find most meaningful in their lives.

Aaron Zhu, a photographer from Walnut Creek, California, appears to be a laid-back millennial living rent-free in a condominium his father owns. His father still does his dishes whenever he visits, even though Aaron is 28 years old. Aaron's greatest aim is to "create something valuable, like a work of art that has feeling, or can change a worldview," so he is currently investing in his photography and video skills. Beforehand, he was a serious skateboarder and video gamer, hobbies he retained from his teen years. Balancing his individual interests, though, Aaron cherishes his family, a value he gained from his upbringing. He described how his family made biweekly trips to San Francisco's Chinatown, where they would shop and then eat with his aunts' families:

> We would go there once or twice a month. I feel there was a routine to it. We'd go grocery shopping, then we go to my aunt's. We'd have dinner, visit with my cousins and leave around nine or ten. The two aunts lived in the same building. We would always eat—either my older aunt or my younger aunt would cook.

Aaron cringed at recalling how those visits regularly consisted of getting a bad haircut from his aunt: "I'd get haircuts almost every time. I never liked the way Aunt cut my hair; she'd do the bowl cut and I wanted the asymmetric hair!" The result of these "routine" trips, even when they included unpleasant haircuts, was family bonding: "[I] grew a connection with my cousins and my aunts. That was the reason for the trips—for us to connect with them. Now I don't mind going to see them." When his mother passed away, his aunts stepped in and again did the cooking for the family. They drove 45 minutes each week to support their widowed brother and Aaron. He recalled that these meals were demonstrations of the family bond:

> Our aunt would come to our house and cook, buy groceries. It was mostly a lot of family time that year, the first year. It was the time the whole family bonded the most, the year

of my mother's death and beyond. It was good to know that family's there when time is tough. Our family has always done things via action. We never tell each other that we love each other. We do it by showing up, by doing something.

From his father's dutiful washing of his dishes and his aunts' weekly cooking for the family, Aaron has come to value family functions where he can be present for his family members. This desire and obligation are a paramount responsibility: "I always try to show up at family functions, life events. I try to be there. I'm always out of the loop, but when they tell me to come, I'll make an effort to do so. I'll always show up for Christmas and birthdays, things like that." If he cannot attend a family meal or event, he "feels guilty, definitely." That is because in his family, "showing up" is a sign that he is there for his family, a visible expression of support and love. Through the regular actions of showing up for meals and events, Aaron demonstrates his adherence to Chinese American familism.

These weekly meals with extended family were rituals that inculcated Chineseness, including family roles and responsibilities. Bruce Cheung, a facilities manager in San Francisco, similarly recounted weekly family dinners at his grandmother's home, which reinforced his first language: "I vividly remember driving from San Francisco to Hillsborough every weekend to go to my grandma's house. We would have dinner once, sometimes twice a week. Everyone spoke Mandarin. I actually learned Mandarin before I learned English." Besides the language spoken, the dinners impressed upon Bruce the hierarchical, gendered norms of the family, because they varied from the usual expectations within his nuclear family:

> Women would prepare the food. Grandma is in the kitchen with the aunts helping [with] various little tasks. We all sit around the round table eating hotpot. Always make it a point to say hi to everyone, not just grandma. After that, all the cousins would play with each other.
>
> My dad always says the eldest eats first. I don't remember him saying that to the immediate family, but when we are all together with everyone else he said that.

Even though Bruce knew that his father did not want to be with his in-laws, he regularly brought his family to these meals and greeted his in-laws properly. His father also insisted on respecting the elderly by letting them eat first.

His father's dutiful respect certainly made an impression on Bruce. At one point in his early 20s, he got into "hippie culture, free spirit stuff," and he complained to his father that he "was so oppressive." But despite his independent spirit, Bruce joined his father's fraternal organization. He was the only young adult member, and he remains "the youngest at the lodge by fifteen years." What makes Bruce's membership in this club even more striking is that the lodge requires formal behaviors, which seem antithetical to Bruce's personality:

> There is a lot of ritual work, memorization. You raise new candidates, and put on ceremonies. [My father] grew up with a lot of proper etiquette and taught me to hold yourself to high standards. So when I was eighteen, I joined the [organization] myself. I became the Worshipful Master, which is the manager of the lodge. My responsibilities include all the communications from the grand lodge around the state or the nation and I report that information to the brethren. I collect their money for their annual dues, I record all the meetings, and just help run the lodge. I've been doing that since I was eighteen.

When asked why he joined what seems like an onerous and ostentatiously organization for a young person, Bruce explained that he did it for his father. He recalled how his father was responsible for his own family and how he started a successful business to support his family:

> I was at the lodge my first three to four years for my father. I think it's because he deserves it. He's taken care of me, what he's done with his business. These past two years made me realize Dad was right about a lot of business-related stuff, a lot how you speak to people, or think about certain topics.

Bruce's closest friends and his fiancée are white, yet his values and actions reflect a Chinese American familism socialized by family dinners. This value system led him to obey his father and become a dedicated member of a group that none of his own generation has joined. The ritual of family meals served another primary function for Chinese Americans: it established a time and place for belonging, so much so that they often did not feel the need for other social institutions, like a church, for identity and community.

The Chinese Americans who did not have the opportunity for weekly meals with extended families had another ritual: transnational trips or domestic reunions. Many of our respondents came from transnational families and took multiple trips to Asia with their parents while growing up. As another example of the rituals of Chinese American familism, these visits reunited extended family members and acquainted the second generation with their ancestors. Their memories of these trips, especially the practices of ancestral veneration at gravesites and temples, were powerful because they usually could not be carried out in the United States:

> Whenever they go to China, every five to eight years, [my parents would] go to the gravesite. They brought me along. I remember I was five years old, and they made

me kneel at a temple close to the gravesite, pray and bow. The second time, when I was in middle school, we went to the rural area and the actual gravesite, and we would bow.

—Henry Zhou, *IT professional from Kent, Ohio*

When I went to Taiwan, we'd go to temples, and light incense. My grandmother was Buddhist, but I don't know what they really are. They're not Buddhists, but we'd go to the Mazu Temple and we would kowtow. My mother would tell me to go pray to this for good grades, and to this one, for prosperity.

—Susan Lau, *museum employee from Providence, Rhode Island*

When we were in Hong Kong, we did the money burning. I didn't believe in that, but we did it out of respect too.

—Larry So, *researcher from Sacramento, California*

These rituals, conducted on trips to their parents' homeland, reinforced Chinese family responsibilities. Marilyn Hong, a medical student from Milwaukee, Wisconsin, described her annual family trips to Beijing, which reinscribed the family members' mutual duties:

We were lucky and got to go back to China every year when I was younger. Maybe when I was older, a little less. I've been to China fifteen to twenty times. Family is important, even family living far away. In general, people do have a lot of respect for older members—the idea [is] they have a lot of contribution to the younger generation's success. I grew up with the idea that the elderly should be respected—that was important.

Other second-generation Chinese Americans also attended family reunions, but in the United States rather than in Asia. These domestic family reunions were more fun for the children, and a large number of adult respondents combined the reunions with family vacations with their siblings and elderly parents. Wendy Foo fondly recalled her grandparents' visits when she was growing up in Rochester, New York, and now she carries on that tradition by reuniting annually with her own parents and siblings. When she was a child, her grandparents came twice a year from Hong Kong to stay with them. During these visits her grandparents taught Wendy and her sisters to play the game of Mahjong. The game became a family monthly ritual and one of her happiest memories. She says that the game is still part of her family reunions: "I remember playing Mahjong a lot when I was little. I played among my family and my grandparents whenever they came to visit; my grandparents would come twice per year. I still play with my family when I go home for Christmas." Regularly playing Mahjong evoked for Wendy fond memories of family, their Chinese values, and her Chinese identity:

> [My grandparents] are from Hong Kong so it made them feel connected to their grandchildren. [They were] imparting values through this game even though we lived in America. That's what I imagined it meant to them. This is something that doesn't exist in America, but is part of my cultural heritage. I felt more Chinese when I played Mahjong. There are other things that made me feel Chinese, but this is the happiest.

Even the physical arrangement and process of playing the game held meaning for her. Sitting and facing one another represents family unity. Taking turns and playing rounds of Mahjong symbolized the transnational visits her grandparents would make to her family and cousins: "The fact that Mahjong has you sit around in a circle and face each other—it's really special family time. My mom's parents would come here and make the rounds to visit us in Rochester and then go back to Hong Kong."

As adults in their late 20s and early 30s, Wendy and her sisters continue this tradition of family reunion trips. Instead of playing games, they now take expensive vacations: they invite their white significant others, and find time in their busy, high-powered careers to go on hiking trips with their parents who pay for them. Wendy observes, "It's important for me and my oldest sister; she had to block off a week. [The family vacation] was something that I have [had] since I was little and I look forward to it." The Foo sisters' significant others also take note of how much the sisters value these trips. Wendy described how her parents send them off:

> My middle sister's boyfriend commented, . . . "You guys take your time together very seriously, holding every minute together." His parents would drop him off [at] the curb and casually say bye. At the airport, [my parents] would park and see me off and say goodbye to me. My parents would wave me off at security until the last minute.

Chinese American familism is expressed in two reunion rituals for Wendy: the game of Mahjong and the annual family vacation. The former represents her Chinese heritage and the latter reflects her family's upward mobility, but both symbolize the ultimate priority of being family.

Another person who prioritized an annual family reunion is Jane Man, the healthcare consultant from St. Louis. Her family was so dysfunctional that her parents did not attend her brother's wedding. She claimed, "We are very disconnected as a family because we're different people. I've never gotten along with my mother. My mother and I were never close because she was constantly yelling and scolding me." Furthermore, Jane complains about their lack of emotional connections and even relational ties: "We don't hug, we don't say I love you, we don't call each other. They forget my birthday fifty percent of the time. My family doesn't like spending time in general." Consequently, she says she has "no desire to have a family or [get] married."

In spite of her strained relationship with her parents, she still attends her extended family reunion, a life-long ritual for Jane. These reunions are diffi-cult to schedule and arrange, as six households with 11 cousins participate. Jane says the families have to share "a big Excel sheet in order to manage the expenses of this reunion." Despite the difficulty of coordinating so many schedules and managing the expenses, Jane continues to prioritize this an-nual ritual for several reasons:

> We have a family reunion for my dad's family for a weekend in the summer. That's run by his side of his family and we see the cousins. We've been doing that since I've been born. My grandpa used to own a house, and for a while, we all stayed in his condo in one spot. Now we're old enough to get hotel rooms. First off, if you don't go, you get a lot of shit from the family for the rest of the year. Since we've been going since we were young, it's a tradition, but it is fun and something we and the cousins like to do.

Jane specifies three reasons that sustain her attendance at the annual re-union: the shame of not attending, the tradition, and the fun.

Two other activities at the reunion are also important to Jane. She succinctly described one of them: "Eat. That's all we do. We just eat. We all say we're preparing food for Toronto and so, we stretch our stomachs. We just show up and eat three or four days straight: Chinese pastries for breakfast, dim sum for lunch, and a giant banquet for dinner." As described in chapter 5, eating meals together represents both family unity and love. When not eating, Jane's family takes this time to visit her grandfather and to visit her grandmother's gravesite. Even though the cousins do not interact much with their grandfather, they make it a point to be physically present: "Part of it is that my grandpa is going to die soon. He's ninety-seven. It's not like he's so crucial because he's nap-ping all the time. It is, for some reason, important that he's around." At their grandmother's gravesite, the cousins go through the motions of the prescribed rituals: "We basically go and bring flowers. We do the incense and bowing. Every family goes up by family and bow. I assume it's paying respects, but I don't know fully why we do what we do. It's super casual.

Then we go to *dimsum*." As she acknowledges, even though the gravesite ritual is "super casual," it remains "important" that her grandmother is visited.

While Jane suggests that she does not like her parents and does not want her own family, she continues to adhere to a Chinese American familism that is remarkable in terms of the extent to which family members feel responsible for one another. As quoted in chapter 5, she declared she would take care of her brother "even if he was a drunk," and she "probably would support her cousins." The annual family reunion taught her these mutual obligations, as her grandfather would pay for everyone's vacation. Moreover, the reunion reinforces Jane's family commitments, even to her parents. She summarizes why her family, ultimately, remains important: "I guess it's who you would think would support you at the end of the day."

Correspondingly, Diana Ngai explained why her sisters and cousins are so important to her, even though they are not emotionally expressive of their love for one another: "We're not super emotive, but there is always an expectation that regardless of whatever happened, we would always stand up for each other and help out." This family norm is symbolized by the family reunion. Diana concluded that no conflict or anger could keep her from being with her family, for whom she has to "show up," even if she has to travel far:

> I can't imagine not showing up. That would be awful. Would you ever be that pissed off? No. There are certain unspoken things where if it's your grandparent's birthday, you will find a way to make it to Canada on that day. You better find a way to make it to Canada.
>
> So these family events feel really important, and you must get together. Whether it's for American holidays like Thanksgiving, Chinese New Year, or [a] grandparent's birthday, it is very important to show up, and at least be there and celebrate with them.

Family get-togethers, whether weekly meals or annual vacations for reunions, serve as *li* rituals. They inculcate virtues of loyalty and obedience, create space for Chinese Americans to fulfill their filial responsibilities, and reinforce the significance of family. As Diana says, these reunions embody her identity: "[Family] just feels like the most fundamental block of who you are. They're the most important thing and you owe them your upbringing. But [you reunite with family] not in the sense of guilt, but genuine desire to be with the folks who help make you who you are." She sacrifices for her family out of genuine desire because, as Chinese Americans often remark, the family "make[s] you who you are."

THE ROTATING POTLUCK: INSTILLING NORMS
OF HOSPITALITY AND RECIPROCITY

Chinese Americans who grew up in predominantly white suburbs spoke of another informal ritual: the rotating potluck meal with other Chinese families in the area. These were casual parties where the immigrant adults had a chance to socialize in their own native tongue and the children would spend time together. Like reunions with family, they served as settings where Chinese hierarchical roles were established, Confucian values of generosity and reciprocity were demonstrated, and a sense of ethnic community was nurtured. Although the second generation does not necessarily have the same immigrant need to have Chinese-speaking spaces where they feel comfortable, they carry on *liyi* values of familism in other contexts.

Marilyn Hong grew up in Milwaukee in the 1990s without many other Chinese Americans or Asian Americans in her neighborhood. When her parents first moved to that city in 1991, her mother had been in the United States for only two years, so when they did meet other Chinese, they made quick connections with them. Marilyn noted, "For my parents, because there weren't that many Chinese people in the community, the ones you meet and feel connection with, you gravitate [toward]. My parents didn't have any non-Chinese friends." Her parents eventually established a regular get-together with three or four other Chinese families in the area. She recalls what they did and why:

> I have a lot of good memories of close friends and our families being close. Once or twice a month, usually, there'd be a potluck. During that time, for both me and my parents, we actually celebrated the things that were Chinese. We would have get-togethers and sing karaoke. For bigger events like holidays, then they'd have ten to fifteen families. It seemed very normal to me.

By singing Chinese songs and celebrating Chinese festivals, the families normalized Marilyn's ethnic identity and sense of community. As she stated, the get-togethers provided fictive kin—cousins, aunts, and uncles who took the place of blood relatives: "Certainly, they were a very important sense of community . . . [W]e didn't have family reunions or cousins in this place, so I feel those experiences were analogous to what people would have with extended family."

As stated, many second-generation Chinese Americans found that their extended family was their main source of community, especially when they were younger. In their absence, these rotating potlucks became their source of community.

At these potlucks, Marilyn "actually celebrated things that were Chinese," which helped her accept her ethnic identity, but her younger brother did not have the same experience. When he was six years old, their family moved to the suburbs, and he grew up without the biweekly Chinese potluck ritual. Subsequently he did not celebrate his Chinese heritage but rebelliously asserted when told what to do, "We live in America." For Marilyn's part, the close networks forged at the potlucks helped with self-acceptance: described how her close network from the potlucks helped her to accept her ethnicity: "My brother didn't grow up in his formative years with the same close relationships with other Chinese friends and family as I did. For me, it came naturally to accept that part of my background." She feels her brother faced greater social marginalization, which led to a "sense of otherness." The potluck community helped her face the racial adversities her family would later encounter in Minnesota. She compared the celebration of "the things that were Chinese" at her family parties with her experiences on the school playgrounds and hallways:

> Certainly, micro-aggressions definitely happened. On the playground, in early elementary school, people [would] pull their eyes in reference to me. People would make a lot of jokes about Chinese last names. Growing up in middle school and high school, socially speaking, no one was overtly saying anything. But being different from [them] in background, you don't mesh with the popular kids. You don't have that background.

In spite of these experiences, Marilyn felt that being Chinese was "very normal," and she attributed that, in part, to the biweekly potluck community.

Along with instilling pride in one's heritage, rotating Chinese potlucks inculcuated respect for elders. Daniel Lu was born in Iowa when his immigrated from Hebei province in the mid-1980s. They, then, moved to Silicon Valley for his father's job, and his childhood was filled with Chinese American families and regular potlucks: "My parents have a strong network of Chinese friends, a lot from Iowa. A lot from Iowa eventually came to California to work. They would get together and do potlucks every two or three months. rotating households." At these potlucks Daniel observed Asian "principles" and appropriate interactions with others of different ages:

> There were definitely certain very Asian principles instilled in me. Respecting your elders was emphasized. Respecting authority, too, was something I was taught. Whenever we went to a potluck, we'd salute them as "ayi." We had to answer them. We made sure to go and say hi to aunts and uncles, grandparents. We made sure we had face time and I talked to them.

The first ritual was greeting one's elders. Daniel's parents taught him to address people by their relational title, whether "aunty" or "uncle." He then had to exchange pleasantries and answer their questions before he play with the other children. The adults, too, acted respectfully in ways that impressed Daniel:

> I also saw the way my parents treated their friends. Although they're on the same level in terms of education, they were younger. A lot of the friends they met were a lot older than them. The way they treated people older was always respectful, accommodating.
>
> Social dynamics at those potlucks showed me about how different people are received and treated.

To illustrate, Daniel described his mom's role at these potlucks. She respected and obeyed the older women who mentored and cared for her, and she modled this behavior for him:

> My mom said, even in Iowa, she came to America as a naïve young woman. A lot of the older women took her under [their] wings and taught her how to cook. So there's a mentoring relationship with those people. Any sort of disrespect towards elders was treated very harshly. Any time I'd talk back would result in punishment.

Along with treating elders with respect, Daniel learned the values of hospitality and reciprocity.

At the potlucks, Daniel observed how the adults worked together to share insights and adapt to their new country. As they cooked, they shared new recipes that were actually Japanese American or Korean American meat dishes. At the same time, they sang Chinese songs from their homeland: "We'd have barbeques: teriyaki chicken and kalbi. Whenever someone brought something, we'd share recipes and teach each other. And a lot of karaoke. There's some classic Chinese songs that I would recognize." He also saw that these families reciprocated the hospitality shown to them: "There's a lot of expectation if you get invited, you have to host yourself. It's always rotating from households." Although not every respondent was as conscious as Daniel of the meanings and values behind these social interactions, most adopted these taken-for-granted ways of relating.

Daniel and his other Asian American friends carry on the reciprocity he learned from the Chinese potlucks. For example, when invited to a party, he always brings food or drink to repay the host's generosity. He explained, "You always bring some sort of food with you, no matter what. I think even now [when] I go to someone's house, I feel obligated to bring something. Even if it is just a party, do I bring alcohol? I feel that I should bring something." Daniel said that he shares this sense of group obligation, hospitality, and reciprocity with other second-generation Asian Americans: "I hang out with a lot of Asians. When I was in Chicago, we had a close group of friends. People would always bring different things. People would just know instinctively, 'We'll bring something.' It was understood." Through these rotating potlucks, norms for right relations in Chinese American familism—respect for elders, hospitality, and reciprocity—are socialized and reenacted.

As Teresa stated in the opening quotation of this chapter, the potluck is "the model. . . . You just see other kids or other families operate." Through the community at the rotating potluck, Chinese Americans develop a sense of face and shame as a way to internalize values. Teresa noted that behaviors were reinforced "in the way you talk about kids." Along with learning behaviors that are modeled, Chinese Americans are taught norms and values through regular conversations with others. In fact, the Chinese character for "face" includes components of people under a roof talking. On one hand, one gains a sense of face, which involves respect from others, when one is praised. On the other hand, one loses face, or is shamed, when faced with critique. The rotating potluck, thus, is a ritualized mechanism of social control as family and friends gather to chat about their children. By knowing that their parents and others talk about them, the children become socially aware and develop a sense of face and shame about proper behaviors.

One other site offers an example of how face and shame operate to instill social norms. The Chinese-language school is the other primary place where Chinese Americans gather, engage in conversation and social comparison, and inculcate Chinese values, especially for education. Nearly every second-generation Chinese American reported attending Chinese-language school, and nearly everyone found it to be a chore. Ostensibly aimed at teaching the students to read and write Chinese, the school was more successful in teaching students how to gain face and internalize shame. Teresa explained how ineffective Chinese school was in teaching the language:

> Every Saturday, you know it was just another school that I had to go to, and it was because it was the same thirty kids from kindergarten all the way through tenth or eleventh grade. In retrospect, two hours a week is not going to be that effective in learning Chinese. You know, we compared ourselves to other families, and our house, it wasn't that strict at all.

Instead, as a ritualized space for competition, Chinese school helped to establish academic standards and norms of achievement for the students.

Mark Chou, who grew up in Naperville, Illinois, reported that he attended Chinese school every Sunday from kindergarten until the end of high school with the "same-aged, Chinese kids." By meeting other Chinese American families, his parents found other students to serve as a measuring stick for Mark. He asserted that the networks developed at Chinese school furthered his own academic achievement, as he began to compete against fellow Chinese Americans:

> At that point, then, their parents and my parents, obviously, they had some similar bond, whether they were from mainland China or Taiwan, or China to Taiwan, they had some bond. And so we began hanging out more, and the competition began, and each [set of] parents wanted to push their kid more.

Educational achievement, although not necessarily a key component of Chinese American familism, is socialized in the same way as respect for elders and group reciprocity. In community spaces, whether at Chinese school or the rotating potluck, Chinese Americans reproduced ethnic values and norms through indirect communication of what is prized and what is not.

TABLE TRADITIONS: HOUSEHOLD RITUALS OF MEANING

Daily, ritualized behaviors of Chinese Americans also reflect familism and demonstrate how respect, care, and mutual obligation are shown to family members. Like other rituals, they are often taken-for-granted, habitualized courtesies. Some of our respondents, though, recognized that these Chinese customs differ from those of mainstream American culture, and explained how they interpreted them. Three conventions of familism involve serving tea and food, seating arrangements while driving, and taking off shoes before entering a house.

Table traditions, as one respondent described them, are Chinese American routines of behavior that reflect tenets of familism: respect for elders and guests, care for those who are younger, and mutual responsibility. These rules may have been directly taught to children so that by the time they are young adults, these Chinese norms would create standards for behavior. Violations of these norms by Chinese Americans may result in rebuke or shaming. Non-Chinese, on the other hand, would receive a pass.

For Chinese meals, especially at restaurants, food is typically served family-style; the group shares meat and vegetable dishes, while each individual gets a separate bowl of rice. Since the tables are usually circular, no one person is at the head and everyone is equidistant to the food. Once a pot of tea is placed on a lazy Susan, a rotating table tray, the courtesies begin with the filling of the empty teacups. Younger members are to ensure that the eldest, as well as guests, always have tea in their cups.

The parents of Kenneth Lam, a student from San Leandro, California, are working-class immigrants without high school degrees. They worked long hours at a bakery and a laundry, so Kenneth and his siblings often fended for themselves. On the one day that his mother did not work, everyone was sure to be present for the family dinner. He recounts:

> Mondays now, it became a tradition that in the family, everyone must come home for dinner. Before, she only had that day off, so we made it a big deal. Monday, Mom comes home, gotta eat dinner with her! I guess through her working and being so busy, it makes us closer in a sense, that we got to make time more precious. Mom's home, so we have to go home and spend that time with her.

Over the years this tradition grew stronger as the family became better off financially. Kenneth's mother not only continued to cook the family meal, but she cooked even more. Her home-cooked meals were avenues to demonstrate her love. By physically caring for her children, she fulfilled her family responsibility:

> My family—we're not rich. We kind of get by. We're not really super well off. But we have Monday night dinners, and now it's transformed to a really big dinner. [My mom] makes ten to eleven courses. It's ridiculous. She invites everybody to come over. We do that every Monday, and she doesn't expect any money or payment. She just offers it to people to come over and eat everything. I know it costs a bit of money to do it, but she's very welcoming.

By inviting her children's boyfriends and girlfriends, Kenneth's mother takes on the role of the gracious host, caring for both family and guests.

Just as parents have the familial role to care for their children by providing meals, the children respond by being grateful and respectful. Younger members are to ensure that the eldest, as well as guests, always have tea in their cups. Wendy Foo, a postdoctoral researcher in astrophysics, shared how she came to become aware of this tea etiquette. She grew up in Rochester, New York, with highly educated Cantonese parents, but in her suburban upbringing, she faced ostracism for being different. She recounted, "They would call me Four Eyes Foo or bullies would say something mean. I remember [when] I was little, I hated my name because it was hard to pronounce." Indeed, Wendy is her pseudonym; her real name is a Chinese name that the children in her suburb had trouble pronouncing.

Even though her grandparents would visit twice a year, she did not learn many Chinese customs. She did recall specifically, however, the tea ceremony at her cousin's wedding, which otherwise was an American church ceremony: "I remember once, my oldest cousin, twenty years older than me, was getting married. We went to his wedding and there was a tea ceremony after the main traditional, American ceremony." Wendy recollected her own involvement in the ceremony but did not fully understand the part that she played:

> I remember giving tea to lots of elders, but not knowing what it meant. I gave it to my cousins who were getting married and my parents. I remember passing tea and my cousins offering it. I just have a passing memory of a tea ceremony, but not remembering my role. I remember drinking tea out of those small cups with being Chinese as well. Somehow, that involvement of tea and respecting your elders was a Chinese custom.

Wendy did not fully understand the symbolism of the tea ceremony, and she remained unclear about what were Chinese customs and what were simply her own family norms. For example, she shared the two key values her parents tried to instill in their daughters:

> I don't know if this is specifically Chinese, but respecting elders was a huge value in my home, and always being thankful. Those were the two values my mom and dad passed on. For respecting elders, they made sure we addressed them at a family reunion by their Chinese name, their title. So I when I was little, I was confused but I had to learn them.
>
> They would whisper in my ear to go to this aunt and make sure to say thank you. I remember that.

As learned by many Chinese Americans through the rotating potluck, the youth are to display respect for their elders by greeting them with their Chinese title. They are also to thank them for any gifts, such as Chinese New Year's red envelopes filled with money.

Eventually, Wendy did come to understand and appreciate the display of filiality behind the wedding tea ceremony. Now she makes sure that she serves tea to her elders whenever she is at Chinese meals:

> When I go out to dim sum with my grandparents or other families, I would serve tea. It would be customary for my sisters and I to serve tea so that my grandmother's tea cup would always be full, or any elder's.
>
> It was customary for us to pour tea for any elder who didn't seem to have tea. It's a sign of respect and caring for them, that they don't have to pour their own tea.

Diana Ngai, who had a tea ceremony at her wedding, was especially conscious of table tradition. Along with serving tea, the host and the younger members are to serve the best pieces of food to others before they help themselves. She explained:

> There are different things to show respect. They're really subtle and not really big. There is a lot of "Let me get food for you," or table tradition. I would always pour tea for my uncles before my sister because they're older. And if you know someone that likes something, you give them extra, and things like that.

At a meal, Chinese humility requires that one puts others before oneself. Chinese hospitality and concern involve giving others extra pieces of their favorite foods. Diana developed such other-awareness through these table traditions.

She shared another example of table tradition, that of fighting for the bill at restaurants. Diana observed that haggling over the check is a norm of honor: "Just to show respect, always offer to pay the bill." Providing a meal, as Kenneth's mother did, meets physical needs and demonstrates taking responsibility for the other's well-being. In the same way, paying for a meal is an act of duty toward family and of hospitality toward guests. Chinese Americans fighting over a bill is a micro-ritual of give and take that enables the host to gain face and to demonstrate concern for others.

Outside the dining room, Chinese Americans maintain other customs that signify filiality and reciprocity. Diana shared her family's seating arrangements while driving with her elder relatives:

> There is also car seating hierarchy in minivans that had three tiers. Grandparents in the front, my mother and aunt in the middle, and kids in the back. And even today, I feel super uncomfortable sitting in the front seat even when my husband is driving. Stuff like that comes back with us. It's how you grew up and [a] social expectation that you would do this.

Besides the functional reason of having children sit in the back of the van, where legroom is least abundant, this seating arrangement reflects who gets the most status in the household. As Diana explains, the deviant who violates the norm gets labeled as socially incompetent, and therefore, that person actually reinforces the norm: "Part of this [expectation] is basic social norms and not being the awkward terrible person that no one wants to hang around." Yet Diana also acknowledges the significance of letting elders sit up front. She claims that it is a way for her to "genuinely love" her relatives:

> And there is also [this pattern] because you genuinely love your aunt, uncles, and cousins, and if you don't do it, then you're not reflecting how much you care for them. You want to make the most of the time you have since everyone is getting older and show that you care.

Along with this love, making children sit in the back acknowledges that those who are older deserve higher status.

A final example of table tradition in the house is taking off one's shoes before entering. Susan Lau explained why she was able to acculturate easily to her white environment in Providence: "Growing up, because I was raised by an unconventional, single mother, we didn't do culturally Chinese things. . . . We didn't have red rhombuses everywhere or pictures of children with envelopes on the wall, and we didn't wrap dumplings for New Year's. I didn't know what Qingming was. We wore shoes in the house."

Serena Zhang said that when her family hosted potlucks at her home in Cleveland, they and their guests would maintain their Chinese culture, including playing games, singing songs, and eating. She also noted that being Chinese meant taking off one's shoes inside a home: "We'd have parties where they invited all their Chinese friends and we'd have thirty shoes at the front door and kids and a potluck. That was really fun. They would rotate [hosting parties] among the families. They would also play Chinese chess and go and sing karaoke." Rotating the parties was a way to reciprocate hospitality and generosity. Likewise, taking off shoes is a sign of respect, indicating that one appreciates the host. By not dirtying up the house, one is considerate and thoughtful of the host's time and efforts.

Through these habitualized, micro-level social interactions—serving tea, sitting in the back of a vehicle, and taking off shoes—Chinese Americans act in culturally scripted ways that reveal their core values of familism. In making sure teacups are filled and that others have their favorite foods, they express love. By taking the backseat of a car, they show respect to elders, offering them a better view and more comfort. And through the simple act of taking off their shoes, they express gratitude for the hospitality of their hosts and reciprocate that generosity as much as possible. Without saying a word, they demonstrate how to relate properly to others.

AMERICANIZED RITUALS: MARKETED, CONSUMABLE ETHNICITY

As described in chapters 3 and 4, Chinese American immigrants transmit and translate familism from its sources in Confucianism and Chinese

Popular Religion to their second-generation children. The values of right relationships within the family continue through rituals of proper behaviors. We have described some of these rituals, including remembering the dead by lighting incense, respecting the elderly by serving them tea, and caring for one's family by reuniting during vacation time. The transmission of Chinese American familism to the third generation differs, however, because the second generation has attenuated knowledge of Chinese culture, and they do not have a migration story of sacrifice by which they can make their children feel obligated to them. Furthermore, the American context of racialized multiculturalism structures what traditions are easily maintained. This selective transmission of culture, which we term "marketed consumable ethnicity," reduces Chinese American traditions to what is fun and tasty.

Chinese Americans carry on celebrating Chinese holidays, such as Chinese New Year and Mid-Autumn Festival, but they tend to reduce these festivals to what is enjoyable and edible. Most Americans view holidays, like the Fourth of July and Labor Day, as three-day weekends for vacations and barbeques, as they have long been removed from the American Revolutionary War or the labor strikes of union workers. Instead, they celebrate these days as federally required time off, and corporations heavily market particular foods and drinks for picnics. Quite similarly, Chinese Americans become distanced from the historic or religious significance of their holidays, and thus see them as simply days of ethnic pride. And in a very American manner, they celebrate their ethnicity with fun activities and special foods, just as Irish Americans revel during St. Patrick's Day and Mexican Americans party during Cinco de Mayo.

Wendy Tong, a mother of two, lists which aspects of Chinese New Year rituals she retains:

> We'll keep customs—anything that's fun, I want them to have fun and to see family. I don't want them to be crazy superstitious. I think having little rituals makes holidays fun, so that's what the customs are for. And they're very customary and traditional. Your mom did it, your grandma did it. It's nice to do, but it's not for thinking bad luck or dragons eating you. It's just about fun and your family's wisdom.

Taboos and rituals to maximize luck are deemed "crazy superstitious" and discarded. Wendy enjoys doing things for the sake of tradition itself—that "your mom did it, your grandma did it." Instead of performing a ritual, such as lighting incense, because of its moral virtue to inculcate respect or its efficacy in enlisting spiritual protection, the ritual is performed as a symbol of ethnic tradition; it comes to represent one's Chineseness in general.

Celebrating holidays for fun rather than to commemorate, lament, and reflect is an American festive choice that shapes which Chinese traditions are retained. One interviewee, Monica Tanemura from Norton, Virginia, described her main purpose in life: "I want a balanced life. You know, like friends, family, fun, and work." Consequently, of all the Chinese New Year rituals—preparing the home, remembering the dead, eating special foods, avoiding taboos, and giving red envelopes (*hongbao*)—the most common custom the second generation passes down is the gifting of red envelopes, because it is similar to Christmas gift-giving and an exciting treat for children. When asked what Chinese customs he will pass on to his own children, Ken Li answered, "Chinese New Year. I'll have that with the red envelopes. I liked getting the money. I'm sure they'll like it too."

With the same orientation, Julia Tom, who is single and does not yet have her own family, thought that she would want to preserve the special foods from Chinese holidays to maintain heritage:

> I think even the holiday stuff, like the mooncakes and then sticky rice, I would like to do that for my kids, too, so they don't lose touch. I've already got out of touch with what the meaning is behind those, really, so I'd like them to have some of it.

In June, Chinese make sticky rice wrapped in bamboo or lotus leaves, called *zongzi*, to celebrate the Dragon Boat Festival and to memorialize Qu Yuan, a poet and patriot. Later, around August, Chinese eat mooncakes to honor Chang E, the goddess of immortality, and to commemorate the overthrow of the Mongol Yuan dynasty. Julia confused the holidays and said that she needed to Google them to get their exact, historic references. For the most part, though, these holidays and special foods have come to represent family gatherings. When asked her views of these festivals, she responded:

> It's just, "Yeah, let's get together!" and then you eat. And maybe you eat certain types of food. I guess they were fun, though. I guess because usually it'd be a lot of good food, or more food than usual. I guess, it's like a Thanksgiving food. People getting together, and maybe family friends or something would gather together.

Chinese holidays, then, are primarily occasions for family to gather, have fun, and eat "more food than usual."

Li practices emphasize what is ultimately prioritized. The continued celebration of Chinese holidays through food and fun highlights the Americanized outlook that Chinese in the United States have adopted. Like other Americans, they have come to value—on a ritualized basis—what they can consume, what they can enjoy, and what they can use as symbols for ethnic pride. Multiculturalism and diversity in the United States observe these aspects of ethnicity and race because they benefit the economic system, such as when the NBA airs commercials with New Year wishes and markets Chinese basketball jerseys. At the same time, this superficial recognition of ethnicity and race in a show of multiracial unity masks the racism and marginalization that second-generation Chinese Americans repeatedly recounted.

CONCLUSION

Chinese American familism is best understood through the relationships valued by the group and the rituals practiced by them. As discussed in this chapter, second-generation Chinese Americans prioritize specific traditions to maintain and pass down. They carry on rites of passage to pay respect to their families and to their Chinese heritage. They establish new traditions in the United States, such as family vacations and rotating potlucks, where they continue to express their group loyalties and family responsibilities. Even on the level of micro-interactions, Chinese Americans exhibit proprieties that confer status on others, such as when they serve tea and food. At different spaces, but at recurring times, they construct what it means to be Chinese American and to value family.

One other way that we examined the *liyi* values and rituals of Chinese Americans was to interrogate ethical relations. Our respondents shared how they related to other persons in their communities and broader society in moral ways. Overall, the great majority of our interviewees asserted that good persons are those who treat others as they want to be treated, who are honest and kind, and who do not harm others. Everyone was politically liberal, as this sample was a highly educated group. Being racial minorities in the United States, they understood social justice to entail equal opportunities for all. Sharon Chung, a nonprofit administrator, expressed the need for Asian American political empowerment:

> I think America is still a place that has an unequal playing field for immigrants, and for people who are different from white, male mainstream. I think within the Asian American community, and the Chinese American community specifically, I buy into this construct of Asian America. It's very much a political construction with the idea that we're banding together to advance and level that playing field—and I think that's the work I'm trying to do.

In sum, this group held ideals of American liberal democracy in supporting freedom, opportunity, and equal rights.

A large portion of this group was concerned with changing the world, making a difference, and fighting for social justice, but even more—all but two—placed their family's needs and concerns as paramount. In doing so, they maintained a Chinese, Confucian perspective. Ben Hao, an attorney from Seattle, described this outlook: "The sort of model I use is concentric circles. Your family is the smaller circle, then friends make up the second circle, and it goes out from there. But I feel like you should take care of the smaller circles first." In this model, one's main source of identity and belonging is one's family.

An ethic that differs from a Confucian concentric circles model hybridizes Chinese familist values with American social justice ones to empower communities. Diana Ngai has mentored two youth for over five years, since she graduated from college. She explains why she has kept such a close relationship with students outside of her own family:

> I just view it as a dual obligation. From my traditional Chinese culture, you care for your family and you work really hard to do well for your family. And then there is the broader, metaquestions of the world. The world around you is really important and it's your job to give back.

Her parents, who were politically active in the 1989 democracy movement in China, encouraged her to reciprocate and "to give back." She described how she saw her mentees: "The kids I mentor now, I saw them even in business school and I hope that one day I get to see their kids and how they develop in the community. So it kind of develops into an extended family, so the world becomes an extended family."

Gary Loo, a nonprofit director in Boston, was asked what is most important to him. As a father of two, he immediately responded, "Being a father. It seems so clear to me that being a father is the important thing to me. I'm so directly responsible for them." Gary's statement demonstrates how Chinese American familism provides not only meaning and belonging but also identity. Although he is a recognized community leader and an accomplished spoken-word artist, he sees himself as a father. Like the other Chinese Americans who stated that being a good parent is their top goal in life, Gary finds his primary identity located in his sense of family.

Just as he saw his primary role is to be a father, he took that familist perspective and brought it to his work:

> My ethics involve imagining any child as my child. Any child could have been my child. In the sense, I would want the best for them, just as every parent wants the best for their child. We have a human responsibility to spread the idea of being safe, to feel like there's a way out in cases of trouble.

By seeing every child as his own, he wants "the best for them." And in adopting others into his extended family, he assumes the "human responsibility" to care for them and give them opportunity.

Second generation Chinese in the United States find their sense of identity and belonging in the ritual practices of Chinese American familism, which range from the significant (i.e. weddings) to the mundane (i.e. Sunday brunches). Further, familism can be extended to those outside one's closest circles. In developing an Asian American ethic of justice, Diana and Gary show how to participate in civil society: by simply seeing others as one's family.

Conclusion

Implications of Chinese American Familism
and Liyi Theory

The World's Newest Majority Religion: No Religion
—Gabe Bullard, *National Geographic*, April 22, 2016

National Geographic ran this startling headline for its feature article in an issue in 2016. The article emphasized American atheism's lack of racial diversity but, curiously, made no mention of the ethnic group most likely to be nonreligious: Chinese Americans. Instead, the article emphasized the global decline of the Western church, omitting those who have long historical ties to "no religion." Thus, the *National Geographic* article misleads in two ways. First, it suggests that "no religion" is the world's newest majority religion. However, most societies probably did not employ the concept of religion in terms of the modern Western paradigm of a belief and belonging system.[1] Hence, members of no religion—those not categorizing themselves as religious—have long been the majority in the world. Nonreligious Chinese, for instance, have been around for millennia, and as shown in this book, Chinese Americans have defended their status as "heathen" and non-religious long before it became a trend among millennials. Second, given that religion is a historicized concept, "no religion" may not be a useful category. The use of more culturally appropriate, historically accurate, and self-determined terms offers more relevant ways to examine and interpret a group's worldviews, ethics, and ultimate value systems: What if *National Geographic* had understood the unaffiliated from the perspective of Chinese Americans, the historically "heathen," whose parents never belonged to a church? It would have led them to consider more culturally appropriate, historically accurate, and self-determined terms and categories to examine worldviews, ethics and ultimate value systems. *Family Sacrifices* reframes the very lens through which to understand the unaffiliated. It begins with the viewpoints of Chinese Americans and employs the lens of *liyi* to understand their transpacific lived tradition of *familism*.

For most of its history, China could have been classified as having no religion; in the 19th-century other Americans deemed Chinese Americans as "heathens" for their lack of Christian faith. Scholars today use more palatable terms to describe the unaffiliated: spiritual but not religious, agnostic, and atheist. But even these terms are ill-suited for understanding unaffiliated Chinese Americans, for they primarily depend on absence. *Family Sacrifices* offers the concept of *liyi* as an alternative to the category of religion to highlight the presence of rituals and ethics of the unaffiliated.

Sociological examination of *liyi*, as a reappropriated Chinese term for theoretical analysis, focuses on how people orient their lives toward their highest priorities. Specifically, it considers their *li*, their dearest practices and rituals, in conjunction with how they establish *yi*, ethical relationships based on their most cherished values. Use of *liyi* as a concept reveals that Chinese Americans may affiliate as nonreligious, but they hold to a moral value system that is coherent, consistent, and rooted in traditions. These values and ethics are ideals, in that Chinese Americans aspire to them, even if they do not always live up to them.[2]

Applying *liyi* to Chinese Americans, *Family Sacrifices* has uncovered observations, narratives, and trends of familism, a value system prioritizing interdependence and right relationships through the meaningful rituals of being family. Through familism, Chinese Americans live out their ultimate priorities, ethics, identity, and belonging. Chinese Americans actively sacrifice for their family, which is their highest priority, and they find meaning in their family ties, their most deeply held relationships. They define themselves and narrate their own identities through family histories and gain a strong sense of belonging through their family rituals. As a lived tradition based in Chinese Popular Religion and Confucianism, Chinese American familism offers this ethnic group a link to their heritage and a direction for their future.

THE GENEALOGY OF CHINESE
AMERICAN FAMILISM

Both the affiliation of Chinese Americans as religious nones and their worldview and ethics have historical, transpacific sources in their unique heritage from China. Chapter 2 identified three distinct but intertwining Chinese classical discourses that shaped this heritage. First, their correlative cosmology, as evidenced by Chinese Popular Religion, assumed a range of gods, spirits, and supernatural forces that allowed for a pluralism of beliefs, practices, and values. Consequently, religious pluralism made identifying with one religious grouping difficult. Second, Confucianism encouraged skepticism about the role of supernatural forces; instead it promoted an agnostic and even atheistic stance toward religious matters. Third, Confucianism promoted a *liyi* Chinese identity, in which Chineseness distinguished itself from barbarianism through the rituals and righteous relations practiced by Chinese. A major aspect of these righteous relations was filiality, in which individuals were to be mutually responsible in their family roles. Given these three discourses, identifying as nonreligious makes much more sense to Chinese than affiliating with one religious grouping.

In recent history, Chinese Popular Religion and Confucianism have been transformed, revealing their historically contingent and politically constructed nature. Through the process of state modernization in the 19th and 20th centuries, politicians deemed practices of Chinese Popular Religion "superstitious," disenchanting the worldviews of some Chinese. Depending on who was in power, the elite have promoted Confucianism as either a political, cultural, or religious ideology. The official policy of atheism of the People's Republic of China, along with formally recognizing five major religions, clearly legitimated certain religious affiliations, including nonreligiousness. Nonetheless, the *liyi* practices and values of Chinese people continued to be inculcated, practiced, and prioritized. For Chinese in the United States, two other factors profoundly shaped their maintenance of traditions: migration and the American religious marketplace. Migration uprooted Chinese from their ethnoreligious cultural context, which supported extended family and ancestral ties. Instead, they found themselves with fewer temples and shrines and fewer calendric festivals that supported Chinese traditions. Chinese Americans, therefore, grow up in a religious terrain where Christianity is privileged and Western understandings of religion circulate. Wong Chin Foo, as the first Chinese American in the 19th century trying to navigate these two cultures, had to make a defense of his "heathen" affiliation in this cultural, religious, and racial context. As a historical bridge between the 19th and 20th centuries, he highlights the transitions that the Chinese American community itself must negotiate.

THE TRANSMISSION AND TRANSLATION
OF CHINESE AMERICAN FAMILISM

In the United States, Chinese immigrant parents apply their cultural toolkits and religious repertoire when raising their own children. Chapter 3 investigated how Chinese American households transmit the *liyi* dimensions of their Chinese Popular Religion and Confucian worldviews and ethics. In this group, education and social class strongly correlate to the religious worldview of Chinese American immigrants. Working-class households tended to pass down the practices of Chinese Popular Religion based on a worldview of fate, luck, and *qi*, whereas professional households socialized their children to affirm Confucian thought that matched their rational, scientific worldviews. The class and professional background of Chinese American parents made a difference as to whether their children would identify as spiritual but not religious, atheist, or agnostic in their nonreligiosity.

For example, almost all the parents of respondents in our sample practiced elements of Chinese Popular Religion, most notably (1) venerating ancestors, (2) adhering to *fengshui* principles of *qi*, and (3) celebrating Chinese New Year. The New Year festivities often included customs and taboos related to luck, prosperity, and health. For many Chinese American working-class families, these practices included belief in supernatural realities and the efficacy of practices to bring about well-being and good fortune. They were consequently more devout than the professional families in adhering to these practices and modeling to their children their religiosity. In contrast, Chinese American professional families maintained these elements for different reasons; they wanted to instill family responsibility through ancestor veneration, maintain good energy via *fengshui*, and celebrate their heritage through Chinese New Year. They saw these rituals as secular customs. Given the religious pluralism and skepticism of Chinese, they could easily hold to the range of meanings and approaches toward their *liyi* rituals.

Even though parents maintained Chinese values and rituals and hoped to instill them in their children, the translation of these *liyi* practices into the American context, particularly those of Chinese Popular Religion, had mixed success. Chapter 4 detailed four major barriers to the transmission of Chinese Popular Religion and to Chinese values and rituals. First, Chinese American families transmitted practices by modeling rituals without explaining them, such that the second generation performed customs without fully understanding the symbols and meanings. Second, the dissonant acculturation between parents and children led to the second generation being more Americanized and less receptive to traditional, hierarchical values. Third, Christian dominance and privilege in the United States rendered Chinese practices exotic and superstitious. Fourth, gendered and racialized experiences further "othered" Chinese traditions as foreign and outdated. In spite of these barriers, Chinese Americans distilled and hybridized what was most important to them from these practices to sustain familism.

THE *YI* AND *LI* OF CHINESE AMERICAN FAMILISM

After discussions of the genealogy, transmission, and translation of Chinese American familism, chapter 5 specified the top goals and aims of this group. Ostensibly, those of different ages had varied goals for their lives. Chinese Americans under 30 tended to be "maximizing world-changers": they valued making the most of their opportunities and careers to make a difference in whatever arena they chose. Those over 30 desired to be "expressive balancers," seeking fulfillment by balancing the various aspects of their lives: work, community, and family.

Tempering these Americanized, individualistic tendencies was a familism that both age groupings of Chinese Americans shared. In fact, family sacrifice is the central narrative by which Chinese Americans make sense of their lives: past, present, and future. The first key element of familism, venerating the past, is to respect and honor one's ancestors and immigrant parents, especially their migration and sacrificial love. The second key element, relating in the present, is giving back to one's parents in culturally appropriate ways: honoring one's family through one's own hard work, maintaining good communication, sharing love through food, and including family in major decisions. The third element, paying it forward, is centering dreams for the future around the family. With the aims of supporting parents, siblings, and cousins and of providing their own children with opportunity, Chinese Americans envision coherent and meaningful lives based on family relations. In these ways, the *yi* of Chinese Americans is an ethic of how to relate rightly with those one considers family.

If the *yi* of familism involves making one's family the highest priority and ultimate responsibility, then the *li* of familism is cherished rituals that Chinese Americans practice to inculcate, reproduce, and embody family values. Chapter 6 identified this group's formal rites of passages, the informal ethnic routines, and the daily table traditions. Rites of passage, such as the wedding tea ceremony and funerals, provide individuals with distinct roles and responsibilities that they are to assume within the family. Ethnic routines, including regular meals with family, transnational visits, and reunion vacations, are the times Chinese Americans find to be the most memorable and significant events of their lives, precisely because they are times to be family together. The rotating house potluck and Chinese school are unique Chinese American institutions for immigrant families in the suburbs. With other families acting as fictive kin, these parties and schools provide spaces for the second generation to learn Chinese norms of hospitality, reciprocity, and face/shame. Finally, through micro-rituals that we call "table traditions," Chinese Americans learn cultural scripts that enact familism: pouring tea as an outpouring of one's love, sitting in the backseat of the car to offer another person higher status, and taking off one's shoes before entering a house to reciprocate hospitality and generosity.

Traditions and rituals change over time, however, and second-generation Chinese Americans pass on their *liyi* values and ethics differently from their immigrant parents for three main reasons. First, the second generation lack a migration story of family sacrifice by which they can make their children feel obligated. Second, the second generation have an attenuated knowledge of Chinese *liyi* traditions, so the foods, customs, and rituals of Chinese Popular Religion are often difficult to reconstruct. Third, racialized multiculturalism further reduces ethnic traditions to what is marketable and consumable in the United States. In other words, Chinese Americans hybridize and Americanize their ethnicity such that the new *liyi* Chinese American identity consists of food and fun.

IMPLICATIONS OF CHINESE AMERICAN FAMILISM

As a racial and ethnic minority group, Chinese Americans face marginalization and stereotypes that negatively affect their concrete, day-to-day lives: their health, well-being, and political standing. An understanding of Chinese American familism offers a fuller portrait of this group by which they can be empowered, develop wholeness, and become more integrated into American society. For Chinese Americans themselves, recognition and validation of their Chinese history, cultural background, and upbringing provide a strong basis for ethnic identity formation and group solidarity. Cross-cultural competence regarding familism can assist those working with Chinese American populations, including those in the fields of mental health and politics. While Chinese American familism relates to every aspect of this community, this section identifies just three implications of Chinese American familism.

Family Sacrifices seeks to give voice to the legacies, struggles, and dreams of second-generation Chinese Americans on their own terms. Too often, mainstream media portrays this ethnic group as an assimilated, model minority or as perpetual foreigners.[3] These stereotypes and other racialized experiences negatively impact the self-image of Chinese Americans, leading to feelings of invisibility or otherness.[4] For example, our respondents often termed their parents' practices of Chinese Popular Religion "weird" and "superstitious" rather than recognizing the cultural depth and historic meaning of these traditions. Having to mark "none" in response to questions of religious affiliation further marginalizes Chinese Americans in the United States, where religious identity historically gave one a place and standing in the community.[5]

For those Chinese Americans who desire to strengthen their ethnic identity, build community, and preserve their traditions, *Family Sacrifices* provides some terminology and a mental map for continuing to do so. In fact, awareness and self-recognition of one's ethnic and *liyi* heritage can become the basis for conscientiously passing down practices. Beyond the label of "nonreligious Chinese American" lies a rich history of moral and spiritual questioning, argumentation, and conviction. A hidden inheritance lies beneath the surface of those habits of the heart that Chinese Americans possess. A knowledge of Chinese Popular Religion, Confucianism, and Chinese American familism enables Chinese Americans to draw from a variety of spiritual and *liyi* sources in an authentic and collective way. This religious repertoire and these *liyi* traditions empower them to appreciate ritual despite skepticism about the spirits they posit; to love and respect parents more fully; and to bring that love and respect not just to their own families but to the broader society as well. Self-recognition, therefore, becomes the basis for identity formation, community building, and the preservation of traditions with can prevent misrecognition and foster interreligious respect.

Chinese American traditions are neither static nor essentialized. As *Family Sacrifices* reveals, Chinese American familism is a dynamic, lived tradition in that the community continually adapts its heritage to new contexts and times. Drawing from their transpacific roots, our respondents hybridize their Chinese and American worldviews to form at times messy and conflicting constellations of hopes and attitudes. While capitalism's multicultural discourse tends to reduce American ethnicity to what is marketable and consumable, Chinese Americans themselves author what they deem valuable, ethical, and worthwhile in their lives. In this process of self-definition and community building, they continue to create moral boundaries for themselves as Chinese Americans.

Nevertheless, cultural conflicts emerge in this process of *liyi* traditioning, and the actual family dynamics of our respondents do not always live up to the idealized relationships of Chinese American familism. In particular, dissonant acculturation between the first and second generations poses conflicts of boundaries and communication.[6] From a Westernized psychological perspective, Chinese American families can appear dysfunctional and discordant. While the first generation may demand obedience and family responsibility, the second generation may long for freedom, autonomy, and individual fulfillment, as especially indicated by our respondents under 30 years of age.[7] As they negotiate these demands, such conflicts can result in higher stress levels, depression, and even suicidal tendencies.[8]

Yet many of our respondents persisted in the rituals and practices of familism, in spite of some of their negative familial experiences, including the dynamics of patriarchy and heteronormativity. Rhonda Woo, a single mother who found the male-centered upbringing of her Chinese American family insufferable, nevertheless maintained that sustaining family rituals with her own son was her highest priority. Cary Yu, a transgender activist who has yet to come out to his father about his queer sexuality due to language barriers, continues to show his devotion to him by sharing meals. Such adherence to familism as a tradition may be perplexing, and even construed as codependent and enabling. However, Rhonda, in rejecting the patriarchy of her own upbringing, seeks to reform the gendered practice of familism and to pass down a healthier, and even woman-centered form of the tradition to her child. Cary's sexuality, though seemingly untranslatable to his immigrant father, does not prevent him from the continued practice of familism. Familism cannot simply be equated to the patriarchal or heteronormative forms of Confucianism. It ought to be understood as a hybridized tradition that continues to live on through Chinese Americans' own adaptations of it, even for their own feminist and queer contexts. Thus, as stated just previously, mental health practitioners ought not to simply reject these familial dynamics as backward or dysfunctional but help Chinese Americans negotiate their multifaceted and changing identities within the practice and ethics-centered context of familism.

Yet, admittedly, like any other tradition, familism has its limits and can legitimate or perpetuate hierarchical and even abusive relationships. Michael Chen acknowledged the nobility of his mother's desire to keep their family together, in spite of his father's gambling: "Part of her I feel thinks it's very noble to do that. To basically sacrifice and say 'You know, even though this is tough for me, I'm going to let this happen.'" Seeing his mother's sacrifice, Michael also forgave his father and concluded, "Just recently, I decided to mentally let all that stuff just go and say, 'Dad, I've forgotten, I'm trying to forget everything that you did, and let's just consider this a fresh start.'" Adherence to familism provided a pathway for Michael, along with his mother, to sacrifice for the sake of moving on as a family. Unfortunately, such adherence allowed them to gloss over the father's abuse. Scott Lai, in spite of being estranged from his abusive father, continued to financially provide for his family. While Scott continued to value familism, it did not necessarily help him to resolve his trauma that led to the estrangement. Understanding the sources and depth of familism can help Chinese Americans like Scott resolve the intergenerational conflicts they face.

Second-generation Chinese Americans may experience hurt and trauma, pain and frustration precisely because their families mean so much to them. Certainly, Chinese American familism, in its actual practice and future iterations, cannot condone such patriarchal relationships and abusive behaviors. Instead, it must develop healthier imaginations of gender and power to adapt the practices and ethics of familism to meet the individual's own needs.

Chinese American familism can foster inward focus on one's family, and it can also provide resources for political empowerment. One aspect of the model minority myth is that Chinese in the United States face racial discrimination but succeed without complaining. This ethnic narrative of success through hard work and family devotion perpetuates the notion that Chinese Americans are passive and uninvolved citizens. On the contrary, the Pew national survey data reveal that "helping others" is a higher goal in life for Chinese Americans than having a high-paying job or free time. A large proportion (42.0%) of Chinese Americans indicated in the Pew Asian American Survey that they did community service. Among our respondents under 30 years old, the majority wanted to use their time, resources, and talents to make a difference in society. Indeed, while Chinese Americans valued caring for the family as their highest priority, that goal did not preclude them from community engagement.

Chinese American familism—in terms of concern for the welfare of one's family—can be drawn upon to spur active participation in political campaigns and social movements across a wide range of ideologies.[9] Throughout their history in the United States, Chinese have long organized themselves to resist racism and exploitation. Along with seeking social justice, equal representation, and civil rights, they have mobilized to secure better conditions for their families.[10] For instance, in the successful Asian Immigrant Women Advocates 1992 worker campaign to win back wages from the dress designer Jessica McClintock, organizers worked with high school and college students to boycott Macy's and McClintock's products.[11] One student drew a cartoon for her high school newspaper that read, "How would you feel buying a $149 dress that your mother made for only $15?"[12] AIWA relied on family responsibility—the consideration of one's own mother as the seamstress—as well as the tactic of publicly shaming to win concessions for workers. Not only do those supporting progressive politics mobilize around the value for family, but Chinese Americans with conservative political visions of the heterosexual Chinese American family do so as well. In one of the largest political demonstrations by this ethnic group in California in the past two decades, Chinese American evangelicals rallied to protest same-sex marriage.[13] This movement is not merely an example of evangelical conservative politics, but also an example of familism in action, as Chinese American Christians banded together around the notion of Christian and Chinese kinship to defend traditional marriage. In like ways, organizers might draw on the language of family to mobilize Chinese Americans around immigration reform and family reunification, healthcare for children and the elderly, and environmental justice.[14] In sum, whether for conservative, liberal, or progressive political agendas in contemporary America, the discourse of familism is a key lexicon through which Chinese Americans take action.

Along with concern for family welfare, Chinese American familism offers an ethic that might be mobilized to spur this community to community engagement. From both their Confucian and Chinese Popular Religion traditions, Chinese Americans can find historic resources for resistance and political empowerment. The Confucian virtue of *ren*, or benevolence and empathy, teaches that responsibility and concern for others should be cultivated to develop one's full humanity. The stories of Guan Gong, the god of literature and one of the most revered deities of Chinese Popular Religion, highlight his values for fair play and social justice. Sharon Chung explained that she works in the nonprofit sector because of such a concern for the community. She observed how her mother volunteered for Sharon's Chinese dance troupe:

> A sense of community is big to me. That is something my mom instilled in me. Even though we didn't have a lot, the fact that she volunteered, that she did things for my whole dance troupe. She thought of it as a community service for the dance troupe, so that, one, I could be a part of it, and, two, she knew the mission was important. The dance troupe brought part of the Chinese culture to the broader community and she was proud of that, of being Chinese.

Both the welfare of her daughter and ethnic pride in the Chinese community motivated Sharon's mother to contribute long hours. Likewise, her great-grandfather started a Chinese school in Mozambique because of his desire to build the community there. As stated earlier, Gary Loo summarized how Chinese American familism can help reimagine one's shared responsibility to others: "My ethics involve imagining any child as my child."

Family Sacrifices, in summary, highlights the worldviews and ethics of Chinese Americans across generations and religious traditons. To be sure, these thick descriptions provide ideal types of those who hold to Chinese Popular Religion or Chinese American familism. Chinese Americans display a great range in how they value family interdependency and to what extent they live up to these values. Nevertheless, the Pew 2012 Asian American Survey and our respondents reveal clear trends in how Chinese Americans prioritize family, gain identity and belonging from family, and find meaning in their familial relationships. Through the concept of *liyi*, these key relationships, moral responsibilities, and ritualized practices are better understood and analyzed.

The appropriation of *liyi* for theoretical purposes has further implications. First, *liyi* points to new directions for extant debates about the category of religion and, relatedly, the secular. That is, *liyi* offers an alternative approach to the binary categories of the religious versus the secular that reinscribe Christian belief-centered categories. Second, *liyi* as a concept may be applied to other groupings, such as American millennials, to better interpret their trend toward nonreligiosity. Third, this study of Chinese American familism and the use of *liyi* as a concept raise further questions for research, especially with regard to the nature of traditions in a postmodern society.

A THEORY OF *LIYI* AND THE STUDY OF RELIGION

Family Sacrifices argues that the category of religion and even the term "religious none" are ill-suited to understanding Chinese Americans and even the changing and diversifying American landscape in which the unaffiliated are increasing. The concept of *liyi* better illuminates the ways Chinese Americans in particular, and even religious nones in general, prioritize and embody specific values, morals, and ethics. As a parallel concept to religion, the application of *liyi* as a theoretical concept highlights emerging trends among the nonreligious and avoids the problematic, binary discourses of religious/nonreligious and secular/nonsecular. In *Imagine No Religion: How Modern Abstractions Hide Ancient Realities,* Carlin Barton and Daniel Boyarin cease relying on the "anachronistic word 'religion'" in order to understand ancient practices more clearly.[15] Similarly, *Family Sacrifices* sidesteps the use of the category of religion to avoid anachronisms and to actively decolonize scholarly visions of Chinese America's practices and ethics.

The Western concept of religion tends to employ a colonizing discourse prone to misrepresent and distort non-Christian groups.[16] In his seminal work, Talal Asad critiques Clifford Geertz's definition of religion, which understands religion from the "standpoint of theology" and belief—of moods and conceptions of the order of existence.[17] The mind does not move spontaneously to religious belief, Asad argues, but conditions of power create the contexts for belief to emerge.[18] The colonial process that categorized and essentialized Chinese as "Orientals" similarly constructed the binary of religion and the non-Western other.[19] The "Orient" provided a mirror image to the "Occident" and reinforced Western superiority; a similar discursive move defined the "heathen" Chinese as opposite to the morally superior American Christian. Orientalist and religious nomenclature, then, justified violence against Chinese and their exclusion during Wong Chin Foo's life in the late 19th century.

To avoid such colonizing and distorting tendencies, some scholars have turned to "the secular" as a more promising category for locating meaningful beliefs, rituals, and practices in contemporary America. Thus, one might surmise that the secular may be a more promising lens through which to understand Chinese American practices and ethics. Kathryn Lofton and Courtney Bender, respectively, broke down binary categories such as the "secular" and "religious" and identified the "religious" in unlikely places.[20] Yet in spite of this helpful examination of the secular, Lofton and Bender mostly mobilized Western definitions of religion in that their subjects find "faith" or provide assent to what they discover in the secular sphere.[21] For example, Bender's ethnographic account shows that the "spiritual but not religious" put their *faith* in scientifically and social scientifically driven data about psychology and metaphysics to make sense of their spiritual lives. As discussed, unaffiliated Chinese Americans, however, tend not to believe or assent to familism but engage in practices driven by ethics and values. Thus, while Lofton locates the "religious" in the secular, *Family Sacrifices* identifies *liyi*—rituals and ethics—in the secular. The category of the secular, unfortunately, may result in circuitous debates that continue to reinscribe, or at least rely on Western Christian definitions of religion.[22] Avoiding the pitfalls of terminology such as "nonreligious" and "secular," *liyi* offers a different entry point altogether in discussing human phenomena.

By integrating both Confucian and Durkheimian emphases on ritual, a theory of *liyi* starts with people's practices to which they are most devoted to interpret values and relationships and employs three assumptions of "no religion" scholarship. First, *liyi* rituals and values are historically situated; Chinese American familism among the second generation in the early 21st century takes a different form from the familism of their immigrant parents. Second, an analysis of lived traditions requires explication of the social and cultural contexts in which they are expressed. Chinese Americans express their familism differently based on class, gender, and the particular religious marketplace where they live. Third, theoretical concepts from one religious culture may be applicable to others. To demonstrate, a theory of *liyi* can be helpful in illuminating the presence of rituals and moral boundary systems among other nonreligious Americans, particularly millennials.[23]

A THEORY OF *LIYI* AND THE STUDY OF AMERICAN MILLENNIALS

In its application, the theory of *liyi* leads researchers to ask different questions about their commitments. Instead of asking "Why are American millennials increasingly nonreligious?," one might ask "What deeply held values are expressed in the rituals to which millennial religious nones devote themselves?" The latter question can help researchers understand, for instance, American millennials' greater desire for social justice and higher levels of activism than previous generations.[24] A concern for *yi*, then, might examine how millennials embody their value for justice (*yi*) in their activism (*li*). The Black Lives Matter movement, for instance, would be a rich site for applying the concept of *liyi* to understand millennial engagement in justice and activism. Looking back to the civil rights movement, some have mourned and inquired about the absence of a vigorous presence of "the black church" in the Black Lives Matter movement. However, nonreligious black millennials engaged in BLM, and those Asian American millennials in solidarity with them, are drawing on a wide range of practices and traditions to empower their activities: Christian spirituality, indidgenous African traditions such as Yoruba, Ifa and Vodou, Buddhist-inspired mindfulness meditation as well as the rituals of familism. How are BLM activists, and those in solidarity with them, using these variegated sources, outside of institutionalized religion, to ground their movement in ideals of justice (*yi*) and methods of activism (*li*)?

Another question framed by a theory of *liyi* is "What practices help nonreligious American millennials maintain their ultimate priorities?" Mindfulness and yoga are increasingly popular practices among Americans, including among the nonreligious, as they seek meaningful practices devoid of religious dogma or belonging to an institution. Such attempts to reorient their lives toward a practice may reflect an unconscious cultural appropriation of Eastern traditions without understanding the meaning or ethics behind the practices and without any responsibility to one's fellow community of practitioners. Indeed, though mindfulness has its roots in Buddhism and yoga in Hinduism, often these practices among millennials gain the most currency when they are presented as explicitly secular practices void of doctrines and history. Even while acknowledging the pernicious Orientalist attitudes that shape the consumption of these practices in contemporary America, scholars can benefit from clarifying how the focus on practice rather than on truth-seeking indicates a growing *liyi* orientation among nonreligious millennials. That is, American millennials practice meditation and yoga (*li*) to live out their values of compassion, kindness, peace, and equanimity (*yi*). To be sure, their practices need to be problematized for cultural appropriation, but *Family Sacrifices* suggests that instead of the category of religion or the secular, scholars can study these millennial practices as *liyi* rituals.

A theory of *liyi* may also be employed to explain the growth of American religious nones among millennials in general. Americans are increasingly living in a landscape of pluralism and skepticism, which drives millennials to become nonreligious, whether it be spiritual but not religious, agnostic, or atheist. That is, American millennials are living more and more in a religious landscape that looks like the ancient Chinese context. Just as the Chinese had three historical strands of discourse that shaped their nonreligiosity, the United States now has similar factors. These parallels include a context of religious pluralism, a postmodern sensibility that encourages skepticism, and identity formation based on values and relationships rather than beliefs and belonging.

Indeed, the nonreligious in America are increasingly living in a context in which pluralism and skepticism are becoming the norm. In one generation the percentage of white Christians in the United States dropped from 81% in 1976 to only 43% in 2016.[25] Growing religious diversity might challenge people's belief systems such that the numbers are less religious overall.[26] Further, postmodernity has heightened Americans' skepticism of universal truths. Affiliation with one religion, then, has clearly declined as the number of religious nones has increased. Additionally, with a heightened mistrust in institutions, Americans affiliate less with religious groupings and more around those with lifestyle affinities.

Rather than a secular age, we suggest that American millennials may be increasingly living in a *liyi* age. American religious nones are leaving churches and, therefore, may be leaving what is understood as religion

China	US
Religious pluralism	Religious pluralism
Religious skepticism	Postmodern Sensibility
Chineseness based on morals/rituals	Identity based on relationships and practices, not beliefs and belonging

Figure 7.1 Chinese and American Contexts

in the Western paradigm. *Family Sacrifices* suggests that a significant portion of these millennial nones hold onto moral boundary systems of *liyi*, practice-centered means of forging right relations, just as Chinese Americans have done historically. Rather than seeing contemporary America as an increasingly secular society, much like the paradigm used to think about a secularizing Europe, scholars would benefit from reorienting their gaze toward the Pacific to see how the U.S. is increasingly a reflection of China, which has historically embraced religious pluralism, skepticism toward the supernatural, and relational responsibilities. That is, even in the study of the unaffiliated, scholars can benefit from the reminder that America is as much a Pacific civilization as it is an Atlantic civilization.[27]

FUTURE DIRECTIONS

Chinese American familism will undoubtedly shift as succeeding generations come of age in different cultural milieus and historical moments. On one hand, Chinese Americans may further acculturate to American individualism and lose reference points to Chinese familism. On the other hand, although later generations in the United States may be further removed from Chinese traditions of the 20th century, globalization and technology may enable them to recover and retain transnational connections. Chinese Americans can easily access more information than ever about traditions and heritages. In addition, nativist politics and xenophobic movements in the United States may initiate greater reactive solidarity among Chinese Americans, in which they would draw together against racist attacks and discrimination. In their efforts for greater representation in the government, media, and other spheres, Chinese Americans may rally around themes of familism to draw strength and numbers. Whatever direction these changes take, they provide multiple opportunities for the research of *liyi*, four of which are entertained here.

If rituals are the primary means by which values and ethics are shaped, what new rituals might be developed to socialize ultimate values and top priorities? A theory of lived traditions such as *liyi*, like theories of religious socialization and religious change, examines both how traditions get translated to succeeding generations and how the traditions themselves change in the process. In the examination of *liyi*, researchers must consider how values and practices that are not prescribed by sacred texts, such as Chinese New Year customs, can be recalled and handed down. In the case of Chinese Americans, how will they continue to adhere to values of the family, especially when later generations do not have a sacrifice narrative of migration to hold the family responsible to one another?

As a tradition undergoes adaptation and hybridization, what core elements are retained and what is added to it? A theory of *liyi* change necessarily entails an intersectional understanding of the transformation of ethnic values and practices. Race, class, gender, and sexuality, we have seen, have shaped the contours and expressions of Chinese American familism. Racialized multiculturalism especially privileges some forms of ethnicity that are consumable and marketable over others. In this framework, how might Chinese Americans maintain a moral boundary system that is not individualized or commercialized but connects them to co-ethnics in deep ways?

How might researchers account for, theorize, and describe the range of beliefs toward lived traditions? This use of *liyi* as a concept analyzes Chinese American familism based on what this group values and practices instead of what they believe. However, we do not intend to suggest that belief, faith, or assent do not matter to Chinese Americans. Whether Chinese Americans strongly believe in the efficacy of their *fengshui* practice or their ancestor veneration often makes a difference in how devoutly they engage in them, and subsequently makes an impact on how familistic they might be. Chinese Americans do have a range of beliefs in their practices of Chinese Popular Religion, from firmly believing in their efficacy to not believing at all in the supernatural. In the latter case, they might conduct these practices out of custom and for the sake of tradition, out of respect for their family, or out of pride in their Chinese heritage. Just as cultural Christians might decorate a Christmas tree and cultural Hindus might celebrate Diwali, cultural practitioners of Chinese Popular Religion adhere to the traditions without belief in them. Theoretical consideration of belief within religious and *liyi* traditions would help greatly in clarifying and analyzing its role and impacts.

How might even major world religions such as Islam and Christianity reorient themselves toward liyi, that is, toward the practice of right relations as opposed to the recitation of dogma? The increasing number of people who identify as "spiritual but not religious" is a sharp reaction to dogmatic and fundamentalist traditions that require belonging and belief for defining strong boundaries. In 2016 Wheaton College ousted its first tenured black professor for wearing *hijab*. Professor Larycia Hawkins was engaging in a practice (*li*) that emphasized right relations (*yi*) in terms of supporting religious freedom. Yet the college, which requested professors to sign faith statements, expected strict adherence from Hawkins that aligned with the doctrine of the school, resulting in significant controversy. Can conservative Christianity, for example, emphasize an orientation beyond accepting Jesus into one's heart, and toward a practice of following Jesus with faith in action? Even such world religions may learn from reorienting their traditions toward a *liyi* orientation.

To conclude, second-generation Chinese Americans recognized that the family sacrifices of their ancestors and immigrant parents made them who they are and gave them inspiration for who they wanted to become. The second generation appreciated the enormous efforts and struggles their family members endured on their behalf, including surviving poverty and political turmoil and especially migrating to a new culture. In acknowl-edging their parents' hard work and resilience, the second generation made sense of their own lives as gifts borne from great costs. In this sense, family sacrifices were their parents' acts of love and devotion made on behalf of the family.

Family sacrifices have another sense as well. Employing an American in-dividualistic perspective, the second generation view their parents as giving up their own personal dreams, careers, and fulfillment for their children's interests. From the Chinese immigrant parents' familist point of view, how-ever, their efforts on behalf of their children and grandchildren are not sacrificial but are simply what they ought to provide and what are norma-tive based on their cultural understandings. In the second sense, family sacrifices are not just the gifts an individual offers to the family unit but also the costs incurred by the family—as a whole group and collectivity—for its individual members.

In our historical moment, tremendous pressures challenge and fracture the family unit in terms of its valuation, its unity, and its strength. As late cap-italism makes increasing demands on workers' time and psychic resources, the family bears the brunt of these costs. When media and consumer markets cater to individual tastes and preferences, the family becomes less cohesive and interdependent. In this light the Chinese American family, as a group, sacrifices for the survival and flourishing of its individual members. That is why *liyi* rituals are so significant for Chinese Americans. In the shared experience of being family, through the recurrent, devoted practice of acting as family, the family itself is renewed. And so the sacrifices of the ancestors have not been made in vain.

APPENDIX A

———— ✺ ————

Research Methodology

Family Sacrifices employs data from two primary sources: the 2012 Pew Asian American Survey and 58 in-depth interviews with second-generation Chinese Americans who stated that they did not affiliate with any religion.

The 2012 Pew Asian American Survey data set includes telephone survey responses from 3,511 Asian Americans sampled nationwide. Of this sample, 728 respondents self-identified as Chinese or Taiwanese. Since several of our in-depth interviews were with Taiwanese Americans, we included Taiwanese in the survey data set for a valid and reliable comparison sample. This survey asked a range of questions about the individual's beliefs, attitudes, and opinions on religious, ethnic, and political matters. For more information about this survey, see http://www.pewsocialtrends.org/2012/06/19/appendix-1-survey-methodology-3/.

Disaggregating this survey's data and identifying the ethnic particularity of Chinese Americans, as opposed to Asian Americans overall, enables us to highlight what is distinctive about this group. Besides having the highest percentage of religious nones, Chinese Americans have a particular spiritual heritage and religious repertoire that we wanted to analyze and detail.

The respondents for the in-depth interviews came from a nonprobability sampling method in which we first contacted individuals whom we knew were second-generation Chinese American religious nones. The second generation are those born in the United States with parents born abroad. Religiously unaffiliated individuals are those who reply "none" when asked if they identify with any religion. These respondents then referred other possible interview candidates to us.

This snowball sampling technique is advantageous in that we were able to access members of a minority group who are generally difficult to reach.

However, we do not claim that our sample is representative. For instance, our sample includes only Chinese Americans who completed a college degree. Nevertheless we find that the themes and trends that emerged from the in-depth interviews are reliably consistent with each other.

The interviews, which took place over a period of five years, lasted about one and a half hours and asked questions about the respondent's (1) family background, (2) ethnic upbringing, (3) religious upbringing, (4) life purposes and meanings, (5) beliefs about the supernatural and reality, and (6) ethics. The respondents were quite open about these topics, and several trends began to emerge early in the interview process.

The respondents consistently spoke of a common upbringing: speaking Chinese at home and eating Chinese food; attending Chinese-language school and facing racial harassment and stereotypes, visiting family often and celebrating Chinese New Year. They almost all spoke about venerating their ancestors, even when their parents were affiliated with major faith traditions.

The respondents shared a range of beliefs about God and their stances toward religious traditions. Often they did not articulate a coherent belief system in the way that Christians might when they have a theological framework about how God relates to the universe and humanity. Instead the sample, especially the agnostics, could only speculate on the supernatural and the nature of reality and rarely held to firm beliefs. By the 10th interview, we recognized that trying to examine religious nones about their beliefs rarely provided much insight on how they understood their own lives. Questions about what was meaningful to them, however, garnered rich, vivid stories and details about their aims and aspirations.

Developing a theory of *liyi* therefore was a result of grounded theory and inductive methods. As narratives of Chinese American familism emerged, we began to focus more on our respondents' values than on their particular beliefs. We also began to look for Chinese terminology that better grasped the Chinese American worldview, and chose *liyi* as a concept to employ. By the last 10 interviews, we were explicitly inquiring about the rituals that Chinese Americans cherished and what these practices meant to them.

The authors and a team of research assistants, including Sharon Lau, Steven Rozzi, and Anastasia Wong, coded each interview transcript around themes. Through this joint process we could make reliable claims about what an individual asserted as well as the trends across our sample. We then identified the themes and topics that were most prevalent and created an ideal type of Chinese American familism, a composite portrait of this group. By no means do we suggest that this ideal type matches any one individual or that any individual embraces all the values and ethics of this group. Rather we suggest that Chinese American familism includes a set of values, narratives, and ethics that offer an ethical way of being and a source of identity for individuals.

APPENDIX B

List of Respondents

Name	Gender	Hometown	Occupation	Affiliation
Michelle Li	F	Landsville, PA	Project manager	Agnostic
Laura Chan	F	Quincy, MA	Marketing professional	Agnostic
Steph Wu	F	Seabroook, MD	College administrative assistant	Agnostic
Rodney Shem	M	Fairfield, CA	Data entry clerk	Agnostic
Kenneth Lam	M	Oakland, CA	College student	Agnostic
Celia Hsiao	F	San Francisco, CA	Artist	Agnostic
Michael Chen	M	San Francisco, CA	Community organizer	Agnostic
Serena Zhang	F	Cleveland, OH	PhD student	Agnostic
Teresa Owyang	F	Los Gatos, CA	Nurse	Agnostic
Benjamin Wong	M	Hillsborough, CA	Vineyard owner	Agnostic
Emily Huang	F	Saratoga, CA	Attorney	Agnostic
Marc Chiou	M	Naperville, IL	Engineer	Agnostic
Tony Chan	M	San Mateo, CA	Analyst	Agnostic
Diana Ngai	F	Palo Alto, CA	Product manager	Agnostic
Derek Qian	M	Fremont, CA	Electrical engineering researcher	Agnostic
Andrea Yao	F	Houston, TX		Agnostic
Sandy Liu	F	Houston, TX	Labor attorney	Agnostic
Chun Shao	F	Irvine, CA	Market research analyst	Agnostic
Jack Wai	m	Richardson, TX	Facebook director	Agnostic
Gary Loo	M	Brookline, MA	Nonprofit director	Agnostic
Henry Zhou	M	Kent, OH	IT professional	Agnostic
Edward Song	M	Calgary, CN	Software engineer	Agnostic

Name	Gender	Hometown	Occupation	Affiliation
David Jong	M	Amarillo, TX	Therapist	Agnostic
Susan Lau	F	Providence, RI	Museum associate	Agnostic
Jodi Shieh	F	Minneapolis, MN	IT analyst	Agnostic
Aaron Zhu	M	Walnut Creek, CA	Photographer	Agnostic
Wendy Foo	F	Rochester, NY	Astronomer	Agnostic
Bruce Cheung	M	San Francisco, CA	Facilities assistant	Agnostic
Tracy Lee	F	Houston, TX	NIH program officer	Agnostic
Ken Li	M	San Jose, CA	Financial analyst	Agnostic
Peter Hsieh	M	Naperville, IL	Computer designer	Atheist
Ben Hao	M	Seattle, WA	Attorney	Atheist
Cheryl Teng	F	Berkeley, CA	College student	Atheist
Scott Lai	M	Columbus, OH	Attorney	Atheist
Larry So	M	Sacramento, CA	Researcher	Atheist
Rhonda Woo	F	Albany, CA	Legal billing clerk	Atheist
Jonathan Hu	M	Albany, CA	Shoe salesman	Atheist
Jane Man	F	St. Louis, MO	Healthcare consultant	Atheist
Daniel Lu	M	Cupertino, CA	Tech project manager	Atheist
Marilyn Hong	F	Milwaukee, WI	Medical student	Atheist
Lila Song	F	Fremont, CA	Software engineer	Atheist
Cary Yu	M to F	Portland, OR	Nonprofit consultant	Atheist
Craig Quan	M	Dallas, TX	Medical student	Atheist
Sophia Wong	F	San Francisco, CA	Personal trainer	Spiritual But Not Religious
Grace Chu	F	Daly City, CA	Student	Spiritual But Not Religious
Wendy Tong	F	Daly City, CA	Acupuncturist	Spiritual But Not Religious
Danielle Hsu	F	Pleasant Hill, CA	Therapist	Spiritual But Not Religious
Irene Hui	F	San Jose, CA	Medical student	Spiritual But Not Religious
Lesley Dong	F	Saratoga, CA	Attorney	Spiritual But Not Religious
Jonathan Pan	M	San Mateo, CA	Analyst	Spiritual But Not Religious
Julia Tom	F	San Mateo, CA	Advertising executive	Spiritual But Not Religious
Karen Lai	F	Alhambra, CA	Design student	Spiritual But Not Religious

Name	Gender	Hometown	Occupation	Affiliation
John Chao	M	Hillsborough, CA	Real estate developer	Spiritual But Not Religious
Erica Tsang	F	Boston, MA	Financial aid director	Spiritual But Not Religious
Sharon Chung	F	Newton, MA	Nonprofit director	Spiritual But Not Religious
Irving Shue	M	Scarsdale, NY	Entrepreneur	Spiritual But Not Religious
Margaret Chung	F	Boston, MA	Graduate student	Spiritual But Not Religious
Monica Tamayo	F	Norton, VA	Physician	Spiritual But Not Religious

APPENDIX C

Interview Questions

A. FAMILY BACKGROUND

1. Where are your parents from?
2. What education did your parents receive? What did your parents do for a living?
3. When did your parents immigrate to the U.S.? Why did they come?
4. Where did you first live in the U.S.? What was it like for your family to immigrate?
5. What are your most vivid memories of being ethnically Chinese? How did your location affect these memories?
6. What Chinese culture did your family maintain, such as language, food, customs?

B. RELIGIOUS UPBRINGING—PARENTS

1. How would you describe your grandparents' religion? Your parents' religion?
2. What religious or spiritual rituals or customs did your parents practice?
3. What other rituals or beliefs related to the supernatural, luck, or fate do your parents hold? How do they practice or reveal them?
4. What religious values and practices do you think your parents attempted to transmit to you? Why?
5. How effective were your parents in transmitting these values and practices?

C. RELIGIOUS UPBRINGING—PARTICIPANT

1. What religious or spiritual rituals or customs did you practice as a child?
2. Why did you practice them?
3. How did you feel about these religious rituals and customs?
4. What strong religious or spiritual beliefs did you hold as a child?
5. Where did you learn these beliefs or teachings?
6. During your youth, did you ever change or convert your practices or beliefs? For what reasons?
7. What other rituals or beliefs related to the supernatural, luck, or fate did you hold as a child?
8. When you were a teenager, who influenced your beliefs and values the most while you were growing up? Why and how?

D. MEANING OF LIFE/VALUES

1. Currently, what is most important to you? Can you give examples of how you live by these values?
2. What do you think is the ultimate purpose in life? How did you come to hold these views about life?
3. What else gives you your greatest meaning in life? How do these things give you meaning?
4. Thinking of the most negative events or circumstances in your life, how did you come to understand and deal with them?
5. Do you believe in life after death? How do you think your belief on this matter affects how you live?
6. Do believe in or practice any Chinese religious rituals or customs currently? If yes, how do they relate to your purposes in life?
7. If no, why don't you believe in or practice these Chinese religions?

E. NATURE OF REALITY

1. How much do you believe in a personal God? How do you think your belief on this matter affects how you live?
2. How much do you believe in any other supernatural force? How do you think your belief on this matter affects how you live?
3. Chinese believe that our lives are governed by luck or karma, that people can enhance their opportunities by gaining better luck. How much do

you believe in this concept? How do your beliefs on this matter affect how you live?

4. Chinese also believe that our lives are governed by fate, that things happen for a reason. How much do you believe in this concept? How do your beliefs on this matter affect how you live?

5. Chinese also tend to be agnostic, in that they can't be sure about things of the supernatural or afterlife. How much do you believe in this concept? How do your beliefs in this matter affect how you live?

6. Partially because of their agnosticism, Chinese may be utilitarian in practicing multiple beliefs and religious rituals. How much do you agree to this concept? How do your beliefs in this matter affect how you live?

7. How do you relate science and technology with your spiritual or religious understandings?

F. ETHICS AND SOCIAL RELATIONS

1. What makes a person morally good or bad, in your perspective? Why?
2. Do you consider yourself a good person? Why or why not?
3. What ways do you show respect in your family?
4. What are your most important responsibilities? How so?
5. Chinese also respect their elders and authorities. To what extent do you respect your elders and authorities?
6. Chinese strongly value their families, as evidenced by the practice of ancestor veneration. Do you practice ancestor veneration? Why or why not? How do you demonstrate filiality?
7. Are there differences in how you relate with your family than with other friends? acquaintances? broader society?
8. Politics?
9. What Chinese values and practices will you want to pass to your own children?

G. GENERAL BACKGROUND

1. What's your education? Work?
2. How would you characterize your closest friends?
3. What groups/organizations are you involved with?
4. On a range from liberal to conservative, how do you identify politically?

NOTES

CHAPTER 1

1. Familism "refers to a collective orientation in which family roles and obligations are highly valued, and the well-being of the family group takes precedence over the interests of each of its members." Many societies hold to this orientation, but Chinese American familism is a distinct ethnic form with its own historical antecedents. C. S. Hartnett and E. Parradom, "Hispanic Familism Reconsidered," *Sociological Quarterly* 53 (2002): 638.

2. In his study of Chinese familism, Lin Yueh-Hwa examines how external, structural factors affect Chinese family dynamics. In contrast, this book considers primarily the values and rituals operating within Chinese American families. Lin Yueh-Hwa, *The Golden Wing: A Sociological Study of Chinese Familism* (London: Routledge and Kegan Paul, 1947).

3. National data about Chinese Americans and Asian Americans come from the Pew Research Center's 2012 Asian American Survey of 3,511 Asian Americans, including 728 Chinese and Taiwanese Americans. Pew Research Center, "Asian Americans: A Mosaic of Faiths" July 19, 2012. http://www.pewforum.org/2012/07/19/asian-americans-a-mosaic-of-faiths-overview/.

4. Becka Alper and Aleksandra Sandstrom, "If the U.S. Had 100 People: Charting Americans' Religious Affiliations," Pew Research Center, 2016, accessed September 25, 2017, http://www.pewresearch.org/fact-tank/2016/11/14/if-the-u-s-had-100-people-charting-americans-religious-affiliations/.

5. Katharina Wenzel-Teuber, "Statistics on Religions and Churches in the People's Republic of China: Update for the Year 2016," China Zentrum, accessed September 25, 2017, http://www.china-zentrum.de/fileadmin/downloads/rctc/2017-2/RCTC_2017-2.26-53_Wenzel-Teuber__Statistics_on_Religions_and_Churches_in_the_PRC_%E2%80%93_Update_for_the_Year_2016.pdf.

6. Pew-Templeton Global Religious Futures Project, "Taiwan," 2016, accessed September 25, 2017, http://www.globalreligiousfutures.org/countries/taiwan#/?affiliations_religion_id=0&affiliations_year=2010&region_name=All%20Countries&restrictions_year=2015.

7. Michael Lipka, "10 Facts about Religion in America," Pew Research Center, August 27, 2015, http://www.pewresearch.org/fact-tank/2015/08/27/10-facts-about-religion-in-america/.

8. Fenggang Yang and Anning Hu, "Mapping Chinese Folk Religion in Mainland China and Taiwan," *Journal for the Scientific Study of Religion* 51, no. 3 (2012): 505–521.

9. Yang and Hu, "Mapping Chinese Folk Religion," 516.

10. Joseph Baker and Buster Smith, "None Too Simple: Examining Issues of Religious Nonbelief and Nonbelonging in the United States," *Journal for the Scientific Study of Religion* 48 (2009): 719–733.

11. Barry Kosmin and Ariela Keysar, "American Nones: The Profile of the No Religion Population. A Report Based on the American Religious Identification Survey 2008," in *American Nones: The Profile of the No Religion Population,* Trinity College Faculty Report (Hartford, CT: Institute for the Study of Secularism in Society & Culture, 2009.

12. Pew Research Center, "Nones on the Rise," October 9, 2012, http://www.pewforum.org/2012/10/09/nones-on-the-rise/#_ftn4.

13. Chaeyoun Lim, Carol McGregor, and Roger Putnam, "Secular and Liminal: Discovering Heterogeneity among Religious Nones," *Journal for the Scientific Study of Religion* 49 (2010): 596–618.

14. Joseph Baker and Buster Smith. "The Nones: Social Characteristics of the Religiously Unaffiliated," *Social Forces* 87 (2008): 1251–1263.

15. Pew Research Center, "Nones on the Rise."

16. Baker and Smith, "None Too Simple."

17. Christel Manning. "Unaffiliated Parents and the Religious Training of Their Children," *Sociology of Religion* 74 (2013): 149–175.

18. Michael Hout and Claude S. Fischer, "Why More Americans Have No Religious Preference: Politics and Generations," *American Sociological Review* 67 (2002): 65–90.

19. Baker and Smith, "None Too Simple."

20. Nicholas Vargas, "Retrospective Accounts of Religious Disaffiliation in the United States: Stressors, Skepticism, and Political Factors," *Sociology of Religion* 73 (2012): 200–223.

21. Peter Berger, *The Homeless Mind: Modernization and Consciousness* (New York: Random House, 1973).

22. Robert Bellah, Richard Madsen, William M. Sullivan, Ann Swidler, and Steven M. Tipton, *Habits of the Heart: Individualism and Commitment in American Life* (Berkeley: University of California Press, 2007).

23. Robert Wuthnow, *After the Baby Boomers: How Twenty- and Thirty-Somethings Are Shaping the Future of American Religion* (Princeton, NJ: Princeton University Press, 2007).

24. Nancy Ammerman, "Spiritual but Not Religious? Beyond Binary Choices in the Study of Religion," *Journal for the Scientific Study of Religion* 52 (2013): 258–278.

25. Fenggang Yang, *Religion in China: Survival and Revival under Communist Rule* (New York: Oxford University Press, 2012).

26. Carolyn Chen, *Getting Saved in America: Taiwanese Immigration and Religious Experience* (Princeton, NJ: Princeton University Press, 2014), 42.

27. Lizhu Fan, "The Dilemma of Pursuing Chinese Religious Studies within the Framework of Western Religious Theories," in *Social Scientific Studies of Religion in China,* edited by Fenggang Yang and Graeme Lang (Boston: Brill, 2011), 87–108.

28. Li Yih-Yuan, *Collected Works of Religion and Mysteries* (Taipei: Lixu Press, 1998).

29. Zhixin Wang, *Introduction to Chinese Religious Thought* (Shanghai: Sanlien Press, 1933).

30. C. K. Yang, *Religion in Chinese Society: A Study of Contemporary Social Functions of Religion and Some Their Historical Factors* (Berkeley: University of California Press, 1961).

31. Wing-tsit Chan, *A Source Book in Chinese Philosophy* (Princeton, NJ: Princeton University Press, 1963), 790.

32. Ben Schwartz, *The World of Thought in Ancient China* (Cambridge, MA: Harvard University Press, 1985, 62.

33. Patricia B. Ebrey, *Confucianism and Family Rituals in Imperial China: A Social History of Writing about Rites* (Princeton, NJ: Princeton University Press, 1991), 11, 49.

34. Chinese Text Project, "Mencius: Liang Hui Wang," accessed October 11, 2017, http://ctext.org/mengzi/liang-hui-wang-i.

35. Eric Hutton, "On the Meaning of *Yi* (義) for Xunzi," M.A. thesis, Harvard University, 1996, 24.

36. Hutton, "On the Meaning of *Yi*," 24.
37. Chinese Text Project, *"Liji, Guan Yi,"* accessed October 11, 2017, http://ctext.org/liji/guan-yi.
38. Hutton, "On the Meaning of *Yi*," 21.
39. Confucius, "Analect 17.18," in *The Analects*, accessed October 11, 2017, http://classics.mit.edu/Confucius/analects.1.1.html
40. Chinese Text Project, "Mengzi: Wen Zhang II," accessed October 11, 2017, http://ctext.org/mengzi/wan-zhang-ii
41. Sima Qian, *Shiji*, 110.2879. See Shao-yun Yang, "Reinventing the Barbarian: Rhetorical and Philosophical Uses of the Yi-Di in Mid-Imperial China, 600–1300," PhD dissertation, University of California, Berkeley, 2014, xxiv–xxv.
42. Yang, "Reinventing the Barbarian," xxiv.
43. As Talal Asad astutely observes, "My argument is that there cannot be a universal definition of religion, not only because its constituent elements and relationships are historically specific, but because that definition is itself the historical product of discursive processes." Talal Asad, *Genealogies of Religion: Discipline and Reasons of Power in Christianity and Islam* (Baltimore: Johns Hopkins University Press, 1993), 29.
44. Emile Durkheim, *Elementary Forms of the Religious Life* (New York: Oxford University Press, 2008).

CHAPTER 2

1. Wong Chin Foo, "Why Am I a Heathen?," *The North American Review* 145 (1887): 169.
2. Stephen F. Teiser, "Popular Religion," *Journal of Asian Studies* 54, no. 2 (1995): 378.
3. Emily Ahern, *Chinese Ritual and Politics* (Cambridge, UK: Cambridge University Press, 1981); Jean DeBernardi, *The Way That Lives in the Heart: Chinese Popular Religion and Spirit Mediums in Penang, Malaysia* (Stanford, CA: Stanford University Press, 2006); Maurice Freeman, "On the Sociological Study of Chinese Religion," in *Religion and Ritual in Chinese Society*, edited by Arthur Wolf (Stanford, CA: Stanford University Press, 1974); Arthur Wolf, *Religion and Ritual in Chinese Society* (Stanford, CA: Stanford University Press, 1974); Yang, *Religion in Chinese Society*.
4. Yang, *Religion in Chinese Society*, 296.
5. Anna Sun, "Theorizing the Plurality of Chinese Religious Life: The Search for New Paradigms in the Study of Chinese Religions," in *Religion and Orientalism in Asian Studies*, ed. Kiri Paramore (London: Bloomsbury2016) 51–72.
6. Chinese Popular Religion also includes the use of spirit mediums of fortunetelling and the petitioning of gods for assistance. Why immigrant families transmit these practices less often is discussed in a later section of this chapter.
7. Evelyn Rawski, "A Historian's Approach to Death Ritual," in *Death Ritual in Late Imperial and Modern China*, edited by James Watson and Evelyn Rawski (Berkeley: University of California Press, 1988), 25.
8. Rawski, "A Historian's Approach," 23.
9. Sue F. Chung and Priscilla Wegars, *Chinese American Death Rituals: Respecting the Ancestors* (Lanham, MD: AltaMira Press, 2005), 22–24; Stephen Teiser, "Religions of China in Practice," in *Asian Religions in Practice: An Introduction*, edited by Donald S. Lopez (Princeton, NJ: Princeton University Press, 2010), 109.
10. Rawski, "A Historian's Approach," 26–27; Schwartz, *The World of Thought*, 99, 115; Teiser, "Religions of China in Practice," 111, 118.
11. The historian Ben Schwartz writes of this ancient religious pluralism, "When one examines the oracle bone inscriptions one is immediately struck by the pervasiveness of what we call ancestor worship. It is not an exclusive religious orientation and is in constant interplay with a concern with spirits of rivers, mountains, earth, wind, rain, heavenly bodies,

and the 'high god' (Ti or Shang-ti). Yet the orientation to ancestor worship is so omnipresent and so central to the entire development of Chinese civilization that it warrants some separate reflection on its possible implications" (*The World of Thought*, 20–21).

12. Rawski, "A Historian's Approach," 24.

13. Chen Qiyou, *Lüshi Chunqiu Xinshi* (Shanghai: Shanghai Guji Chubanshe, 1984), accessed October 11, 2017, https://plato.stanford.edu/entries/chinese-metaphysics/.

14. Rawski, "A Historian's Approach," 24–25.

15. Stevan Harrell, "The Concept of Fate in Chinese Folk Ideology," *Modern China* 13, no. 1 (1987): 90–109; Chan, *A Sourcebook in Chinese Philosophy*; P. Sangren, "Fate, Agency, and the Economy of Desire in Chinese Ritual and Society," *Social Analysis* 56, no. 2 (2012): 117–135.

16. DeBernardi, *The Way That Lives*.

17. Rawski, "A Historian's Approach," 25.

18. Mary Fong, "'Luck Talk' in Celebrating the Chinese New Year," *Journal of Pragmatics* 32, no. 2 (2000): 219–237.

19. Charles Taylor devotes himself to answering the question of how it became widely possible *not* to owe one's allegiance to transcendent goals after that possibility was precluded for so long in the West. He queried, "Why was it virtually impossible not to believe in God in, say, 1500 in our Western society, while in 2000 many of us find this not only easy, but even inescapable?" Charles Taylor, *A Secular Age* (Cambridge, MA: Harvard University Press, 2007), 26.

20. Confucius, "Xian Jin" (Book 11), verse 12, in *Analects*, translated by James Legge, reprinted in Donald Sturgeon, ed., *Chinese Text Project*, 2011, accessed April 2015, http://ctext.org.

21. Confucius, "Shu Er" (Book 7), verse 21, in *Analects*, in Sturgeon, *Chinese Text Project*.

22. Xunzi, *Xunzi*, chapter 21, translation by Dubs, quoted in modified form in Joseph Needham and Ling Wang, *Science and Civilisation in China: Volume 2* (Cambridge, UK: Cambridge University Press, 1956), 27.

23. Confucius, "Yong Ye" (Book 6), verse 22, in *Analects*, in Sturgeon, *Chinese Text Project*.

24. Needham and Wang, *Science and Civilisation*, 13.

25. Xunzi, *Xunzi*, chapter 17, quoted in Needham and Wang, *Science and Civilisation*.

26. Quoted in Needham and Wang, *Science and Civilisation*, 374.

27. Wang Chong, *Lunheng*, translation by Forke, quoted in Needham and Wang, *Science and Civilisation*, 375.

28. Ebrey, *Confucianism*, 89.

29. Ebrey, *Confucianism*, 93.

30. Ebrey, *Confucianism*, 66.

31. Randall Nadeau, "Divinity," in *The Wiley-Blackwell Companion to Chinese Religions*, edited by Randall L. Nadeau (New York: John Wiley and Sons, 2012), 393.

32. Yang, *Religion in China*.

33. William Theodore De Bary and Richard Lufrano, eds., *Sources of Chinese Tradition*, 2nd ed. (New York: Columbia University Press, 1999), 568.

34. Mencius, *Mengzi*, "Teng Wen Gong I" (Book IIIA), chapter 4, translated by James Legge, reprinted in Sturgeon, *Chinese Text Project*.

35. Tsukamoto Zenryū, *A History of Early Chinese Buddhism: From Its Introduction to the Death of Hui-yüan*, translated by Leon Hurvitz (Tokyo: Kodansha International, 1985), 827.

36. Kenneth Ch'en, *Buddhism in China, a Historical Survey* (Princeton, NJ: Princeton University Press, 1964), 75, 142–144.

37. Paul A. Cohen, *China and Christianity: The Missionary Movement and the Growth of Chinese Antiforeignism, 1860–1870* (Cambridge, MA: Harvard University Press, 1963), 26.

38. Cohen, *China and Christianity*, 54.

39. Wong, "Why Am I a Heathen?," 172.

40. Wong, "Why Am I a Heathen?," 174.
41. Wong, "Why Am I a Heathen?," 178.
42. Ronald Inglehart and Wayne E. Baker, "Modernization, Cultural Change, and the Persistence of Traditional Values," American Sociological Review 65, no. 1 (2000): 19–51.
43. Peter Berger, *The Sacred Canopy: Elements of a Sociological Theory of Religion* (Garden City, NY: Anchor Books 1967); Jose Casanova, *Public Religions in the Modern World* (Chicago: University of Chicago Press, 1994).
44. Sor-Hoon Tan, "Modernizing Confucianism and 'New Confucianism,'" in *The Cambridge Companion to Modern Chinese Culture*. Cambridge, England: Cambridge University Press, 2008. 135–154.
45. Thoralf Klein, "Political Religion in Twentieth Century China and Its Global Dimension," in *Globalization and the Making of Religious Modernity in China*, edited by Thomas Jansen, Thoralf Klein, and Christian Meyer (New York: Brill, 2014), 52–90.
46. Prasenjit Duara, "Knowledge and Power in the Discourse of Modernity: The Campaigns against Popular Religion in Early Twentieth-Century China," *Journal of Asian Studies* 50 (February 1991): 67–83.
47. Goosaert, "1898."
48. Tan, "Modernizing Confucianism," 140.
49. Fenggang Yang, "What about China? Religious Vitality in the Most Secular and Rapidly Modernizing Society," *Sociology of Religion* 75, no. 4 (2014): 567.
50. Daniel Overmeyer, "From 'Feudal Superstition' to 'Popular Belief': New Directions in Mainland China Studies of Chinese Popular Religion," *Cahiers d'Extreme Asie* 12 (2001): 103–126.
51. Tu Wei-Ming, *Confucian Traditions in East Asian Modernity: Moral Education and Economic Culture in Japan and the Four Mini-Dragons* (Cambridge, MA: Harvard University Press, 1996), 8–9
52. Fenggang Yang and Anning Hu, "Mapping Chinese Folk Religion in Mainland China and Taiwan," *Journal for the Scientific Study of Religion* 50, no. 3 (2012): 518.
53. Anning Hu and Fenggang Yang, "Trajectories of Folk Religion in Deregulated Taiwan: An Age, Period, Cohort Analysis," *Chinese Sociological Review* 46, no. 3 (2014): 80–100.
54. Timothy Smith, "Religion and Ethnicity in America," *American Historical Review* 83, no. 5 (1978): 1155–1185.
55. Sheba Mariam George, *When Women Come First: Gender and Class in Transnational Migration* (Berkeley: University of California Press, 2005); R. Stephen Warner and Judith G. Wittner, *Gatherings in Diaspora: Religious Communities and the New Immigration* (Philadelphia: Temple University Press, 1998).
56. Chen, *Getting Saved in America*; Pyong Gap Min, *Preserving Ethnicity through Religion in America: Korean Protestants and Indian Hindus across Generations* (New York: New York University Press, 2010); Fenggang Yang, *Chinese Christians in America: Conversion, Assimilation, and Adhesive Identities* (University Park: Pennsylvania State University Press, 1999).
57. Pew Research Center, "Asian Americans."
58. Phillip Connor, "Increase or Decrease? The Impact of the International Migratory Event on Immigrant Religious Participation," *Journal for the Scientific Study of Religion* 47, no. 2 (2008): 243–257.
59. Min, *Preserving Ethnicity*.
60. Carolyn Chen and Russell Jeung, *Sustaining Faith Traditions: Race, Ethnicity, and Religion among the Latino and Asian American Second Generation* (New York: New York University Press, 2012).
61. Chen, *Getting Saved in America*, 86–87.
62. Chen and Jeung, *Sustaining Faith Traditions*, 3-4.

63. Russell Jeung, *Faithful Generations: Race and New Asian American Churches* (New Brunswick, NJ: Rutgers University Press, 2005).
64. Nazli Kibria, *Becoming Asian American: Second-Generation Chinese and Korean American Identities* (Baltimore: Johns Hopkins University Press, 2002), 160.
65. Roger Finke and Laurence R. Iannaccone, "Supply-Side Explanations for Religious Change," *Annals of the American Academy of Political and Social Science* 527 (1993): 27–39.
66. Rodney Stark and Roger Finke, *Acts of Faith: Explaining the Human Side of Religion* (Berkeley: University of California Press, 2000).
67. Finke and Iannaccone, "Supply-Side Explanations," 28.
68. Yang, *Religion in China*, 87.
69. Chen, *Getting Saved in America*, 62.
70. Rebecca Y. Kim, *God's New Whiz Kids? Korean American Evangelicals on Campus* (New York: New York University Press, 2006).
71. Jerry Park, personal correspondence about Pew data. Park observes that for those Chinese American families who arrived after 1965, 21.6% of immigrants, 19.1% of the second generation, and only 10.2% of the third generation are Christian. These figures indicate that the acculturation does not lead to Christianization.
72. Khyati Y. Joshi, *New Roots in America's Sacred Ground: Religion, Race, and Ethnicity in Indian America* (New Brunswick, NJ: Rutgers University Press, 2006).
73. Wong, "Why Am I a Heathen?," 175–176, 178.

CHAPTER 3

1. "Welcome to Naperville Video," accessed March 18, 2016, https://www.naperville.il.us/about-naperville/
2. Chinese place statues of lions, also known as *fu* dogs, to frame doorways and to protect homes.
3. Actually, according to Chinese folklore, a mythical beast named "Nien" (a homonym for "year") would attack villagers every spring. Lights are left on all night and firecrackers are lit for Chinese New Year to ward off the beast.
4. *Yu Tao Gao*, or taro root cake, is made into round pieces to represent wholeness. The word *gao* is a homonym for "tall," so the cake symbolizes growth for the new year.
5. Whole steamed chicken that includes the head symbolizes completeness and prosperity.
6. Longevity noodles, which are long, represent long life.
7. Berger, *The Sacred Canopy*.
8. Joseph Baker and Buster Smith, *American Secularism: Contours of Nonreligious Belief Systems* (New York: New York University Press, 2015).
9. Elaine Howard Ecklund and Christopher Scheitle, "Religion among Academic Scientists: Distinctions, Disciplines, and Demographics," *Social Problems* 54, no. 2 (2007): 289–307.
10. Herbert J. Gans, "Symbolic Ethnicity: The Future of Ethnic Groups and Culture in America," *Ethnic and Racial Studies* 2 (1979): 1–19.
11. Stephen Merino, "Irreligious Socialization? The Adult Religious Preferences of Individuals Raised with No Religion," *Secularism and Nonreligion* 1 (2012): 1–16.

CHAPTER 4

1. *Joong*, or *zongzi* in Mandarin, is glutinous rice wrapped in leaves and steamed. It's eaten to commemorate the death of Qu Yuan, a patriotic poet who drowned himself.
2. R. Stephen Warner, "The Role of Religion in the Process of Segmented Assimilation," *Annals of the American Academy of Political and Social Science* 612 (2007): 102–115.
3. Gwun Yam, or Guan Yin, is the Buddhist Goddess of Compassion.
4. Chen, *Getting Saved in America*, 2014.

5. Vincent Goossaert, "Mapping Charisma among Chinese Religious Specialists," *Nova Religio: The Journal of Alternative and Emergent Religions* 12, no. 2 (2008): 12–28.
6. Baker and Smith, *American Secularism.*
7. Marjorie Gunnoe and Kristin Moore, "Predictors of Religiosity among Youth Aged 17–22," *Journal for the Scientific Study of Religion* 41, no. 4 (2002): 613–622.

CHAPTER 5

1. Bellah et al., *Habits of the Heart.*
2. Pew Research Center, "Millennials: A Portrait of Generation Next," February 24, 2010, http://www.pewresearch.org/topics/millennials//.
3. Among all Americans between 18 and 29, 22.2% are married (data from 2010); 13.5% are married and live with their children. And 21.3% of all millennials live with their children.
   Wendy Wang and Paul Taylor, "For Millennials, Parenthood Trumps Marriage," Pew Research Center, March 9, 2011, http://www.pewsocialtrends.org/2011/03/09/for-millennials-parenthood-trumps-marriage/
4. More than half (54.0%) of millennials have at least some college education. See Pew Research Center, "Millennials."
5. Compared to 75.0% of Gen X, 86% of millennials say it's important for their work to "give back." Sylvia Ann Hewlett, Laura Sherbin, and Karen Sumberg, "How Gen Y and Boomers Will Reshape Your Agenda," *Harvard Business Review*, July–August 2009, https://hbr.org/2009/07/how-gen-y-boomers-will-reshape-your-agenda.
6. Likewise 77.0% of millennials are in regular contact with parents. Among 25- to 39-year-olds in the United States, 85.0% communicate weekly, and 37.0% daily. Clark University, "New Clark University Poll: Grown-up Millennials Are Closely Connected to Parents," November 6, 2014, https://clarknow.clarku.edu/2014/11/06/new-clark-university-poll-grown-up-millennials-are-closely-connected-to-parents/.
7. Overall, millennials are more likely than Gen X or Baby Boomers to believe that they should bring their parents to live with them. Pew Research Center Social and Demographic Trends, "From the Age of Aquarius to the Age of Responsibility: Baby Boomers Approach Age 60," Accessed 5 March 2019 http://www.pewsocialtrends.org/2005/12/08/baby-boomers-from-the-age-of-aquarius-to-the-age-of-responsibility/
8. More than three in five Americans (63.2%) communicated with (by phone, email, or letter) a sibling at least once a month, and 35.0% at least once a week. Larry Bumpass and James Sweet, "A National Survey of Families and Households (NSFH): Wave III, 2001–2002," University of Wisconsin Center for Demography and Ecology, accessed July 22, 2017, http://www.ssc.wisc.edu/nsfh/content3.htm.

CHAPTER 6

1. Rosemary Gong, *Good Luck Life: The Essential Guide to Chinese American Celebrations and Culture* (New York: HarperResource, 2005).
2. Gong, *Good Luck Life.*
3. Standing chopsticks in rice at mealtimes is considered rude, because doing so is to be reserved for the ancestors.

CONCLUSION

1. Brent Nongbri, *Before Religion: A History of a Modern Concept* (New Haven, CT: Yale University Press, 2013); Carlin Barton and Daniel Boyarin, *Imagine No Religion: How Modern Abstractions Hide Ancient Realities* (New York: Fordham University Press, 2016).
2. Chinese Americans, as well as Asian Americans, find themselves popularly represented as a model minority because of their economic success, work ethic, and strong families.

Several works in Asian American studies have unpacked the myth of this stereotype. We do not want to perpetuate this image, but instead offer a broad profile of Chinese American familism as an ideal type of one moral boundary system. See Madeline Hsu, *The Good Immigrants: How the Yellow Peril Became the Model Minority* (Princeton, NJ: Princeton University Press, 2015); Ellen Wu, *The Color of Success: Asian Americans and the Origins of the Model Minority* (New York: Oxford University Press, 2015).

3. Mia Tuan, *Forever Foreigners or Honorary Whites? The Asian American Experience Today* (New Brunswick, NJ: Rutgers University Press, 1999).

4. Jean Tsai, Yu-Wen Ying, and Peter Lee, "Cultural Predictors of Self- Esteem: A Study of Chinese American Female and Male Young Adults," *Cultural Diversity and Ethnic Minority Psychology* 7, no. 3 (2016): 284–297; Soryoung Kim, "Intergenerational Conflict and Its Role in Suicidal Ideation among Chinese American and Japanese American College Students," PhD dissertation, University of Hartford, 2002.

5. Will Herbert, *Protestant, Catholic, Jew: An Essay in American Religious Sociology* (Chicago: University of Chicago Press, 1955).

6. Min Zhou, "Growing Up American: The Challenge Confronting Immigrant Children and Children of Immigrants," *Annual Review of Sociology* 23, no. 1 (1997): 63–95.

7. May Tung, Chinese Americans and Their Immigrant Parents (Binghamton, NY: Haworth Press, 2000).

8. Wei-Chin Hwang, Jeffrey Wood, and Ken Fujimoto, "Acculturative Family Distancing (AFD) and Depression in Chinese American Families," *Journal of Consulting and Clinical Psychology* 78, no. 5 (2010): 655–667; Paul Jose and Carol Huntsinger, "Moderation and Mediation Effects of Coping by Chinese American and European American Adolescents," *Journal of Genetic Psychology* 166, no. 1 (2005): 16–43; Kim, "Intergenerational Conflict."; Weichao Yuwen and A. C. Chen, "Chinese American Adolescents: Perceived Parenting Styles and Adolescents' Psychosocial Health," *International Nursing Review* 60, no. 2, (2013): 236–243; Jose and Huntsinger, "Moderation and Mediation Effects.";

9. Leaning politically liberal, Chinese Americans overwhelmingly support the Affordable Care Act, increased federal assistance for college, and setting stricter emissions limits to prevent climate change Karthick Ramakrishnan, Janelle Wong, Taeku Lee, and Jennifer Lee, "Asian American Voices in the 2016 Election," National Asian American Survey, Fall 2016, accessed October 4, 2017 http://naasurvey.com/wp-content/uploads/2016/10/NAAS2016-Oct5-report.pdf.

10. Michael Liu, Kim Geron, and Tracy Gee, *The Snake Dance of Asian American Activism* (Lanham, MD: Lexington Books, 2008).

11. Jennifer Jihye Chun, George Lipsitz, and Young Shin, "Intersectionality as a Social Movement Strategy: Asian Immigrant Women Advocates," *Signs* 38, no. 4 (Summer 2013): 917.

12. Michelle Lin, "The Garment Workers Justice Campaign," accessed October 11, 2017, http://www.umich.edu/~snre492/Jones/jessica.htm.

13. Ulysses Torassa, "Thousands Protest Legalizing Same-Sex Marriage: Asian Americans, Christians Rally in Sunset District," *San Francisco Chronicle*, April 26, 2004.

14. The in Oakland's Chinatown organized tenants through arts and culture. Their poster artwork depicted various family members threatened by eviction, including a child holding a key. Stop Chinatown Evictions Coalition, poster, *Found SF*, accessed October 4, 2017, http://www.foundsf.org/images/f/fe/Stop_Evictions_of_Our_Elders_poster.jpg.

15. Barton and Boyarin, *Imagine No Religion*, 1.

16. As J. Z. Smith observes, "religion" is "not a native category.... It is a category imposed from the outside on some aspect of native culture." J. Z. Smith, "Religion, Religions, Religious," in *Critical Terms for Religious Studies*, edited by Mark Taylor (Chicago: University of Chicago Press, 1998), 269.

17. Geertz's work in *Interpretation of Cultures* represents a social scientific method through which religion could be understood. In his analysis of "thick description," he defined religion as a system of symbols that create long-lasting "moods and motivations" that create certain "conceptions" of the "order of existence," and these conceptions are cloaked in the "aura" of "facticity" so that the moods and motivations seem uniquely real. In Talal Asad, "Anthropological Conceptions of Religion: Reflections on Geertz," *Man* 18, no. 2 (1983): 237–259; Asad, *Genealogies of Religion*.
18. Catherine Bell thus sought to make a turn from religion as belief to an understanding of religion as ritual, just as Durkheim theorized. Catherine Bell, *Ritual Theory, Ritual Practice* (New York: Oxford University Press, 2009).
19. Edward Said, *Orientalism* (New York: Vintage, 1979); Charles Long, *Significations: Signs, Symbols, and Images in the Interpretation of Religion* (Aurora, CO: Davies Press, 1999).
20. Kathryn Lofton, for instance, argues that devotees of Oprah Winfrey not only consume Oprah's product recommendations but consume Oprah herself, as a spiritual icon of modernity. In the secular sphere of television and capitalist culture, moderns find their "salvation" through Oprah. The "secular," Lofton writes, is "not an absence of religion." Kathryn Lofton, *Oprah: The Gospel of an Icon* (Berkeley: University of California Press, 2011), 109See also Courtney Bender, *The New Metaphysicals: Spirituality and the American Religious Imagination* (Chicago: University of Chicago Press, 2010).
21. The religious historian Brad Gregory, who has criticized a Durkheimian definition of religion for engaging in a confessional faith in the secular, still depends on the idea of religion as a faith, some form of assent, a system of belief and belonging. Brad Gregory, "The Other Confessional History: On Secular Bias in the Study of Religion," *History and Theory* 45, no. 4 (2006): 132–149.
22. Lofton's and Bender's logic echoes Charles Taylor's definition of secularization in *A Secular Age* that depends on absence, particularly the decline of Western Christendom in the modern world. That is, Taylor's understanding of secularization depends on, first, identifying itself in relationship to the decline of religion as a system of belief and belonging.
23. Millennials are those born after 1980 and the first generation to come of age in the new millennium.
24. Pew Research Center, "Millennials."
25. PPRI, "PRRI Releases Largest Survey of American Religious and Denominational Identity Ever Conducted," *Cision*, September 6, 2017, http://www.prnewswire.com/news-releases/prri-releases-largest-survey-of-american-religious-and-denominational-identity-ever-conducted-300514391.html.
26. Daniel Cox, "Religious Diversity May Be Making America Less Religious," *FiveThirtyEight*, August 23, 2016, https://fivethirtyeight.com/features/religious-diversity-may-be-making-america-less-religious/.
27. Gary Okihiro, "Toward a Pacific Civilization," *Japanese Journal of American Studies* 18 (2007): 73–85.

BIBLIOGRAPHY

Ahern, Emily. *Chinese Ritual and Politics*. Cambridge, UK: Cambridge University Press, 1981.

Alper, Becka, and Aleksandra Sandstrom. "If the U.S. Had 100 People: Charting Americans' Religious Affiliations." Pew Research Center, 2016. Accessed September 25, 2017. http://www.pewresearch.org/fact-tank/2016/11/14/if-the-u-s-had-100-people-charting-americans-religious-affiliations/.

Ammerman, Nancy. "Spiritual but Not Religious? Beyond Binary Choices in the Study of Religion." *Journal for the Scientific Study of Religion* 52 (2013): 258–278.

Asad, Talal. "Anthropological Conceptions of Religion: Reflections on Geertz." *Man* 18, no. 2 (1983): 237–259.

Asad, Talal. *Genealogies of Religion: Discipline and Reasons of Power in Christianity and Islam*. Baltimore: Johns Hopkins University Press, 1993.

Baker, Joseph, and Buster Smith. *American Secularism: Contours of Nonreligious Belief Systems*. New York: New York University Press, 2015.

Baker, Joseph, and Buster Smith. "The Nones: Social Characteristics of the Religiously Unaffiliated." *Social Forces* 87 (2008): 1251–1263.

Baker, Joseph, and Buster Smith. "None Too Simple: Examining Issues of Religious Nonbelief and Nonbelonging in the United States." *Journal for the Scientific Study of Religion* 48 (2009): 719–733.

Barton, Carlin, and Daniel Boyarin. *Imagine No Religion: How Modern Abstractions Hide Ancient Realities*. New York: Fordham University Press, 2016.

Bell, Catherine. *Ritual Theory, Ritual Practice*. New York: Oxford University Press, 2009.

Bellah, Robert, Richard Madsen, William M. Sullivan, Ann Swidler, and Steven M. Tipton. *Habits of the Heart: Individualism and Commitment in American Life*. Berkeley: University of California Press, 2007.

Bender, Courtney. *The New Metaphysicals: Spirituality and the American Religious Imagination*. Chicago: University of Chicago Press, 2010.

Berger, Peter. *The Homeless Mind: Modernization and Consciousness*. New York: Random House, 1973.

Berger, Peter. *The Sacred Canopy: Elements of a Sociological Theory of Religion*. Garden City, NY: Anchor Books, 1967.

Bullard, Gabe. "The World's Newest Major Religion: No Religion." *National Geographic*, April 22, 2016. Accessed October 2, 2017. http://news.nationalgeographic.com/2016/04/160422-atheism-agnostic-secular-nones-rising-religion/Casanova.

Bumpass, Larry, and James Sweet. "A National Survey of Families and Households (NSFH): Wave III, 2001–2002." University of Wisconsin Center for Demography and Ecology. Accessed July 22, 2017. http://www.ssc.wisc.edu/nsfh/content3.htm.

Casanova, Jose. *Public Religions in the Modern World*. Chicago: University of Chicago Press, 1994.

Chan, Wing-tsit. *A Source Book in Chinese Philosophy*. Princeton, NJ: Princeton University Press, 1963.

Chen, Carolyn. *Getting Saved in America: Taiwanese Immigration and Religious Experience.* Princeton, NJ: Princeton University Press, 2014.

Chen, Carolyn, and Russell Jeung. *Sustaining Faith Traditions: Race, Ethnicity, and Religion among the Latino and Asian American Second Generation.* New York: New York University Press, 2012.

Chen Qiyou, Lüshi Chunqiu Xinshi (Shanghai: Shanghai Guji Chubanshe, 1984), quoted in Perkins, Franklin, "Metaphysics in Chinese Philosophy", The Stanford Encyclopedia of Philosophy (Winter 2016 Edition), Edward N. Zalta (ed.), https://plato.stanford.edu/archives/win2016/entries/chinese-metaphysics/.

Ch'en, Kenneth. *Buddhism in China, a Historical Survey.* Princeton, NJ: Princeton University Press, 1964.

Chen Qiyou, Lüshi Chunqiu Xinshi (Shanghai: Shanghai Guji Chubanshe, 1984), quoted in Perkins, Franklin, "Metaphysics in Chinese Philosophy", The Stanford Encyclopedia of Philosophy (Winter 2016 Edition), Edward N. Zalta (ed.), https://plato.stanford.edu/archives/win2016/entries/chinese-metaphysics/.

Chinese Text Project. "*Liji*, Guan Yi." Accessed October 11, 2017. http://ctext.org/liji/guan-yi.

Chinese Text Project. "Mencius: Liang Hui Wang." Accessed October 11, 2017. http://ctext.org/mengzi/liang-hui-wang-i.

Chinese Text Project. "Mengzi: Wen Zhang II." Accessed October 11, 2017. http://ctext.org/mengzi/wan-zhang-ii.

Chun, Jennifer Jihye, George Lipsitz, and Young Shin. "Intersectionality as a Social Movement Strategy: Asian Immigrant Women Advocates." *Signs* 38, no. 4 (Summer 2013): 917–940.

Chung, Sue F., and Priscilla Wegars. *Chinese American Death Rituals: Respecting the Ancestors.* Lanham, MD: AltaMira Press, 2005.

Clark University. "New Clark University Poll: Grown-up Millennials Are Closely Connected to Parents." November 6, 2014. https://clarknow.clarku.edu/2014/11/06/new-clark-university-poll-grown-up-millennials-are-closely-connected-to-parents/.

Cohen, Paul A. *China and Christianity: The Missionary Movement and the Growth of Chinese Antiforeignism, 1860–1870.* Cambridge, MA: Harvard University Press, 1963.

Confucius. *The Analects.* Accessed October 11, 2017. http://classics.mit.edu/Confucius/analects.1.1.html.

Connor, Phillip. "Increase or Decrease? The Impact of the International Migratory Event on Immigrant Religious Participation." *Journal for the Scientific Study of Religion* 47, no. 2 (2008): 243–257.

Cox, Daniel. "Religious Diversity May Be Making America Less Religious." *FiveThirtyEight*, August 23, 2016. https://fivethirtyeight.com/features/religious-diversity-may-be-making-america-less-religious/.

De Bary, William, and Richard Lufrano, eds. *Sources of Chinese Tradition.* 2nd ed. New York: Columbia University Press, 1999.

DeBernardi, Jean. *The Way That Lives in the Heart: Chinese Popular Religion and Spirit Mediums in Penang, Malaysia.* Stanford, CA: Stanford University Press, 2006.

Duara, Prasenjit. "Knowledge and Power in the Discourse of Modernity: The Campaigns against Popular Religion in Early Twentieth-Century China." *Journal of Asian Studies* 50 (February 1991): 67–83.

Durkheim, Emile. *Elementary Forms of the Religious Life.* New York: Oxford University Press, 2008.

Ebrey, Patricia B. *Confucianism and Family Rituals in Imperial China: A Social History of Writing about Rites.* Princeton, NJ: Princeton University Press, 1991.

Ecklund, Elaine Howard, and Christopher Scheitle. "Religion among Academic Scientists: Distinctions, Disciplines, and Demographics." *Social Problems* 54, no. 2 (2007): 289–307.

Fan, Lizhu. "The Dilemma of Pursuing Chinese Religious Studies within the Framework of Western Religious Theories." In *Social Scientific Studies of Religion in China*, edited by Fenggang Yang and Graeme Lang, 87–108. Boston: Brill, 2011.

Finke, Roger, and Laurence R. Iannaccone. "Supply-Side Explanations for Religious Change." *Annals of the American Academy of Political and Social Science* 527 (1993): 27–39.

Fong, Mary. "'Luck Talk' in Celebrating the Chinese New Year." *Journal of Pragmatics* 32, no. 2 (2000): 219–237.

Freeman, Maurice. "On the Sociological Study of Chinese Religion." In *Religion and Ritual in Chinese Society*, edited by Arthur Wolf, 19–41. Stanford, CA: Stanford University Press, 1974.

Gans, Herbert. J. "Symbolic Ethnicity: The Future of Ethnic Groups and Culture in America." *Ethnic and Racial Studies* 2, no. 1 (1079) : 1–19.

George, Sheba Mariam. *When Women Come First: Gender and Class in Transnational Migration.* Berkeley: University of California Press, 2005.

Gong, Rosemary. *Good Luck Life: The Essential Guide to Chinese American Celebrations and Culture.* New York: Harper Resource, 2005.

Goossaert, Vincent. "1898: The Beginning of the End for Chinese Religion." *Journal for Asian Studies* 65, no. 2 (2006) 317–335.

Goossaert, Vincent. "Mapping Charisma among Chinese Religious Specialists." *Nova Religio: The Journal of Alternative and Emergent Religions* 12, no. 2 (2008): 12–28.

Gregory, Brad. "The Other Confessional History: On Secular Bias in the Study of Religion." *History and Theory* 45, no. 4 (2006): 132–149.

Gunnoe, Marjorie, and Kristin Moore. "Predictors of Religiosity among Youth Aged 17–22." *Journal for the Scientific Study of Religion* 41, no. 4 (2002): 613–622.

Harrell, Stevan. "The Concept of Fate in Chinese Folk Ideology." *Modern China* 13, no. 1 (1987): 90–109.

Hartnett, C. S., and E. Parradom. "Hispanic Familism Reconsidered." *Sociological Quarterly* 53 (2002): 636–653.

Herbert, Will. *Protestant, Catholic, Jew: An Essay in American Religious Sociology.* Chicago: University of Chicago Press, 1955.

Hewlett, Sylvia Ann, Laura Sherbin, and Karen Sumberg. "How Gen Y and Boomers Will Reshape Your Agenda." *Harvard Business Review*, July–August 2009. https://hbr.org/2009/07/how-gen-y-boomers-will-reshape-your-agenda.

Hout, Michael, and Claude S. Fischer. "Why More Americans Have No Religious Preference: Politics and Generations." *American Sociological Review* 67 (2002): 65–90.

Hsu, Madeline. *The Good Immigrants: How the Yellow Peril Became the Model Minority.* Princeton, NJ: Princeton University Press, 2015.

Hu, Anning, and Fenggang Yang. "Trajectories of Folk Religion in Deregulated Taiwan: An Age, Period, Cohort Analysis." *Chinese Sociological Review* 46, no. 3 (2014): 80–100.

Hutton, Eric. "On the Meaning of *Yi* (義) for Xunzi." M.A. thesis, Harvard University, 1996.

Hwang, Wei-Chin, Jeffrey Wood, and Ken Fujimoto. "Acculturative Family Distancing (AFD) and Depression in Chinese American Families." *Journal of Consulting and Clinical Psychology* 78, no. 5 (2010): 655–667.

Inglehart, Ronald, and Wayne Baker. "Modernization, Cultural Change, and the Persistence of Traditional Values." *American Sociological Review* 65, no. 1 (2000): 19–51.

Jeung, Russell. *Faithful Generations: Race and New Asian American Churches.* New Brunswick, NJ: Rutgers University Press, 2005.

Jose, Paul, and Carol Huntsinger. "Moderation and Mediation Effects of Coping by Chinese American and European American Adolescents." *Journal of Genetic Psychology* 166, no. 1 (2005): 16–43.

Joshi, Khyati Y. *New Roots in America's Sacred Ground: Religion, Race, and Ethnicity in Indian America.* New Brunswick, NJ: Rutgers University Press, 2006.

Kibria, Nazli. *Becoming Asian American: Second-Generation Chinese and Korean American Identities.* Baltimore: Johns Hopkins University Press, 1900.

Kim, Rebecca Y. *God's New Whiz Kids? Korean American Evangelicals on Campus.* New York: New York University Press, 2006.

Kim, Soryoung. "Intergenerational Conflict and Its Role in Suicidal Ideation among Chinese American and Japanese American College Students." PhD dissertation, 2002.

Klein, Thoralf. "Political Religion in Twentieth Century China and Its Global Dimension." In *Globalization and the Making of Religious Modernity in China,* edited by Thomas Jansen, Thoralf Klein, and Christian Meyer, 52–90. New York: Brill, 2014.

Kosmin, Barry, and Ariela Keysar. "American Nones: The Profile of the No Religion Population. A Report Based on the American Religious Identification Survey 2008." In *American Nones: The Profile of the No Religion Population.* Trinity College Faculty Report. Hartford, CT: Institute for the Study of Secularism in Society & Culture, 2009.

Li, Yih-Yuan. *Collected Works of Religion and Mysteries.* Taipei: Lixu Press, 1998.

Lim, Chaeyoun, Carol McGregor, and Roger Putnam. "Secular and Liminal: Discovering Heterogeneity among Religious Nones." *Journal for the Scientific Study of Religion* 49 (2010): 596–618.

Lin, Michelle. "The Garment Workers Justice Campaign." Accessed October 11, 2017. http://www.umich.edu/~snre492/Jones/jessica.htm.

Lin, Yueh-Hwa. *The Golden Wing: A Sociological Study of Chinese Familism.* London: Routledge and Kegan Paul, 1947.

Lipka, Michael. "10 Facts about Religion in America." Pew Research Center, August 27, 2015. http://www.pewresearch.org/fact-tank/2015/08/27/10-facts-about-religion-in-america/.

Liu, Michael, Kim Geron, and Tracy Gee. *The Snake Dance of Asian American Activism.* Lanham, MD: Lexington Books, 2008.

Lofton, Kathryn. *Oprah: The Gospel of an Icon.* Berkeley: University of California Press, 2011.

Long, Charles. *Significations: Signs, Symbols, and Images in the Interpretation of Religion.* Aurora, CO: Davies Press, 1999.

Manning, Christel. "Unaffiliated Parents and the Religious Training of Their Children." *Sociology of Religion* 74 (2013): 149–175.

Merino, Stephen. "Irreligious Socialization? The Adult Religious Preferences of Individuals Raised with No Religion." *Secularism and Nonreligion* 1 (2012): 1–16.

Min, Pyong Gap. *Preserving Ethnicity through Religion in America: Korean Protestants and Indian Hindus across Generations.* New York: New York University Press, 2010.

Nadeau, Randall. "Divinity." In *The Wiley-Blackwell Companion to Chinese Religions,* edited by Randall L. Nadeau, 369–395. New York: John Wiley and Sons, 2012.

Needham, Joseph, and Ling Wang. *Science and Civilisation in China: Volume 2.* Cambridge, UK: Cambridge University Press, 1956.

Nongbri, Brent. *Before Religion: A History of a Modern Concept.* New Haven, CT: Yale University Press, 2013.

Okihiro, Gary. "Toward a Pacific Civilization." *Japanese Journal of American Studies* 18 (2007): 73–85.

Overmeyer, Daniel. "From 'Feudal Superstition' to 'Popular Belief': New Directions in Mainland China Studies of Chinese Popular Religion." *Cahiers d'Extreme Asie* 12 (2001): 103–126.

Pew Research Center. "Asian Americans: A Mosaic of Faiths." July 19, 2012. http://www.pewforum.org/2012/07/19/asian-americans-a-mosaic-of-faiths-overview/.

Pew Research Center. "Millennials: A Portrait of Generation Next." February 24, 2010. http://www.pewsocialtrends.org/2010/02/24/millennials-confident-connected-open-to-change/.

Pew Research Center. "Nones on the Rise." October 9, 2012. http://www.pewforum.org/2012/10/09/nones-on-the-rise/#_ftn4.

Pew-Templeton Global Religious Futures Project. "Taiwan." 2016. Accessed September 25, 2017. http://www.globalreligiousfutures.org/countries/taiwan#/?affiliations_religion_

id=0&affiliations_year=2010&region_name=All%20Countries&restrictions_
year=2015.

PPRI. "PRRI Releases Largest Survey of American Religious and Denominational Identity Ever Conducted." *Cision*, September 6, 2017. http://www.prnewswire.com/news-releases/prri-releases-largest-survey-of-american-religious-and-denominational-identity-ever-conducted-300514391.html.

Ramakrishnan, Karthick, Janelle Wong, Taeku Lee, and Jennifer Lee. "Asian American Voices in the 2016 Election." National Asian American Survey, Fall 2016. Accessed October 4, 2017.

Rawski, Evelyn. "A Historian's Approach to Death Ritual." In *Death Ritual in Late Imperial and Modern China*, edited by James Watson and Evelyn Rawski, 20–34. Berkeley: University of California Press, 1988.

Said, Edward. *Orientalism*. New York: Vintage, 1979.

Sangren, P. "Fate, Agency, and the Economy of Desire in Chinese Ritual and Society." *Social Analysis* 56, no. 2 (2012): 117–135.

Schwartz, Ben. *The World of Thought in Ancient China*. Cambridge, MA: Harvard University Press, 1985.

Smith, J. Z. "Religion, Religions, Religious." In *Critical Terms for Religious Studies*, edited by Mark Taylor, 269–284. Chicago: University of Chicago Press, 1998.

Smith, Timothy. "Religion and Ethnicity in America." *American Historical Review* 83, no. 5 (1978): 1155–1185.

Stark, Rodney, and Roger Finke. *Acts of Faith: Explaining the Human Side of Religion*. Berkeley: University of California Press, 2000.

Sturgeon, Donald, ed. *Chinese Text Project*. 2011. Accessed April 2015. http://ctext.org.

Sun, Anna. "Theorizing the Plurality of Chinese Religious Life: The Search for New Paradigms in the Study of Chinese Religions." In *Area Studies and Religion: History and Practice*, edited by Kiri Paramore. forthcoming.

Tan, Sor-Hoon. "Modernizing Confucianism and 'New Confucianism.'" In *The Cambridge Companion to Modern Chinese Culture*, edited by Kam Louie, 135–154. Cambridge, UK: Cambridge University Press, 2008.

Taylor, Charles. *A Secular Age*. Cambridge, MA: Harvard University Press, 2007.

Teiser, Stephen F. "Popular Religion." *Journal of Asian Studies* 54, no. 2 (1995): 378–395.

Teiser, Stephen. "Religions of China in Practice." In *Asian Religions in Practice: An Introduction*, edited by Donald S. Lopez, 88–122. Princeton, NJ: Princeton University Press, 2010.

Torassa, Ulysses. "Thousands Protest Legalizing Same-Sex Marriage: Asian Americans, Christians Rally in Sunset District." *San Francisco Chronicle*, April 26, 2004.

Tsai, Jean, Yu-Wen Ying, and Peter Lee. "Cultural Predictors of Self-Esteem: A Study of Chinese American Female and Male Young Adults." *Cultural Diversity and Ethnic Minority Psychology* 7, no. 3 (0000) : 284–297.

Tsukamoto Zenryū. *A History of Early Chinese Buddhism: From Its Introduction to the Death of Hui-yüan*. Translated by Leon Hurvitz. Tokyo: Kodansha International, 1985.

Tu, Wei-Ming. *Confucian Traditions in East Asian Modernity: Moral Education and Economic Culture in Japan and the Four Mini-Dragons*. Cambridge, MA; Harvard University Press, 1996.

Tuan, Mia. *Forever Foreigners or Honorary Whites? The Asian American Experience Today*. New Brunswick, NJ: Rutgers University Press, 1999.

Tung, May. *Chinese Americans and Their Immigrant Parents*. Binghamton, NY: Haworth Press, 2000.

Vargas, Nicholas. "Retrospective Accounts of Religious Disaffiliation in the United States: Stressors, Skepticism, and Political Factors." *Sociology of Religion* 73 (2012): 200–223.

Wang, Wendy, and Paul Taylor. "For Millennials, Parenthood Trumps Marriage." Pew Research Center, March 9, 2011. http://www.pewsocialtrends.org/2011/03/09/ii-comparing-millennials-with-gen-xers/.

Wang, Zhixi. *Introduction to Chinese Religious Thought*. Shanghai: Sanlien Press, 1933.

Warner, R. Stephen. "The Role of Religion in the Process of Segmented Assimilation." *Annals of the American Academy of Political and Social Science* 612 (2007): 102–115.

Warner, R. Stephen, and Judith Wittner. *Gatherings in Diaspora: Religious Communities and the New Immigration*. Philadelphia: Temple University Press, 1998.

Wenzel-Teuber, Katharina. "Statistics on Religions and Churches in the People's Republic of China: Update for the Year 2016." China Zentrum. Accessed September 25, 2017. http://www.china-zentrum.de/fileadmin/downloads/rctc/2017-2/RCTC_2017-2.26-53_Wenzel-Teuber__Statistics_on_Religions_and_Churches_in_the_PRC_%E2%80%93_Update_for_the_Year_2016.pdf.

Wolf, Arthur. *Religion and Ritual in Chinese Society*. Stanford, CA: Stanford University Press, 1974.

Wong Chin Foo. "Why Am I a Heathen?" *North American Review* 145 (1887): 169–179.

Wu, Ellen. *The Color of Success: Asian Americans and the Origins of the Model Minority*. New York: Oxford University Press, 2015.

Wuthnow, Robert. *After the Baby Boomers: How Twenty- and Thirty-Somethings Are Shaping the Future of American Religion*. Princeton, NJ: Princeton University Press, 2007.

Yang, C. K. *Religion in Chinese Society: A Study of Contemporary Social Functions of Religion and Some of Their Historical Factors*. Berkeley: University of California Press, 1961.

Yang, Fenggang. *Chinese Christians in America: Conversion, Assimilation, and Adhesive Identities*. University Park: Pennsylvania State University Press, 1999.

Yang, Fenggang. *Religion in China: Survival and Revival under Communist Rule*. New York: Oxford University Press, 2012.

Yang, Fenggang. "What about China? Religious Vitality in the Most Secular and Rapidly Modernizing Society." *Sociology of Religion* 75, no. 4 (2014): 564–578.

Yang, Fenggang, and Anning Hu. "Mapping Chinese Folk Religion in Mainland China and Taiwan." *Journal for the Scientific Study of Religion* 51, no. 3 (2012): 505–521.

Yang, Shao-yun. "Reinventing the Barbarian: Rhetorical and Philosophical Uses of the Yi-Di in Mid-Imperial China, 600–1300." PhD dissertation, University of California, Berkeley, 2014.

Yuwen, Weichao, and A. C. Chen. "Chinese American Adolescents: Perceived Parenting Styles and Adolescents' Psychosocial Health." *International Nursing Review* (2013): 236–243.

Zhou, Min. "Growing Up American: The Challenge Confronting Immigrant Children and Children of Immigrants." *Annual Review of Sociology* 23, no. 1 (1997): 63–95.

INDEX